BRAIN TUMOR
A Love Story

a memoir by
Kathy Eliscu & Ted White

Authors' Note: The stories in this book reflect the authors' recollection of events. Some names, locations, and identifying characteristics have been changed to protect the privacy of those depicted. Dialogue has been recreated as closely as possible from memory.

Brain Tumor: A Love Story
Copyright © 2024 Kathy Eliscu & Ted White

ISBN: 978-1-63381-388-5

All rights reserved. No part of this book may be reproduced in any form or by any electronic or mechanical means, including information storage and retrieval systems, without permission in writing from the author, except by a reviewer, who may quote brief passages in review.

Cover background photograph © Ted White, *Whirling Waters*.

Designed and produced by:
Maine Authors Publishing
12 High Street, Thomaston, Maine
www.maineauthorspublishing.com

Printed in the United States of America

*For Beth
and our many loved ones.
Thank you for showing up in your own perfect way.
It was just right.*

TABLE OF CONTENTS

A Note to the Reader xv

Prologue 1
    2011, Southern Maine 1

PART 1 5
    Background 5

Chapter 1 7
    2005 7
    2011 8

Chapter 2 10
    Ted—Ides of March, 2011 10
    On the Way to the Sherwoods Reunion 12
    Fallingwater/Failing Leg 16
    The Sherwoods 17
    Maybe Rabies, Maybe Not 19

Chapter 3 24
    Maybe Herpes 24

Chapter 4 31
    Calling All Possibilities 31

Chapter 5 34
    Lots of Shakin' Going On 34
    Dr. Emery 35
    The Mystery Continues 36

PART 2 39

Chapter 6 41
- Boston 41
- MGH Admission 43

Chapter 7 46
- Thrown into the Storm 46
- Are We Worried? 48
- Father John 50
- Heading Home for the Weekend 52

Chapter 8 56
- Back to Boston 56
- Alfred Hitchcock's The Birds—Redux 58
- Biopsy Day 59
- Will Curry, aka Dr. McDreamy 62
- Post-Biopsy 63

Chapter 9 65
- Reprieve 65
- Two Doctors, a Social Worker, and Starbucks 66
- Revisiting My Wonderful Case of Denial 69

PART 3 71

Chapter 10 73
- Shock 73

Chapter 11 79
- Beth 79
- Butterfly Corner 80
- Gathering Information 82
- Everyone's Got an Opinion 83

Chapter 12 86
- Butterfly Corner Revisited 86
- The Day Before the First Radiation Treatment 89

Chapter 13 92
- Cancer 92
- Treatment 94

Chapter 14 97
What Helps 97
Good Bill Hunting 98
Beginning of Annulment 99
Radiation Oncology Appointment 100
The Social Ladder—Filled with Love and Food 100

Chapter 15 105
The Inn at Home 105
Just Another Day 108
Living with Cancer 109

Chapter 16 110
Gasps 110
The Immortal Brain of Ted White 110

Chapter 17 114
A Clean House, Prayers, and Final Radiation 114
Methylating Factor 117
Bob, Lubec, and Rails 117
Me: Bitch 118

Chapter 18 120
Visit to Ted's Mom 120
Take Care of Yourself 120
More Boundaries 123

Chapter 19 125
Novocure 125
Insurance Blues 127

Chapter 20 130
Keeping My Big Mouth Shut 130
Friends 131
Fear 131
Beth and the Magic Flute 133

Chapter 21 135
California and the Sherwoods 135
Good, Bad, Ugly 138
Pancakes with the Catholics 139
The Mall and the ER 140

Chapter 22 143
Unreliable Life 143
If We're Not in the ER, It Must Be a Good Day 144
Who Is It with the Chemo Brain? 145
The Cold War 147
Changing the Game Rules 148
And Then There's This 149

Chapter 23 151
On Dying and Helping 151
Winter 2011 Approaching 152
Flutes Can Be Hazardous to Your Health 153
The Holiday Season 154
Fat Enlightenment 157
Urgent Care 158
Christmas 2011 158

Chapter 24 160
Post-Christmas—Getting Ready for the South 160
Then Came the Flood 162
Happy New Year 164
Hello, God? It's Me—Lunatic Woman 165
Beth 167
Almost There, Pre-Trip 168
Ted's MRI 169

Chapter 25 171
Going, Going, Gone! 171
On the Road Again 173
En Route to New Bern 174
Arriving in New Bern 175

Chapter 26 177
Our Cottage 177
New Bern—A Town with History 179
Syrup on That/Cottage Life 179
St. Paul's Catholic Church 182
Tough Morning in NC 183
The Amazing Ambivalence of Walking 184
I'll Be Nicer 185

Chapter 27	188
Learning to Hear Nothing	188
Greenville	189
A Walk to Remember and a Photo Not To	190
Taking the Guilt Trip	192
Chapter 28	193
Out of Nowhere	193
Early February	196
Chapter 29	199
Valentine's Day Approaching	199
Valentine's Day 2012	201
At the Cottage	201
Ted's Take	202
Chapter 30	205
Mail-Order Medicine	205
I See the Light and It Is Good	206
Chapter 31	210
Ash Wednesday—Later and Beyond	210
Logistics	212
Chemotherapy Day 4	213
Roots	214
Exploring	215
Weekend Company	216
Walking Can Be Tough Stuff	218
Contemplation	223
Morehead City	227
Chapter 32	230
A Few Moments for My Soul	230
Getting Ready to Leave NC	231
Last Night in New Bern	232
Maine	233
Of Joy and Sorrow	234
Chapter 33	244
2013	244
Marks of Illness	245

Chapter 34 252
   More Angels 252

Chapter 35 255
   Who or What's Got My Back? 255

Chapter 36 260
   Harsh Reality 260

Chapter 37 266
   Now I Just Feel Like Job 266

PART 4 271

Chapter 38 273
   Hospice, Room 106 273
   Saint Becky 279
   Next Morning 280
   On the Home Front 280

Chapter 39 286
   Choices 286
   A Different Kind of Day 287
   From Gosnell to God 292

PART 5 295

Chapter 40 297
   Reality 297
   Grieving People 302

Chapter 41 306
   Plodding Along 306
   Back Home in Maine 308
   The Universe as We Know It 310

Chapter 42 312
   Anniversary in Heaven 312

Chapter 43 316
   January 2016, Southern Wandering 316
   Spring, Summer, and Onward 317
   Home Again 318

Chapter 44 324
    Early 2017 324
    Frustration and Gratitude 325
    Cold Weather Coming... 327
Chapter 45 328
    Love, Guilt, Changes 328
    Fall Realization 330
Chapter 46 332
    2019 and Beyond 332

Epilogue 336
Acknowledgments 339

A NOTE TO THE READER

Brain Tumor: A Love Story is written in two voices: Kathy's and Ted's. Separate typefaces are used throughout to differentiate between the two.

Kathy's voice is typeset in Garamond Premier Pro Regular.
Ted's voice is typeset in Futura PT Medium.

PROLOGUE

April 2011, out-of-state hospital
 "Are we worried?" I ask the doctor, in front of Ted, fully expecting him to say,
 "Oh, no. Nothing a round of antibiotics can't treat."

2011, SOUTHERN MAINE

A woman pulls into a parking space at a grocery store, leaving her husband in the car to rest. He doesn't feel well. She needs to buy dishwasher detergent. Late last night she used up the last of it. In fact, the amount she used in that last run was a little short. But never mind, she thought. Good enough. And it's worth the stop tonight because lately, being efficient is not only helpful for the running of the household, but also for her peace of mind. Something about organization being next to godliness, or however that goes.

Now, holding her list—detergent and a few other items—she breezes through the electronically opening doors, almost too fast for the speed of these older grocery store doors she's walked through for decades at her neighborhood market. She's on a mission.

Milk. Fruit? Definitely low. She's off to a good start. She doesn't want to keep her husband waiting long.

First, she hits the produce section and picks out some berries and a couple of bananas. Then she heads to the dishwashing/laundry aisle. On her way, she passes the cereal aisle. Does he have his bran flakes for the morning?

Poor guy. Even while sick, he still loves his bran flakes. She pulls a box off the shelf, begins to study the SKU information below that box and the larger box next to it on the shelf. She starts comparing prices, but then snaps back to reality, reminding herself that he is in the car. Sleeping? Maybe. Needing to use a bathroom? She throws the smaller box she's holding into the cart, price be damned, and picks up her pace a little, continuing down her list and moving more quickly through the next couple of aisles. When she finds herself passing the yogurt section, she is surprised and overwhelmed at the choices and beautiful colors on the labels, as if seeing color for the first time. The cooler temperature of the air at the dairy section is refreshing. She figures what the heck, I'll get a bunch of different-flavored Greek yogurts. Nonfat and full of protein. She feels happy in this moment. The containers are so pretty, with colorful pictures of different fruits on the labels. Raspberry. Blueberry. Peach. She notes again that she feels lighter, mood-wise, than in the past couple of weeks. There's a hint of a spring in her step as she moves down the aisle, navigating her cart in the relative emptiness of the store at this hour. She continues through the store, tired eyes scanning the hurriedly written list she made on the back of an old CVS receipt from her purse: milk; already got the fruit; uh-huh, uh-huh, yup, and then heads to the checkout. She pulls out the credit card that pays her back some points or money or something—not important now, she thinks. She just wants to get to her husband, make sure he's OK, and get him home.

    She hurries to the car and sees that he has put the seat back and is sleeping. He wakes up, happy to see her. Thank God. She feels her shoulders relax, and she takes a deep breath, smiling at him as she loads the groceries into the backseat. They go home.

    He gets into the house with some effort, and she goes back to the car and carries in the groceries, something he used to do. She's careful how she lifts and how much she carries at a time, as she has not fully recovered—possibly never will—from a neck and back injury of a few years earlier. That happened in the "old days" before he was sick, when he was able to do all the heavy lifting and more rigorous chores. But still, after shopping and knowing he was OK in the car? She has that successful feeling. They're home. Safe.

    They have supper and watch an episode of *Doc Martin* together, then he goes to bed. She stays up answering emails from friends and family who ask for updates and express their love and concern. She gets lost in it, and quite late, goes to the kitchen for a quick snack before bed. In the kitchen, she washes a piece of fruit over the sink full of dishes. I'll do them tomorrow, she thinks. Then she decides she will do them tonight, so they'll be clean and ready in the morning. And as she gets the last plate into the bottom rack, she realizes—she never got the dishwasher detergent.

PART 1

BACKGROUND

Ted and I met in 2001. I was at work in a hospital clinic when the staff door opened and I was introduced to a doctor—Ted White. I was unimpressed. The background to our brief hello is that I was already sad that the female doc with whom I'd been working closely was leaving. This man was her replacement, so I was already resentful.

"So. You must be the new doctor," I said, barely looking up from a chart.

Much later, as we reviewed this first meeting, I would give my side of the encounter. Ted, this new doctor, would insist I was flirting with him.

"I thought you were boring, and I wanted the old doctor to stay," I'd say.

Thus began a friendship based on humor, and soon we found common ground: disillusionment with the current way medicine was being driven by the insurance industry; bureaucracy in healthcare; a way of caring for our patients that felt genuine, even if it meant a healthy skepticism of some of the new cookie-cutter ways of treatment. I was at the end of divorce proceedings, and Ted's marriage was nearing its end. We both were quite sad about having to say goodbye to relationships fraught with much difficulty. In staff meetings, Ted and I began to share unspoken jokes with a simple look, and we began to share lunch breaks when it worked out, timewise. Then he found out he had prostate cancer that required surgery. I did the only thing I could when he told me: I hugged him. During his surgery, I drove around the hospital area playing hymns on my car's tape deck, windows closed, and singing my prayer for him. It was a rough go after the surgery, with a lot of blood loss, but he recovered.

We each began to find in each other a listening ear, lots of humor, and eventually, he didn't seem so boring after all. It wasn't long before I learned an important lesson about initial impressions. Ted became quite sexy in my eyes, in a sense regrettable, as I was not looking for a relationship. True, I had, some months earlier, fleetingly asked God to send me "a gentle man."

During the upcoming year, Ted and I started dating, meeting each other's families, going on trips together—those kinds of building blocks of a relationship I had not formerly experienced with that level of joy.

At the same time, at home, I had been left with one of the cutest puppies in the world, a cairn terrier named Rebel, but here I was, a single parent, working full-time, a dog that was essentially untrained, and an owner—me—who knew nothing about dogs. He was a pup I'd inherited from a previous marriage. When I went to work during the day, he was gated safely in the laundry room/downstairs bathroom, a large but unexciting space, with his toys, food, water, bed, and so on, and I'd get home at the end of the day, exhausted, to find a puddle almost every time. Even when I wasn't out, he was not well trained.

Overwhelmed, I sobbed at the next well-visit at my vet's office.

"I don't know what to do," I told him. "I'm just not cut out for this."

The vet gave me guidance and support, told me how he retrained his own dog, and told me if I really couldn't handle it, that he knew someone who might be willing to take him.

I went home and hugged and hugged my dog, crying, and realized I couldn't give him up. Ted showed me, step by step, how to help the dog along in a more social way, assisting with the techniques of training, and before too long, I was able to bring the dog up to speed, at least enough. The dog gave—and received—much love and happiness for years and years. Ted, a good and caring man. A gentle man.

CHAPTER 1

2005

We are living together in Ted's nearby farmhouse with my son, Will, who is approaching his senior year of high school. Will and Ted have already established a solid relationship. Will is happy about the move, and he has the new, semi-finished wing of the farmhouse as his own. We are a

> **2002—IN BED**
>
> "This isn't funny anymore," I said, after an intensely loving romp in bed.
> "It isn't even fun," he said.
> And we laughed, realizing that the fun and attachment we had for each other was no longer merely a fling.

growing family, in this way. Our children and grandkids and other relatives and friends come up to spend time with us here and there. We are happy together. We get each other. Independent yet quite connected.

Our lives are made up of everyday, ordinary things. Walking the dog. Making shopping lists. Calling relatives and friends on birthdays. Cooking scrambled eggs and making toast. Fetching bills from the mailbox at the bottom of the driveway. Bickering about spending too much money on a piece of electronics.

Ted and I have dinner dates with other couples from time to time, outings together, family gatherings both planned and spontaneous…a couple of trips each year to visit Ted's beautifully aging, feisty mom on Long Island, New York, who only recently gave up the community bowling league, where she was a top scorer at age 90-something. We take weekend car rides, go to movies; we sing at church in a small group on Sunday afternoons, usually singing harmony with each other, after which Ted and I typically go to supper at one of our favorite local restaurants with our friends. Ted and one of the regulars enjoy a perfect Manhattan at the start of our now-traditional Sunday meal. I sip my Sunday Pepsi with extra ice, no fruit. Ted orders a fish selection, and I go for their special salad with grilled shrimp. The warm restaurant rolls are crispy on the outside, soft and warm in the middle. We go through lots of butter. And we know all the servers by name. We sang a harmonious chorus of "Happy Birthday" to one of them when we found out she was turning 30 that day.

In our workplace, at staff meetings, Ted and I exchange subtle glances and in-jokes. There's nothing sexier than being united against a common enemy: the continually ridiculously "improving" administrative practices. We try to keep our relationship under wraps at work, but one Friday afternoon we are called into the boss's office to find that someone has accused us of PDA in the staff room, which is ludicrous, saying he "was nuzzling your neck." Oh, please. He was probably whispering that someone farted. That passes, although our resentment that someone would make up a lie, or possibly interpret something innocent in this way, lingers. Nevertheless, we continue by day in the workplace. In bed at night, we snuggle like two bears, free from scrutiny.

Our wonderful grown children, scattered from North Carolina to Maine, are quite attentive to us, as are our extended families out of state. Ted has a son, Randey, and I have two daughters, Cassie and Sally, and a son, William. There are in-laws and grandkids. We are a well-blended, loving family. In 2008, we marry.

2011

At the start of 2011, Ted is planning his upcoming retirement from our workplace, probably sometime in the late spring or early summer. I am out of nursing, after 30-plus years of a wonderful career. I'm a young retiree, due to a car accident in 2007 resulting in chronic pain, which ultimately stopped my career. But as any nurse will tell you, you are never out of nursing, no matter what. Your heart is forever there. Currently, I work about ten to fifteen hours a week at the local office of a well-known weight loss company, filling lightweight grocery orders (mostly snacks) and stuffing pamphlets into envelopes. It's a terrifically fun atmosphere, with great people around me. And I write from home, something I started earlier in my adult life, only now I have a regular humor column in a magazine in southern Maine. And I have been working, for years, on a light, fluffy novel.

All this is to say we have a good life, having found each other later in life when we weren't looking for anyone. Grateful for the time we have together, and especially for our wonderful children. I can't help wondering how it took so long to meet my good match.

"I wish I had met you when we were younger," I often say to Ted.

And his answer is always the same: "You wouldn't have liked me then. I was an asshole."

The long list of what attracts me to him can be pared down to the important points: his sense of humor, his gentleness, his sincere love of my family, his wisdom, his brilliant brain, his humility, his laidback attitude, which is a great match for my more anxious nature. I love the way he smells like pistachios, how he kisses me and comes up behind me in the kitchen to put his arms around me and moves his hips into mine, starting to dance, and I love how he snuggles me at night. We sing together, in more ways than just vocal. I do not wish my previous life to be different. But now, with Ted, I am fully living a life shared with a man whom I find to be quite extraordinary. He saved my dog, in a sense, but also saved me in my very soul, and became a loving second dad to my children.

I like to think that what has brought him to me is my great ass.

Here is our story.

CHAPTER 2

TED—IDES OF MARCH, 2011

Dream:
I'm part of a small group of men and women involved in some sort of training program. Seems like we are all fairly young adults, maybe 30-ish. There are about fifteen of us, mostly men, some women. I'm aware that at least one of the women is attractive and I wonder whether she and I might get to know each other during the training, might hit it off. We're offered an opportunity, so it seems, to undergo a sort of special training program. The program is organized and led by a bunch of older men who seem somehow menacing, like Mafia types. The training is to take place at a location about a mile down a road, at a compound of houses/buildings surrounding an open courtyard, which is paved. The road goes straight downhill, fairly steeply. As we are deciding whether to do this, one of the other men asks the leaders/bosses some question, something about whether we will be allowed to have our own pens, or something. The basic idea is how much autonomy or freedom we will have during the process.

"Of course you will," the head guy reassures us.

So, we descend the road, all downhill, until we are all assembled in the courtyard surrounded by the buildings. The scene is dark, nighttime, and everyone is dressed in black. Seems like the men are wearing suits and the women are well-dressed for business also. Getting down to this point has been arduous somehow, and we are anxious, standing in little groups, with the trainers/bosses standing around the outside of us. In other words, we're surrounded by them.

The man in our group who had asked about whether we could keep our pens takes note that we do not have them and is alarmed, and reminds the head guy that he'd said we could have them. He smiles very darkly.

"Well, that is no longer true," he says, "and we can't."

Somebody, maybe I, points out to our group that if they could lie about that, they could lie about anything, including whether we'd even be allowed to leave, if we want to.

"Oh no, you can leave anytime," the man says.

Several of us immediately decide to get out of there, it's too frightening, and we start to leave. The trainers/bosses try to talk us out of it, and all but two of us change their minds and decide to stay.

Two of us walk out of the compound, and I'm in the lead, but then someone comes running out and pleads with the other guy to stay and he reluctantly goes back in, obviously scared.

I start climbing back up the hill, which is steep. I'm surprised how hard it is to climb up. I come to an old VW bus, and for some reason I can't just stay on the paved road from that point. Instead, I have to clamber up a rock wall, about ten feet high, that runs along the road, and then make my way up the top of the rocks, with the road below to my right.

I finally get to the top, where there is another house, kind of like a gatekeeper's place at the entrance to the long road down into the compound I've just left. I remember the gatekeeper from seeing him on the way in. He looks kind of like Harpo Marx, but with shorter hair. Something menacing about him.

As I come to the area of his house, there is a chain-link fence, and suddenly someone comes crashing through the fence, near me, begging for help, trying to get away from the gatekeeper. Then I'm inside the fence, approaching the house, still trying to get the hell out of there. The gatekeeper appears and starts coming for me.

I take off, but there's more fence before I can get away, and a sharp drop on the other side of the fence. As I'm trying to get through the fence, the gatekeeper charges at me, running at me. I wait until the last instant, then step aside and grab him as he goes by, shoving him through the fence and over the drop. He goes through the fence but manages to hang on to the top of the wall before falling down the cliff. He grabs for me, and I realize we are in a fight to the death. We start to fight.

I wake up.

The setting of the dream: I've announced I'm retiring from the hospital where I've been working, in southern Maine, the psychiatric center where I've practiced for the past decade and more and retiring from psychiatry. Some thoughts associated with the dream: Trying to get out of here is really hard and, in some ways, feels like a fight to the death. Sounds trite, but who am I, what is my identity, if I'm not a psychiatrist? It's been 40 years since I started practice. Also, is the next step of my life the ending of it? At 70, I have begun to feel old in a way I never have before. Someone said recently that old age is the only part of your life you don't get a chance to reflect on. I'm not sure about the gatekeeper guy, who he represents, but probably the part of myself that doesn't want to leave. Why is he like Harpo? To throw in a comical element? Make him ridiculous? VW bus? One of my favorite patients has an old VW. Sometimes I've thought I'd like to open a private practice and take several patients with me, and he'd be one of them, certainly.

This was the latest of several nightmares I've had in recent weeks. Before this time, I have not had nightmares since I was very young, not at all. In fact, it's very, very unusual for me to recall any dreams at all.

So, here's the truth of how it all began, or at least some version of it.

ON THE WAY TO THE SHERWOODS REUNION

Friday, April 8, 2011
Life's been going pretty damn well. I'm going to retire this summer, at the end of July. The paperwork is all turned in. Kathy and I are on our way to a Sherwood reunion, hosted by Allan and Dee. The Sherwoods is an a cappella men's singing group, which I have been a part of since college days at Cornell.

We're driving, taking a somewhat different route than last time we did this, first down through Pennsylvania and then into Maryland, for starters. There are a couple of reasons for the route. One is, I want to see where my friend Bob grew up, in Cumberland, MD. Bob is my longtime dearest friend, more of a brother. Impossible to count or to measure the conversations that have passed between us in the past 40 years, since we worked in the former juvenile jail which the University of California, Davis, had converted into the center of their mental health department. Bob grew up in Cumberland. He went from there to Harvard and then on to make a life as a clinical psychologist in northern California, but in so many ways Cumberland has remained in his blood, and it seems important to me to visit the place where he started out in life. The other reason for driving this route is that as long as we are in this part of the country, we want to visit Fallingwater, Frank Lloyd Wright's wonderful creation in the woods. My brother Kendall so admired Wright's Fallingwater that for one of his projects when he was an architecture student at Cornell, he built a model of the house and, to me, his model was a wonder in itself. That would have to have been around 1961, and I've been wanting to see the original ever since. So here we are, on our way.

Small Town, PA
The first day is a long one, from Maine to a small town in PA's Lehigh Valley. It is an understatement to say that this town is not a pretty place. It's a dreary, down-at-the-heels spot along the Delaware River, 150 miles or so north of Philadelphia. The kind of place which in the middle of town, on the main street, a shop window features mannequins wearing pornographic underwear, on a drizzly Saturday evening when most of the shops in town are closed and locked. Ordinarily, that would not be too shocking, but somehow, in a place like this, it is. The weather, the night we get there, is dreary and overcast, with some light rain. We are hungry and tired. We ask the desk clerk at the motel for suggestions about a restaurant for dinner and are directed to a place about ten blocks away. Kathy and I walk through the drizzle and find the place, which turns out to be very loud, with second-rate food and poor service,

but substantial prices. It's what you get when the desk clerk you ask is about 22 years old.

Saturday, April 9, 2011
Early in the morning I take a shower and am heading back into the room to get dressed when, all of a sudden, my right leg starts to jerk and twitch uncontrollably. Actually, it probably starts with the abdominal muscles on my right side, then progresses down to my hip. Kathy is still in bed, but awake. I say something to her, like, "Something weird is happening to my body!" I am scared, really scared. She quickly bundles me back into bed and covers me. The warmth helps, maybe, a little, but the jerking continues for, I don't know, a minute, two minutes, five minutes, and then it subsides as quickly as it started. We wonder what to do. Continue the trip? Head for home? Look for a hospital, on a Saturday morning in this nowhere kind of place? There does not appear to be any significantly large cities nearby, that is, nowhere that is likely to have a medical center of any size, and calling 9-1-1 seems unnecessary. I feel fine after the jerking stops. We decide to continue the trip and hope for the best.

I have no clue what's going on, only that when I get him into bed and bundle him up, things subside. I breathe a sigh of relief and try to put it out of my mind.

So, off we drive across Pennsylvania, southwestward, down through Harrisburg and south into Maryland, stopping for lunch in Shippingport before sliding below the Mason-Dixon line (is that where that is?!!!) and then along the PA–MD border and into Cumberland at last. Cumberland's an old railroad town, and I see now why Bob has always disparaged it and done his best to outrun the place but has remained tied to Cumberland all his life. Miraculous that his family, his grandfather, chose to settle there, about the only Jews around in this coal-speckled, redneck, Appalachian place. The area is, geographically speaking, genuinely lovely, once you overlook the mess created by railroads and coal. Steep green mountainsides pile up from the Potomac River, which divides this tiny strip of Maryland from West Virginia at that point. One can almost hear the Civil War troops making their way to death or victory down in the valleys below. I find the city itself pretty ugly. We enter from the east, the poorest and most run-down part of town. Almost immediately, we are caught on the wrong side of the tracks, literally. The rail lines run right through the middle of the city, east to west. The trains are long and slow, and it seems that just as one finishes passing through town, another train bears down from the other direction. We sit for at least 45 minutes in one place, before deciding to take another street, which deposits us in a small shopping center a bit east. Eventually, we make our way back out of town via the interstate west, never really getting to see most of Cumberland at all, and missing entirely Bob's childhood home, to which he'd given directions.

Westward, we run into mountains and fog. The fog becomes very dense as we gain altitude in the mountains. In some places, it's almost impossible to see the road at all, but what we can see is lovely, and one could even say majestic. I had no idea this part of the country was so beautiful. We continue along the border between West Virginia and Maryland, angling northwestward back into Pennsylvania, to an inn we'd booked for the night, a bit south of Fallingwater.

The inn is as graceful and comfortable as the town of Cumberland had been seedy. We have a room on the second floor, filled with Victorian furniture. The view out the window consists mostly of the air-conditioning equipment on the first-floor roof, which sounds ugly, but somehow is not. The inn sits at the nadir of a long and steep valley on US Route 40. The road at that point swoops down from both east and west for a couple of miles, so that by the time the cars and trucks hit bottom, they are really tearing along. You do not want to spend much time out on the front porch because of the roaring traffic, but back inside it's quiet and warm. There is a magnificent dining room, and the food is first-rate.

After a sumptuous meal, we sleep well, until I have to get up to pee around 2 a.m. and am hit by another seizure, very much like the first. We begin to suspect that my being chilled has something to do with triggering these things. Back in bed, and warm, my body settles down again and I am able to sleep some more.

Like a couple of medical detectives, we try to piece this together. Is he chilled? Or overheated? The ability of our medically trained minds to rationalize, as I look back on it, is striking. One thing we do agree on is that we don't want him to go to a small local hospital where the level of care might be inferior. He wants to wait it out. Maybe it will go away. The scared part of me thinks that seems, well, just fine. I somehow manage to shut worry thoughts off and scrunch down a little deeper into the comforting protection of the fluffy bedding.

FALLINGWATER/FAILING LEG

The inn's dining room offers a full breakfast, as good as the previous night's dinner. We check out and find ourselves meandering over back roads, through steep and lush countryside, bearing northward, ultimately following a medium-sized river that leads to Fallingwater. I have no more seizures that morning. The weather is cool and clear. The home, Fallingwater, is breathtaking. We follow a tour guide, a young Asian man who teaches us more about art and architecture in an hour or so than either of us have ever known before. He has an amazing store of knowledge about the place, the people, and the times when the home was built. Kathy and I decide then and there that we will move in and spend the rest of our lives here.

We stay for a couple of hours before heading west again, angling up through Pennsylvania, southwest of Pittsburgh, before turning more directly westward, across the Ohio River at Wheeling and a straight shot across the fairly boring piece of farmland called central Ohio.

We have much more driving ahead of us. Time and geography pass, and by the time we arrive at our hotel, we are both more concerned, as Ted's right leg is now slightly weak. We both should have realized that this symptom, out of the blue, is quite serious. Maybe we do but cannot admit it even to ourselves.

He is a physician; I am a nurse. Denial is a powerful thing. The mind can be a terrible thing to listen to.

At this stage of our lives, though not spring chickens, we are still newlyweds, married for just three years. There are a lot of things I might have expected when he stepped out of that shower stall in the hotel room, but a leg spasm was not one of them.

THE SHERWOODS

We check into our hotel and make it to Allan and Dee's place in time for dinner. I mentioned above that we are on our way to a Sherwood reunion. The group got started in 1956 with a collection of undergraduates affiliated with the Cornell University men's glee club. Generally speaking, in those days we sang with twelve members, equally distributed over the four vocal parts. We sang for fraternity events and for various other public functions. We sang once in Carnegie Hall, and we toured Europe and the Caribbean. We recorded several albums of our music at that time. In the world of a cappella singing, we were well known and admired. As members graduated, other people were taken on through a system of tryouts. The group continued as an active part of Cornell life until the early 1970s. About 25 or 30 years ago, one of the members of the Sherwoods, along with his wife, bought and operated a resort on the shores of Lake Winnipesaukee in New Hampshire. They offered their resort for a week in September for the Sherwoods to come and put on a musical production. We stayed in the cabins at their resort, took most of our meals together, socialized, drank, laughed, ate, told stories, and most of all, made music. The format was that we would rehearse each day toward a performance that was to take place on the upcoming weekend. In different years, the venues of the performances changed. One year the performance might be at the lodge at the resort where we were staying, and the next year we might perform on a stage in town. Most of the music we sang derived from our undergraduate years, although as years went by, we began to experiment with newer and more challenging pieces.

Most of the Sherwoods are married or involved in other serious, long-term relationships. Over the years, our wives and/or partners became a very important part of our gatherings each time we got together. We became intimate friends, not only with the guys with whom we'd shared the college experience so many years before, but with the friends and lovers and spouses who came with them to the reunion gatherings.

For the first few years of these Sherwood "reunions," we gathered in New Hampshire, and in June of every year in Ithaca, New York, for the Cornell University reunions, concluding with a well-attended, well-received performance in the resonant marble entryway to Goldwyn Smith Hall, in the center of the campus.

In later years, we started to branch out and have reunion get-togethers and concerts in other cities around the country. Seattle. Philadelphia. Boston. Other parts of the West Coast. This year we were meeting in the Midwest.

If you are ever invited to dinner at Al and Dee's, you would be well advised not to pass up the experience. They are both as thin as rails, yet they both eat mightily and heartily and well, and with great enjoyment. Allan has been involved for years with a weight-loss program, which, I guess, is how he maintains his trimness. Well, along with his jogging. They both talk about food a lot. A lot! Nearly all the time. But they stay thin. Go figure.

Anyhow, food and good wine and dear friends on a Sunday evening in April, warmth and good cheer, is made the more dear because two of our Sherwood friends have died in the past year. Some things are simply wrong, and that was one of them. Simply wrong.

So here we are gathered, eating and drinking and renewing the friendships. I slide into a place on the couch listening in on lively conversation, sipping some of Allan's good wine, when it happens again: first my right shoulder, then progressively down my right side, jerking, twitching. There is something really frightening about your body doing what you ask it not to do. At first, I try to hide the movements, but one of my friends notices (how could he not?), so I tell him these things have been happening for the past two days, about three or four times now, and I'm not yet sure what is causing it or what to do about it. Peter, also a physician, is quite concerned.

There's a pattern about Sherwood gatherings. Rehearsals begin at 9 a.m., led by our leader, who has the idea that various stretching, bending, and twisting exercises help to open the airways, and he may be right in this, but in any case, that is how we begin. Gradually we add tone exercises, scales, in unison and then in harmonies. After 15 minutes of this, we get into working on a song, usually an old favorite, maybe a Cornell song, "Give My Regards to Davy" or "Strike Up a Song to Cornell" or something, before we move on to something more challenging. We'll keep working for the next four hours or so. In the later parts of rehearsals, we tackle more difficult and newer work, maybe something we've seen only one or two times previously, or not at all. There are breaks, there is laughter, teasing. We all join in the fun, much of the time, but still, the rehearsals are a lot of work. By the time rehearsal is over, around one p.m., everyone is tired and hungry. At that point the group breaks up. One bunch goes off to lunch, the other heads for the golf course. Our leader, I think, goes back to his room and works on music.

At least, that is the typical way that things go. We rehearse that way every day for six days. By the fifth day or so we have hammered together, somehow, a pretty good program of 12 to 15 numbers to perform on stage. They're not perfect, but also not bad, and our audiences are appreciative. It's hard work, yes, but we also have fun with it.

So that's the way things are supposed to go, and they almost always do.

But not this time. Not for me.

MAYBE RABIES, MAYBE NOT

Monday, April 11, 2011
What follows is a very peculiar week. Surreal. Awful. More awful for Kathy than for me.

On Monday morning, our first Sherwood rehearsal is to begin at nine, but I have a seizure, sitting on the john, early in the morning. We decide to take me to the hospital, a solid teaching hospital nearby. I am interviewed by an intern or medical student or resident, someone very young in a white coat. I tell her about the symptoms I have been having and am immediately put in a hospital gown and, over the next several hours, am seen and examined by a succession of medical students, interns, residents, and staff physicians of various kinds.

My husband, ever the patient guy, retells his symptoms and medical history over and over without complaint in the ER, as I try to sleuth my way to a plausible explanation that might hold the word *curable* in its paragraph, doing my best to block out this frightening scene: nurses and doctors in their scrubs, machines beeping, phones ringing, the faded yellow curtain that pulls around the bed but never completely enough to offer privacy, the patient pull-cord hanging off the wall, unattached to Ted's cot, the IV poles in waiting, the white line-embossed paper pillow covers on the crinkly plastic-coated pillows, all visible signs of cold, hard hospital culture. The genuine kindness of the staff doesn't offset the setting.

Until that time, I still am not as concerned about my seizures as I probably should be. Certainly, the professional people who are attending to me in the hospital are concerned. During the course of the day, I have a CT scan, lung and abdominal X-rays, physical examinations, blood tests, and late in the day a lumbar puncture. Then they send me for an MRI of my brain. I have several seizures during that day, all of the same kind as the previous ones. Unfortunately, only one or two of these are witnessed by doctors or other medical people.

Among other tests, a PSA test is run for metastatic prostate cancer, in case the prostate cancer Ted had 10 years earlier has spread. The doctor returns with the results—negative, meaning no sign of spread, and I feel my pulse slow back from rapid to normal, and my subconscious allows my breathing to relax, my shoulders to find their proper resting position.

Among the huge range of explanations is one that involves a hobby of Ted's.

Ted and his brother Rob, an artist, have shared a lifelong interest in animal skulls and bones. They each have a small, interesting collection. It sounds creepy, but think of it as having a two-shelf museum of natural history in your home. By the way, neither of them ever goes out and hunts in order to get these souvenirs.

A few weeks before we left Maine, our wonderful neighbor, Sam, came up the driveway early one morning, just as I was leaving for work, carrying something that turned out to be a dead mink he had found along the road when he was driving the school bus that morning. Sam knows that I collect animal skulls.

This all happens when I am out of the house. Initially, our neighbor suggests putting it in our kitchen freezer. Naturally, I go berserk when I find out Ted considered this for even a moment.

At first, I just pack it in ice in a box in the garage. After a day or so, I locate a taxidermist. He lets me know over the phone that I'll have to get a permit from the state game warden, which I do. Who knew you can't just pick up roadkill? But in Maine you can't legally do that, not even a squirrel or a bunny. After some discussion on the phone, the wildlife authorities decide that I have no criminal intent and that they can send me a permit by mail. It arrives in another day, and on a brisk Friday I drive an hour out into the boonies to find the taxidermist's house and place of business. He gives me the mink's head, but I can tell by feeling it that the skull has been smashed by whatever had hit the thing on the road, so I end up tossing it away anyway.

Ted says I will get a small piece of mink pelt out of it, not something I want or would use. What I don't know, until we are in the ER, is that while at the taxidermist's, Ted had touched the specimen (yuck)—and without putting on gloves (stupid).

Dead minks, apparently, raise the possibility of rabies. Rabies is rare, very rare, in humans, with only a smattering of cases each year in the United States, but rabies is also uniformly lethal, so this possibility generates a lot of excitement among the hospital staff. It is decided that I will have to be prophylactically treated. That treatment consists of four deep intramuscular injections of IgG (gamma globulin) in my thighs, for starters, followed by several more shots, spaced out over the next couple of weeks, of rabies vaccine.

The rabies shots will mean several more stops on the way home, and after getting home. We still have no idea what is going on in Ted's brain, or if the mink incident is related.

And that's when a doctor comes into the room with one of those serious doctor looks on his face, tells us the radiologist has seen my MRI and has immediately called him up, saying she's seen something really "messed up" on my scan, isn't sure just what it is, but it isn't good. He says it's the first time she has ever called him like that, an indication of the depth of her concern. He says I should plan to remain in the hospital for a bit, until they can sort it out. Of course, we quickly agree to the hospitalization, although the news comes as quite a shock.

Sometime during that first evening in the ER, our Sherwood friend Peter (the physician) and his wife, Marcia, call me on my cell phone, then come over to check on Ted—and me, as it turns out. The expression someone would "give you the shirt off their back" must have originated with these people. There is no saying no to them coming over to help in any way they can, as they would prove over and over in the ensuing months, in ways big and small.

The doctors have the kind of look we are to see for months to come, a look I detest, for it always looks like the doctor is saying "I have grave news to tell you" in his or her eyes. And that is exactly what the look means. They can't disguise the information, but why, I often wonder, do they have to look that way and be so blunt with information, even though done with a kind, soft voice? I wish I had a buck for every time a doctor, starting a consult or even a new treatment, says, "I don't have to tell you how serious this is." We know how serious it is. Would it be so terrible to say, "Well, this is how we can treat/track/whatever this kind of illness is" and not look so damned tragic? Each time, that uttered sentence basically translates to, "You are going to die of a dreadful illness, and I can barely look you in the eye because you are a physician and so am I, and we both know this is probably the worst news I can tell you." Of course—and I believe this from the bottom of my heart—each of these people feels terrible about what is going on in Ted's brain. Truly awful. It must be the toughest thing ever for a physician to say to anyone. And there is not a one of them who isn't compassionate and wonderful. I'm just saying it's disheartening to hear from essentially everyone we meet "how serious this is."

"I don't need to tell you how serious this is."

Then don't.

That night, in the ER, before Ted is moved to the medical neurology floor for further workup, Peter takes me aside and strongly suggests I go back to the hotel. There has been some thought that if Ted gets a private room, I can stay with him. I do not want to leave him. He isn't happy about me leaving, either, but Peter and Marcia are both gently twisting my arm, and remind me I need to get rest, which is almost impossible to do in a hospital.

At the time, I am a little annoyed by their not-so-subtle suggestion. Ted and I have not been apart for a single night since long before we married, and it doesn't seem right. We are both scared and upset, although Ted starts agreeing with Peter that I should go back and see him the next morning. It takes a good friend to see things a little objectively and give advice when called for.

It's a tough thing to do. But about an hour later, at close to midnight, I drive back to the hotel, unlock the door to our room, and let myself into the loneliest room in the hotel.

CHAPTER 3

SHHH!

We laughed together, so much. At two in the morning, early on in our relationship, one of us started chuckling about something, which got us both laughing over whatever started it. "Shhh!" the other said, gently, indicating to go back to sleep, thereby inducing more laughter. The "Shhh" joke was one of our favorites, prompting so many times one would hurriedly, competitively say it first after a goodnight kiss. Or just say it aloud while lying together. Our lives, like so many loving mates, included lots of continuous running gags. I had not experienced anything like it before. "This is what happy feels like," we often told each other.

MAYBE HERPES

I do not learn until a day or two later that the doctors, especially the infectious disease specialists, are most concerned that I might have acquired a brain infection from a virus known as herpes simplex, very similar to what causes cold sores. Cold sores are not serious, but a brain infection with the same virus is almost always fatal if not treated very actively. This is the major reason that they want me to remain in the hospital. I am told I must be kept under close watch at least until they get the results back of the viral culture of my spinal fluid, which has been sent to an out-of-state national lab. They estimate it will take three to four days for the culture results to be reported. They administer intravenous (IV) acyclovir, a drug used to treat serious viral infections. Meanwhile, I am also given lorazepam at bedtime to help me sleep, but no other medication at this time. Over the next few days, I am seen by several more specialists and have more medical tests, including an EEG (brain waves), the results of which are apparently normal. I continue to have one or two of my right-sided seizures every day. Kathy stays with me each day I'm in the hospital, and several of my Sherwood friends visit also. Kathy keeps me supplied with mystery novels from a nearby Barnes & Noble. This time is God-awful for both her and me, but in some respects it's harder for her. My denial and anxiety management have generally been more effective than hers, and anyway, I do not have to deal with the possibility of losing my dear spouse, with all the terror and grief that brings. Somehow the possibility of dying seems easier to take than losing a wife or a husband.

There is one other contender for diagnosis. The chief of neurology seems particularly taken with the possibility that I might have Creutzfeldt-Jakob disease, or CJD. He points out several times that this disease is often characterized by myoclonic jerking, which is one way to characterize the symptoms I am having. In addition to twitching and jerking muscles, CJD causes very rapid mental deterioration, loss of memory, personality changes, loss of the ability to speak, seizures, and death, usually within six months or so. There is no known treatment. CJD is essentially the same as Mad Cow Disease. The neurologist does not seem deterred by the fact that, aside from the jerking muscles, I do not have any of the other hallmarks of CJD. He mentions the possibility of this disease in a kind of abstract, off-the-cuff, intellectual sort of way that leaves me feeling pretty much uncared about, and terrified. I think that most physicians, who spend so much of their lives dealing with illness and death, must have particular diseases that they fear more than others. For me, CJD is the most dreaded. This neurologist is simply running down what doctors call a "differential diagnosis," which is a listing of possible diagnoses to account for the signs and symptoms afflicting the patient he/she is treating. Unfortunately, his patient in this case is also a physician whose wife is a nurse, so his dispassionate recitation of his thoughts is disturbing and downright terrifying, even though he concludes that CJD is unlikely.

In retrospect, it is interesting that more consideration is not given to the possibility of a brain tumor. I am, at one point, seen by a neurosurgeon on the staff and by a nurse practitioner who also works with the neurosurgery service. They review my scans and other lab tests and conclude with great assurance that I do not have cancer. I remember being taught when I was in medical school that any new onset of seizures in an adult is a sign of a primary brain tumor until proven otherwise. So I am both surprised and greatly relieved to hear from the neurosurgery service that this is not among their considerations for me.

When Ted tells me about the doctor's concern regarding CJD, I see he is trying his best to be calm. But I can see how anxious he is. I do my best to reassure him. There is a lot of denial going on these days.

The next couple of days move along, with me staying at the hotel at night, connecting briefly with our friends, and clinging to Ted by day, as much as one can cling in a hospital room. Phone calls to relatives are the norm, prayers abundant, tears plentiful. We are scared. Ted's condition does not seem any worse. Maybe this is what keeps us from completely crumbling. That, and the fact that we have never been in a hospital filled (with the exception being an occasional doctor) with such an overtly caring staff. They are, with little exception, wonderful. Even the housekeeping staff stops in daily to make sure everything is satisfactory.

One day, looking for the cafeteria, I find myself at an intersection of hallways. An orderly stops to ask if I need help. I recognize him as the young man who transported Ted two days earlier from the ER to Radiology for his brain imaging tests. Now, I tell him I am looking for the cafeteria, and he gives me a look of pity.

"You want to eat in the cafeteria?" he asks, sporting a frown.

"Yes. Why?"

"Well, there's much better food nearby," he says.

I ask him to point me in the right direction.

"I'll take you," he says, and he walks me down one corridor after another after another, to the hospital entrance, *outside* and down a short street until we are at the corner. He points across the intersection. I'm blown away at the extent of his kindness.

Meanwhile, my seizures are happening several times a day. Most of them don't last very long and don't cause me any particular distress, other than some temporary anxiety until I sense they are winding down. In all other ways, I feel perfectly normal and healthy. At the end of each day, I have to persuade Kathy to go back to the hotel and get some sleep. The nurses are great, with one or two exceptions. Overall, it is, like most hospital stays, a pretty boring experience for me.

Ted's first roommate is discharged, and a new one appears soon after. He and his female companion are very loud and constantly bickering. We hear every snipe through the thin curtain. I find the nurse and ask if there is any way Ted can be moved to another room, and I tell her why. I'm concerned Ted won't be able to sleep at night. In ten minutes, a team of nurses are in the room, moving him out and down the hallway to a private room. Just like that. Done.

An orderly walked me outside; a nurse made a peaceful place for Ted. And I am now becoming more conscious of the way little things matter.

At one point during the first couple of days in the hospital, Kathy rounds up a Catholic chaplain and brings him to my room. Kathy is very devout in her Catholic faith. I would have to describe myself as something more of an agnostic. The priest is a gentle and intelligent and sensitive man. After he has gathered a sense of what is happening with me and with us, he asks me if I would be interested in having a blessing from him. He tells me that he would like to offer me a ritual called "the Sacrament of Anointing of the Sick." This catches me by surprise, but I tell him that, yes, I would like that. I'm not sure I can remember all that he and I and Kathy discuss, but ultimately, he places some oil or holy water on my forehead and says some prayers. I do not learn until later, after he has left, that the ritual he has visited on me was what used to be known as the "Last Rites" or "Extreme Unction." My vision of the Last Rites is one in which a parishioner very near to death, lying in bed, is prayed over by a priest as a final benediction before dying.

After the Anointing of the Sick is done, and despite Ted realizing that it used to be called Last Rites, he seems calmed and moved by the experience.

The priest also leaves a written sheet with prayers on it, which I cherish and use so often and for so long that it becomes worn in the creases. In time, and in times to come, Ted asks me to read them aloud at night when we are in bed.

In the days that follow, I go to a nearby Catholic church where Father is, so I can attend mass, and afterwards I join a small group to recite the rosary, something others do routinely. I find it extremely comforting…and unnerving, because I am a convert to Catholicism and don't have the order of the rosary in memory yet. At one point, one of the others nods to me to take a turn. I mumble something to indicate I have no idea what to do next. We move on to the next person, and it's OK. Faith is, after all, a process. I'd baby-stepped around my faith for decades before finding what feels like home.

Late Wednesday afternoon, a neurology resident, a young woman, brings bad news. They have been expecting all day that my culture results would come in from the lab, but they have just received word that it is going to be tomorrow, not today. Kathy and I have been expecting me to be discharged that evening. The news is crushing. It means another night of uncertainty. It also means another night when Kathy and I will be separated. Sometime in the middle of the evening, we agree it is time for her to go back to the motel, although our parting is intensely sad and difficult. We both have tears. Somewhere around mid-evening she leaves, and I watch from my seventh-floor window as she makes her way, walking alone under the streetlamps, to the parking lot.

I am beyond exhausted. I know that the minute I hit the bed, I'll be out cold. I see him watching me from his window as I go to the parking garage, and I wave and throw kisses, hoping to give him a chuckle.

After a bit of time, I see her car come out onto the street, make the left turn at the corner and slowly disappear.

And that is exactly the moment that a different neurology resident shows up to tell me that lo! the culture results have just come in after all, and they are negative for herpes. I can go home now, if I choose, or I can stay the night and go in the morning. Are you kidding?!!!!!!!!

OOOPS. I'm leaving out one critical part of the narrative. In between Kathy's leaving and the good news from the other resident, the night nurse has slipped me my nighttime lorazepam. My sleeping pill.

The hospital telephones are not equipped to make long-distance calls, and the cell phone Kathy carries has a 207 area code, for Maine, so I initially have no way to call her to tell the good news. At the time, I have no cell phone of my own. I have always hated telephones of all kinds, and cell phones in particular. I have been known to maintain to my friends that in my estimation, civilization ended with the invention of the telephone. So it is ironic that here I am, scrabbling around on a Wednesday evening, looking for some way to get in touch with my sweet wife to tell her to come rescue me from this hospital. One of the nurses comes to my rescue, loaning me her cell phone to call Kathy. The nurse and I get me ready: IVs out, into real clothes, all that. I am wobbly from the lorazepam, and the nurse really wants to get me a wheelchair, but I am pretty insistent that I am going to walk out under my own power. Surprisingly, she yields to that and comes along with me on the elevator and across the lobby until she can turn me over to the next shift, waiting at the curb in her Honda Element with the Maine plates.

I get to the hotel just in time to get Ted's call. I have a quick diet soda to pump a little caffeine into my system, refusing multiple offers from our friends to accompany me or pick Ted up instead of driving there myself. I can be stubborn. I head back, reassuring our friends I am "fine" to pick him up at that hour.

I'm not fine. I am barely OK to drive, I am so exhausted—the kind of tired that makes the road lights fuzzy, the kind of tired that stings your eyes to keep them open, the kind of tired that makes objects on the side of the road look like they are starting to move. I have no business driving. But I'm ultra-careful, and the caffeine kicks in just enough. I drive those few miles and get back to find a slightly loopy Ted waiting with the nurse in the lobby.

Rescued!

It's wonderful to have him next to me, and we're both starting to feel some relief. After all, if it were something serious, they wouldn't have discharged him, right?

And tucked away in my purse is a paper of prayers that would remain close at hand for years to come.

Back at the hotel I find a group of our friends sitting around, sharing beers and laughs. The only advice I have been given on leaving the hospital, by the various doctors and nurses, is that I should return to Maine and consult my primary care physician. That is the obvious thing to do. In the meantime, however, there are the Sherwoods, the music, and the concert.

For the next few days, Ted participates in Sherwood rehearsals and performances quite well. We both worry that he might have a seizure during a performance, but he continues the week as best he can. We'd missed many of their planned activities, such as museums and similar outings. But we make it to the ice cream trip with our friends. Mocha chip for me and black raspberry chocolate chip for Ted—good memories we will carry with us, turning the trip just a little bit sweeter. Calories don't matter. Ted is out of the hospital, and we have reason to celebrate. During the week, our friends also ceremoniously present Ted with a T-shirt from a museum tour we'd missed out on. The Sherwoods—"men in green"—still sing beautifully in multi-harmony. And they all look pretty sharp in their performance outfits, which include the classic green Sherwood jackets.

We intermittently get phone calls from the hospital doctors as test results start coming in. So far everything is negative. There are many tests the results of which won't be in for some time. We know eventually he'll have to see a neurologist for follow-up, once we get home.

I am still having seizures a couple of times a day, partially controlled by a low dose of lorazepam. On Thursday morning, I get up as usual and go to rehearsal. That evening we sing a few numbers for a fried chicken dinner. A group of young singers from a local college also perform.

On Saturday evening, we have the stage at a local community center for our full performance. We do a good job. Correction: We do a *wonderful* job. The group from the other college also gives a great performance on stage and are quite wonderful.

The seizures continue, low level, but not during his performances on stage, and we feel more and more certain there will be some explanation, and we are very relieved to hear it isn't a brain tumor. In fact, I now have another idea.

Meanwhile, we take in the hugs, laughs, and warmth of our dear friends.

CHAPTER 4

CALLING ALL POSSIBILITIES

Ted comes from a large family. His father died in his 60s of a heart attack, following many years of serious health problems. He'd been standing in line at Sears in the tool department, his favorite place, buying yet another screwdriver for his tool collection, when he collapsed. Ted's mom, as of this initial accounting of our story, is 97 and probably in better shape than most women half her age. A natural athlete, and active in sports all her life, she has, simply put, great genes. Ted has two sisters and two brothers, all in pretty good health at the time of this writing.

I got to thinking about an old family story. Apparently, Ted had had a life-threatening illness when he was a tot: scarlet fever, which is caused by the strep bacterium. Today, it is usually taken care of easily with antibiotics. But when young Ted got it, it was during WWII. All the antibiotics available back then were diverted to the troops. My mother-in-law had to watch her little boy suffer with this illness, with its high fevers, and hear the doctor tell her he might not make it. But he did.

Now, my mind starts racing. I'm good at that when I'm anxious.

You see, Ted's friend Bob (introduced previously by Ted) had polio as a child, and as he got into his later years, developed post-polio syndrome, which increased certain symptoms. Now I'm wondering…is it possible that there can be a post-*scarlet fever syndrome* that causes neurological symptoms? It's an illness that can sometimes affect the nervous system, among other parts of the body. Perhaps it can cause symptoms later? I am giddy with the thought that, quite possibly, I am on to something.

Perhaps I should say that subconsciously I hope and pray that we will find out it is a benign condition related to his childhood scarlet fever. I excitedly tell our friends about my theory. At a follow-up appointment, I even tell one of the doctors, who thoughtfully wonders aloud at the possibility. That would sure wrap things up nicely. A little seizure activity we could deal with. A life-threatening illness? I'll pass on that, thanks.

And once again, I unfold the paper of prayers before I go to sleep.

Our sojourn with the Sherwoods comes to a close. My birthday is on the Sunday we are slated to leave. As a birthday activity on the trip back, I want to visit a toy museum I've read about. Routing ourselves there, in a small town, we find the best and seemingly only place to have a birthday lunch is Tim Horton's. But I don't care. I am so happy Ted and I are together, and so relieved that the most serious of possible medical illnesses have been vanquished.

We make it to the museum and enjoy our time there despite a well-meaning tour guide who doesn't get our hints that we are happy to explore on our own for a while. Every time we escape to the next room, she's at our side in seconds, giving us lots to quietly giggle about. We realize too late that we could have chosen an "independent" tour option.

Sometimes, the wrong choice provides more laughs.

On Monday the eighteenth we spend the night in a B&B in western Pennsylvania. That is a peculiar experience. We arrive at the B&B in the late afternoon and find the door unlocked and no one around. There is a note that says we can call a certain telephone number, and someone will come to get us checked in. When we call the number, however, no one is available to greet us in person, and indeed no one comes for about a half hour.

"Have some cookies while you wait," the woman on the phone says. We find the fresh chocolate chip cookies, eat, wait, eat, and wait some more.

The place is owned by a married couple, middle-aged, who do not seem to be at all interested in running a B&B. It is a nice enough establishment, warm and comfortable. We drive down to the place where we had spent the night before we went to Fallingwater and have dinner at their excellent restaurant. Sleep comes easily after a long day of driving. Around four o'clock in the morning, I am awake and decide to get up and read in the room next to ours, a small library. It is quite cold in the house, so I wrap myself in a small blanket in the reading room and have a seizure while sitting there in the chair. I go back to bed after a while. There are no more seizures that day. After a pretty good home-style breakfast at the B&B, we drive across Pennsylvania to the Philadelphia area.

A side trip is arranged by Peter and Marcia, to get Ted's next rabies booster at a nearby hospital near their home.

Peter assures me that I can be in and out of the hospital in a very short while, so it will not delay our trip. As it turns out, we spend more than two hours getting that single injection. Finally, at the end of a very exhausting day, we are able to get to my son Randey's in New Jersey, arriving around eight p.m., very tired and very hungry. I have a seizure in their house very soon after arriving.

The next morning, I get up around 5:30 a.m. and find Randey downstairs. We sit and talk and have coffee. The house is a bit cold, in the mid-60s, the way they like to keep it, and I am chilly but say nothing, although I should have. Predictably, I have a seizure after an hour or so, sitting with Randey in his living room. Later, I do not shower or clean up much, but rather decide we will just have breakfast with Randey and his wife Maryellen at a nearby restaurant, then drive straight home to Maine. After breakfast, saying goodbyes in the parking lot, a very icy wind is blowing, and I have another seizure standing there.

We climb in the car and head for home to pick up the dog from the kennel and get back to normal. And set up a doctor's appointment.

Reinforced by love and pancakes, we hit the road.

CHAPTER 5

LOTS OF SHAKIN' GOING ON

Wednesday, back home in Maine
4/20/11

Looking back, it is still a little amazing to me that my powers of denial have remained so strong. I still do not give much importance to this odd, weird new thing that is happening to my body. My concept is that we will return home and life will go on in a fairly normal way. I will return to my work and continue until my chosen date of retirement, July 28th. I know that I require more medical investigation to figure out a good diagnosis, but at this point of our return to Maine I am not thinking that anything terribly serious is happening. On our first full day home, I go to work at the clinic, just exactly as I had before we left on our trip. I have no seizures all day. I feel I have to tell a few key people about what has been going on, and I do so, telling the clinic directors and a few others about the seizures.

I wonder if the doctors have all made a terrible mistake. This fantasy is reinforced by a weird event: When we return to Maine after the out-of-state hospital admission, we send for Ted's X-rays. When they arrive, Ted puts them into his computer to look at them. He can find nothing that looks like the initial studies he'd been shown. Then we notice that the name in the top corner of the X-ray is the same as his, but the date of birth is different. He calls the hospital immediately, and they apologize for sending the wrong ones. While we wait for the correct ones to arrive, oh, how I pray that they have mixed up the studies in the hospital and maybe, just maybe Ted's brain is, in fact, healthy.

On 4/21 and the next several days, I have a daily seizure or two. I have something of an aura with one of them. Otherwise, things are uneventful. I continue to work half days.

On the 27th, I get home around 5:30 or 6:00, go for a run, which feels good, then stop to talk with Sam in front of his house for a bit. Kathy comes by and expresses concern that I might be chilled. She is, of course, worried that a chill might precipitate a seizure, but although I am beginning to chill a little, I have no sense that a seizure is in the offing. Nonetheless, I walk up to our house with her. It is far from the last time I have to learn to pay attention to her good judgment, as opposed to my usual false bravado. Sure enough, I have a seizure in the kitchen, affecting my right shoulder and hip, lasting for a minute or two, then it is gone without a trace.

The same thing happens after I go for a run the next day. It strikes me in the kitchen as I am cooling off.

So far it seems that my seizures are precipitated by exercise (running, yard work) or by being chilled. Some of them, however, come out of nowhere, without warning. They have all been pretty mild, involving only the right side of my body, mostly the lower right leg.

DR. EMERY

Dr. Emery, our internist, listens to Ted's saga and looks over the records.

"You need to see a neurologist," he says, and of course we nod, knowing that would be the next step.

None of us skips a beat.

"Boston."

It seems obvious that the best course is for me to go to Massachusetts General Hospital or the Dana-Farber Cancer Center, as I've already undergone a thorough inpatient evaluation at a major academic medical center. Consequently, I make an appointment at Mass General in the Epilepsy Clinic. The appointment is for May 16th, two weeks down the line. Just a week and a day before my 71st birthday.

Dr. Emery's office sends the request for this next step over to insurance for Ted. In the new world of complicated insurance, we are grateful for our wonderful Dr. Emery—for his caring, concern, and expertise in this and all situations we've encountered. In Maine, we call this kind of person "good people." Our Dr. Emery is good people.

THE MYSTERY CONTINUES

4/29/11
Early morning (5:15 a.m.). I get out of bed, pee, get out of my damp T-shirt and put on a Capilene shirt and sweatshirt and sweatpants, carry the dog downstairs, and put him out the front door. I am feeling chilled and a bit sweaty. There is some tightness in the middle of my back on the right side, then in my hip, like a mild cramp. That lasts 5–10 seconds, then the clonic jerking begins: hip, abdominal muscles, not so much the shoulder, but some. I try to relax, be calm. With difficulty, I make my way with the dog into the laundry room and get him fed, while the seizure continues. Overall, it seems to be less intense and briefer than some, and the aftereffects on my walking and arm use are less intense, but for an hour or so afterward, I keep feeling like it can come again at any moment.

Saturday, April 30, 2011
I wake up feeling good. About 9:00 I go out for a run, but I have a seizure about a half mile out. It is fairly brief and not profound. There is some discoordination affecting my right leg for a while afterward, but then I am able to continue my run. I complete about 1½ miles with no further problem. I have taken 0.5 mg lorazepam early in the morning, in an attempt to prevent both seizures and anxiety.

Thursday, May 5, 2011
I've had no seizures since last Saturday. Although I am anxious about it, I decide to chance it and go for an early morning run. That precipitates a seizure after about a quarter mile or so. It is a chilly morning. The seizure is a typical one. I walk back home, after waiting five minutes or so to allow my right leg to come back online.

Note: I've been taking lorazepam 0.5 mg bid (twice daily) for the past week but cut back to 0.25 mg for the past two doses, beginning yesterday morning. I don't know why I decreased the dose. Basically, I just don't like to take medicine. No, that's disingenuous. What I don't like is facing the reality that something is going very wrong with my brain and body. There is something very disturbing about having parts of your body take on a mind of their own.

On Friday, May 6th, I mow the lawn, which, even with a self-propelled gasoline-fueled engine, is moderately hard work for me on a hot day. Immediately after finishing the lawn, I have the worst seizure yet, by far. It involves my entire right leg in maximal extension, including my foot in maximal plantar extension, almost painful, followed by erratic jerking movements for perhaps several long minutes. I cannot be certain there is not some minimal involvement of my left leg, but this may have been just reflexive. Arm and shoulder involvement, if any, is minimal. The power of the thing is enormous, it seems to me, an order of magnitude stronger than anything I have ever experienced to that point. After the seizure subsides, my right leg is completely paralyzed for another couple of minutes, from hip to toes. I have no sensory changes, but I absolutely cannot move any part of my right side from the hip down. Very gradually I regain use of the leg. I am fairly panicky. There's a lot of commotion around me, it seems. Sam, our wonderful neighbor, comes over, and Kathy is there. She brings me a tablet of lorazepam, 0.5 mg, a pretty low dose but hopefully enough to settle my body down a bit. I take a shower, cautiously, and we go to the ER for evaluation. After some while, the lorazepam kicks in and I feel more normal. The ER's recommendation: Continue lorazepam, try to move up the date to see the neurologist at MGH. They also offer local neurology services.

Another long day. Kindness from our neighbor.

By this time, with the seizures occurring a couple of times each day on most days, we have both gotten used to them. They are still disturbing, but less so, and neither of us harbors any dire suspicions about their origin. One might think we'd be more alarmed at the possibilities of serious illness. But somehow, we aren't. I'm even looking forward to the upcoming appointment at MGH to sort things out.

025 # PART 2

CHAPTER 6

BOSTON

May 16, 2011

For the past couple of weeks, I've been aware that I'm kind of weak when I'm sitting down and try to lift my right leg off the floor straight out in front of me. I have not had any real seizures in the past two days. I continue the lorazepam as prescribed. My last dose was at 6 a.m. This morning we will be driving to MGH (Massachusetts General Hospital) in Boston for my appointment at their Epilepsy Clinic. Maybe we can at last get to the bottom of this.

I've packed a small overnight bag with some basics in it, just in case they want to run some tests and we need to stay overnight somewhere. Ted reluctantly takes a few items, as well.

The drive from Maine to Boston is uneventful, except for the crazily hectic, confusing area around the hospital and various medical buildings where we need to park. There is not one, but several parking garages and multiple huge buildings. I grew up near NYC, yet here I find myself feeling a little overwhelmed.

We make our way to the Epilepsy Clinic, hand in the paperwork, receive more paperwork, and after a brief wait, we are called to see the doctor.

It's a Monday afternoon. I've brought with me all my medical records from the initial out-of-state workup, including CD versions of the various scans that have been done, and I present them to the resident whom I see first. At first, he seems unsure of what to make of them. He does not appear overly concerned, however, which to me offers some degree of reassurance.

A big YAY goes through my mind.

After looking at my scans, he wants to consult with a more senior doctor. That doctor, however, takes a look at the records and the CTs and MRIs and almost immediately says that he wants me to be hospitalized that afternoon for further studies. He is quite insistent about it.

"You have to go into the hospital. These are tumors," the doctor says, in a thick Irish accent.

No hesitancy, no question. Emergency admission.

The look on the doctor's face is alarming. It may seem odd, after all we had been through, but this is the first moment I let myself realize that I am seriously ill.

We are stunned. I cannot remember the conversation that follows. I only know that I want to run.

LIAR!! LIAR!! We're leaving and we're never coming back to you, you bad, bad doctor!!! screams my child-heart's internal voice. My pulse is racing. My mouth is dry. I am sweating. For the briefest of moments, my grown-up mind tells me maybe it will be OK after all, but the reprieve is only seconds long.

My stomach is churning. My mouth has that bad anxiety taste. It cannot be something bad. I won't allow it. Please, God, let me turn back the clock to yesterday, when this all felt like an adventure in curiosity. How can this be happening?

Every cell of me screams. And yet I sit, just where I am supposed to sit, on the plastic clinic chair, tears filling eyes, wishing to be anywhere but here. Aching for us to be back in our idyllic world of complaints about work and annoyances about long restaurant waits. I claw, desperately, to retrieve the comfort of denial.

Deep down inside, I know this is very, very bad. And as kind as everyone is being to us, every step of the way, it does not change the feeling of doom.

MGH ADMISSION

Kathy and I agree to the hospitalization, of course, and here begins one of the more awful and surreal and frightening weeks of our lives.

Ted and I walk over to Admitting, and I leave him in capable hands while I tend to other essentials.

I go to the car to get his bag, find out about overnight parking, and where I can stay, somewhere close to the hospital. It all happens very fast, and in this huge environment, I am so lost. There is an information desk with wonderful, knowledgeable people. And I soon discover that if I stand pretty much anywhere in the swiftly moving cacophony of people in this virtual city of a hospital, trying to figure out where I am or which turn to take, someone will come along and ask if I need help. Some are uniformed, others look as lost as I feel, some are being pushed in wheelchairs, and some are chatting and snacking as they move, all intersecting in a mighty bustle of this indoor perfect storm.

The scared, tiny child within doesn't go away easily, but I feel compelled to act with some amount of dignity, at least some of the time. To do otherwise is to fall completely apart. This is possibly the corniest thing I have ever said: I have to be strong for Ted. At least to his face. I cannot fall to pieces, not now, at least not the way I fear, and end up in a mental hospital at a time when he needs me. But there are times when I think this will, in fact, happen. That's how awful and how crazy I feel. Wishful thinking...that I could go to an emotional place of unreality and skip over what is coming.

> **THAT LOOK**
>
> Soon after we started dating, Ted joined our small but enthusiastic contemporary Catholic church song group. A few years into the experience, the group was going strong, with occasional special "appearances" in Maine. I don't know that Ted and I planned it—maybe we did, in a way—but after a while we started to give each other something of a playful look while singing and harmonizing. A little sexy. Yeah. I know we were in church, but we loved singing together, and he was 100% into it.

Somehow—and I don't even know how—I manage to get a hotel room across the street at the (former, as I edit this) Holiday Inn, where the angels of Heaven have blessed the staff with the gift of "love thy neighbor." They are so phenomenal, so truly exceptional, that in every single revision and editing of this manuscript, I break down and weep at this part.

Every single person who works there is living, walking proof of the Holy Spirit.

After checking into the hotel, getting our overnight bags, and getting the car secured again, I call the kennel about keeping the dog longer. I notify our close friends and relatives of what is happening.

My younger daughter, Sally, living in Brooklyn, NY, says she is coming up, that she will be there the next day.

Randey and Maryellen make plans to come to Boston from the Philadelphia area.

My older daughter, Cassie, who lives in North Carolina with her husband, Paul, and the children, also volunteers. Nearly everyone I talk to in the ensuing hours and days is willing and ready to drop everything for us and do whatever is needed to ease our distress. It is overwhelming and humbling. The Holy Spirit is not just breathing on us; it is infusing itself into us. I sometimes wonder if these people in our lives know how important, how holy they truly are.

After getting settled into the hotel, I go across the street to find Ted in his room, in the older part of the hospital, the Neurology floor, a locked unit requiring a buzzer for entrance. He is in a double room with a middle-aged man who is not doing well, who is emotionally upset post-surgery and beginning treatment for his illness. Ted has the window bed, so I walk by his roommate every time I go in or out of the room, with only the standard thin hospital curtain separating us. Nothing is secret.

Ted's nurses and doctors, all wonderfully caring and gentle, bring updates of high-tech tests being ordered, scheduled in a predetermined sequence, alarming to us. Yet this is what is needed in order to find out exactly what is wrong and get him treated. But right now, in the thick of it? I want nothing more than "out."

These people know what they are doing with tests, and test they do. Each one brings us closer to an exact diagnosis of what those tumors are all about. Treatment options aren't even part of the dialogue at this point. Test. Wait. Another test. Wait. Repeat. Expert care, but oh, how frightened we are.

The neurology section of the hospital itself can be quite upsetting at times, due to the nature of the complex illnesses of the patients. The patient in the bed next to Ted is agitated and distressed, and his wife is upset because he is not cooperating with the discharge plan and treatment. She has her hands full. From another room, a female in her early 20s rhythmically screams out from her medically related nightmare of some sort, adding to the horror of the atmosphere, reflecting my internal agony.

In our moments together, between the frequent visits from medical staff, Ted and I discuss what is going on, reality-checking our understanding, both plunged into our personal black hole of terror.

I stay with Ted late into the evening that first day. I don't remember eating. We snuggle in his starchy single hospital bed, not caring if that's permissible. No one seems to mind. We hug each other, weep in fear, and give brave reassurances, until we both realize that I need to go back to the hotel, that he needs to sleep, and so I leave. We cry together some more. We don't want to part. It breaks my heart to leave him, but eventually, I take yet another lonely walk back to a bed where my Ted will not be.

I am kept semi-sane by calls with our people, and the knowledge that the best help—love—is on the way.

CHAPTER 7

THROWN INTO THE STORM

What appears here to be a chronological account of my entry into what the writer Christopher Hitchens, writing about his own cancer, called "Tumorville," is in fact an assemblage of bits and pieces of writing which I put together after the fact. I have tried in this to be as accurate as I can in recording not only the events, but also the feelings and emotions that went with them.

I am hospitalized at MGH late on a Monday afternoon in May. My medicines are changed, and I am given something new and specific for seizures, to replace the lorazepam. I don't know whether it is that medication or something else, but within a couple of days I am almost completely unable to walk. The hospital gives me a walker with which I can manage to stay upright, but only with great difficulty. I feel like a marionette with loose strings. Physical therapy is brought in to try to help me, but this is of limited success. Most of the time I stay in bed.

Kathy and I, of course, are terrified. Our lives have changed so radically within only a couple of days. Doctors and nurses and various sorts of medical technologists are in and out of my room in a nearly continuous stream of white coats. My physical condition has deteriorated dramatically since I entered the hospital, and no one offers any explanation for this. Just one month ago, I was completely healthy and active. I was used to running several miles at a time, several times a week. I was looking forward to getting my kayak out in Casco Bay for the summer. Then the seizures started in my right leg, and now I am essentially a bedridden invalid. Everything has happened so fast, there is no way for us to catch our breaths.

The days this week seem to blend together. Each day brings more tests, tests that are subspecialties of other tests, tests I've never heard of and still can't recall names of. I struggle to navigate this enormous hospital. I eventually find the cafeteria and a snack bar that has freshly made sandwiches. I discover a couple of nearby restaurants, which enables me to bring in food for Ted that's a little more exciting than hospital standard fare. I find a Verizon store and buy him a cheap cell phone so we can talk to each other after hours and so he can call family and friends at will. Now, a cell phone seems to him like a good idea to keep in touch with the outside world.

Despite the wonderful (and yes, discounted) hotel accommodations, I am somewhat concerned about money at this point, so I look into a lower cost housing setup a few very steep blocks away. It's quite a trick to get in touch with the people who run the place, and I trek from one block to another, all uphill, until I find it. I wait for the manager, and after a long wait, someone else helps me, with warm apologies. In spite of the fact that it would be a significant savings (we have no idea how long Ted will be in the hospital at this point), I go with my gut: I'm already settled into the Holiday Inn, the staff is amazing in every way, and it is just across the street from the hospital. I need to be able to look out my hotel window and at least see the building that houses my husband. Now, I start walking back to the hospital, and pull out my cell phone to call our internist back home. Later, I won't even remember why I called because the week is such a blur, but it may have been to renew one of my own medications. Walking downhill toward the hospital, I am overcome with tears as I tell the nurse that I'm not in Maine, and I share briefly what's going on with Ted, to update our doctor. Here I am, heading back to see Ted, walking downhill on a sidewalk in Boston, outright sobbing and trying to retain some semblance of control. The nurse on the phone is so kind and supportive…a woman who knows what to say to a distraught person on the other end of the line. It does not feel like a business call any longer; it's as though I am talking to a close friend. It's weird to be taking care of business and erupt into tears, my new unwanted companion.

I wonder if that phone nurse has any idea how much of a difference she has made.

My memory for this week is very hazy.

The week, for me, proceeds with lots and lots of lab tests and MRIs and CT scans. Randey and Maryellen and Sally and Kathy are all very attentive and very loving, despite their fears and apprehensions. Kathy describes this as one of the worst weeks of her life. I can well believe that it is worse for her than it is for me, because I am kept busy with all the medical investigations. But I also feel so depleted and tired and scared and am having so much trouble moving my body around that I am preoccupied with that as well.

At some point, the medicine I am being given for seizures is changed to a drug called Keppra. That works a lot better for controlling my seizures and has fewer side effects than what I had been given before, so that gradually I learn how to walk all over again. Still, it's a miserable week. Somewhere along the way, it is discovered that I have a thyroid nodule, so now that has to be investigated as well. I am frightened and sad and anxious. Even now, it fills me with fear and grief to write this, and tears come to my eyes several times a day unless I force myself not to think about what is happening.

ARE WE WORRIED?

I walk into Ted's tiny shared hospital room to see the back of a doctor sitting on the end of the bed, talking to Ted in a low voice. When I join them, the doctor is explaining the findings of the latest test. He is a very kind, pleasant man. It's hard to imagine anything but goodness coming from him.

I catch the end of his sentence. It contains words that sound an alarm to me, although I cannot hold onto what they are. I rush forward, toward Ted's hospital bed, where Ted is wearing the standard issue hospital gown, and where the doctor sits, at the foot of the bed, facing him. They both turn to me.

"Are we worried?" I ask the doctor, in front of Ted, fully expecting him to say, "Oh, no. Nothing a round of antibiotics can't treat."

"Yes," he looks at me with incredible kindness but a most serious intent, "we are worried." Talk about your shock and awe.

No, no, no, no! my brain shouts. But my words are more mellow, as I ask what is going on.

The doctor gives me the bad news: All the tests conclusively show that Ted has a serious type of brain tumor. How aggressive it is, and the exact nature of it, we do not yet know for certain, but the doctors all agree it is looking like the worst possible type. He will need a brain biopsy to confirm the exact diagnosis.

My brain goes on internal crazy mode.

Even the kindest of physicians cannot make this all go away. But...his compassion, in every expression he reveals, and all his words, envelop us in grace.

The week is a nightmare for both of us. My daughter Sally has taken an immediate leave from her job in New York as a special education teacher to come stay with me in Boston. Here is my truth, looking back: I don't know how I would have gotten through the week without her.

I am a mess, yet I must be, as best as I can, a rock and comfort to Ted, who is also a mess. He and I are reduced to a couple of four-year-olds, emotionally. We cry on each other, we hug, I run around the city of Boston to buy distractions to make him more comfortable—books, things like that, the very tasks also providing a distraction for me as well. I can't eat, which is just ridiculous for me—me, who never, ever loses her appetite. I'm going all day, forcing myself to make a pretense of eating now and then. Sally is essentially mothering me. She is at my side, coaching me through the day. She and I sleep in a king-size bed together at the hotel.

One morning, very early, I hear her saying, "Mom? Mom?" and gently waking me. As I come to, I hear moaning. It is coming from my own throat—a fearful, anxious, heartbroken sound that has awakened her. After a minute, awake and crying, I realize I had subconsciously reached into a place where deep sadness and impending doom merged in my sleep.

I am exhausted, hungry, stressed, and frightened out of my mind. Ted and I are both confused. Some of the medications Ted needs to take probably account for his confusion. For me, it's a different kind of confusion that evolves, probably a profound stress response of some kind. My preoccupation with his illness takes over as my new baseline; everything done, said, thought, links with the new awareness of Ted being ill. It's overwhelming. I am constantly getting lost in the hospital, and emotionally, I am all over the place, too. The person I have come to rely on—Ted—is now fairly helpless, lying in a hospital bed, being pumped with medications to get his seizures under control, still having trouble walking well. The switch to a different medication has improved his functioning somewhat. But it will be days before the original medication works its way out of his system. Meanwhile, I feel a combination of under- and over-caffeinated, like what it felt like when I worked the night shift at one of our local hospitals decades ago. We're quite a pair.

Do our children have any sense at all how they have comforted us? The expanse of their love and caring is beyond description.

FATHER JOHN

This week, a wonderful priest, Father John, comes in to talk with us. I have requested this, recalling how helpful it was to both of us at the first hospital, weeks ago, when the priest came to Ted's room. Father John suggests we go down the hallway with him to a visitor's area, away from the semiprivate room and its innate lack of privacy.

We talk and tell him our story. He listens. Ted and I both cry at times. Ted talks about his growing-up years in relation to church and religion. He says that in recent months, he's been hearing hymns in his head (he grew up Presbyterian). Then, he says that although he has no answers spiritually, and doesn't really know what he believes, but one thing he is sure of is that when he and I eventually leave this world, he wants to be with me forever.

Ted and I have already talked about going through a formal process of annulment of previous marriages to get our marriage blessed in the Catholic Church. When we got married, it was performed by a minister, so previous marriages had not been an issue. Annulment in the Catholic Church involves seemingly endless paperwork on both our parts and that of the church personnel. Father John suggests that when we get back home and can, we talk to our priest to get help in processing this as soon as possible. What surprises me is how ardent and adamant Ted is in this conversation. Prior to his hospitalization and illness, any time Ted and I have talked in intellectual terms about death, he's seemed very much at peace with the concept of being just a blip in the universe, a small thread of a human passage in time, with little concern for what comes after death. Now this feels different. Urgent.

After more than an hour of talking with the priest, we stand up. The priest says he is impressed with how much Ted and I love each other, that it's beautiful to witness. He gives us long, gentle hugs, holding us. Perhaps he is saying prayers over us. We will never forget his warmth and kindness.

Afterwards, I ask Father John for the sacrament of reconciliation for myself. I go to the chapel with him, and we sit at the back, off to the side for privacy, and I spill my guts, searching my brain for every sin I can remember, including some I've probably confessed more than once. I have a need to wipe it all away, to be cleansed. Maybe some part of me, knowing the time ahead is going to be very trying, feels a need to be as ready and right with God as possible; I don't know. Some reading this might not understand it, but it feels right to me. I want to be patient through this, calm even, and although I don't form the thoughts in my head, I think I need to be "lined up" to receive all the help from above I can get. Intellectually, it seems strange, even to me, and I don't believe that's how God works. But it's coming from a place deep inside, perhaps a scared, needy place.

Father John talks with me about a phrase used in AA in reference to times when it's difficult to deal with one's emotions and the challenge of being as loving as we'd like to be when under stress: HALT: Hungry, Angry, Lonely, and Tired. It's easy for me to see, afterwards, that the times when I feel cranky, it's usually because I am hungry, angry, feeling lonely or in fear of future loneliness, or am tired. I would find out that there would be other triggers for feeling overwhelmed by the day's events, and that I could not expect perfection out of myself or others. I spend a few minutes in the chapel after that, letting things sink in. Soon, I see Father John bustling about. Others are milling about, too. Maybe there is going to be a mass. I get up to leave, and he comes over to me in the aisle and asks if I want to receive Holy Communion. I say yes, and a moment later, right there, in the middle of the aisle, with people gently moving about, I receive the sacrament.

Then, it's back to Ted, comforted beyond measure by the kindness of this humble priest who took the time to truly minister to us in this, our hour of crisis.

HEADING HOME FOR THE WEEKEND

I am scheduled for a brain biopsy on Friday this week, May 20 (tomorrow). By this time, the diagnosis of glioblastoma, a primary malignant brain tumor, is pretty well established. The biopsy will be the definitive test.

My cousin, a pediatric neurologist in Boston, stops by the hospital and spends time with us in his kind, soothing way. He is very present for us, offering an open invitation to call on him as needed.

We are nervous about the biopsy but reassured that we have the absolute best neurosurgeon available. Even the wife of the patient in the next bed, upon hearing us talk about the neurosurgeon, smiles widely about this Dr. Curry, whom we've not yet met.

"He has golden hands," she says.

This is encouraging, since a brain biopsy is no walk in the park. Particularly in Ted's case, there is high risk because the primary tumor is sitting on his left motor strip, a most sensitive area to work with, neurologically.

One minor mistake—or even a non-mistake—and Ted could be paralyzed on his entire right side. For the same reason, the tumor is inoperable, as trying to remove the bulk of it would most likely cause paralysis, which would leave him open to complications that could shorten his life even more. For example, it might cut out lung expansion on that side, leaving him vulnerable to pneumonia—and, of course, there are any number of other surgical risks.

There is a problem, however, as we approach Friday. Due to several life-threatening emergencies and consequent use of the operating rooms, Ted's slot gets bumped. It's frustrating for us and staff as well, but they are experiencing so many immediate emergencies that, in the end, we are told the biopsy can't be done until Monday. Ted is being sent home with clear instructions to return Sunday for readmission, with surgery scheduled for Monday morning.

The doctors are very clear that since the biopsy must be done, it's in Ted's best interest to leave the hospital and return Sunday, because the less time in hospital, the less chance of picking up an infection of some sort. Logical, disappointing, but we agree. So, with Ted quite unsteady on his feet and using a walker, we start the trip home. The first challenge is making our way outside to the car. I deposit Ted with a security guard while I go get the car.

I feel vulnerable. Randey and Maryellen have left, and Sally has returned to New York. Basically, I am in charge of a six-foot-tall husband who is unsteady as hell. Taking care of my injured neck and back seems like enough. But...

Tag. I'm it.

On the way home from Boston to Maine, Ted's cell phone rings, just as I'm driving us across the Piscataqua River bridge, which spans from New Hampshire into Maine.

With a mixture of anxiety and relief, we leave the hospital. We are an hour out of Boston when we receive a phone call from the office of the neurosurgeon, telling us that our medical insurance company is declining to pay for the brain biopsy. Can you believe it?! Their point of view is that they will only cover services that are rendered in our local area, i.e., in and around Portland.

There follow several more phone calls between us, the surgeon, my primary care doctor, and the medical insurance company. All these calls take place over cell phones as we hurtle north on I-95 toward home. It doesn't seem to make any sense to me at all to do all the preparatory work for a brain biopsy, only to be told that the biopsy will not be covered by our medical insurance when everything else has already been covered. To start the workup all over again in our "local area" would mean duplicating many of the studies and examinations, thus greatly increasing the cost. This is, of course, part and parcel of the idiocy of the American medical insurance industry and one of the major contributors to the inflation of medical costs in this country. Telephone calls go back and forth as we cruise up the interstate. Someone even suggests I come in through the Emergency Room at Mass General on Sunday evening, complaining of a bad headache. In the face of a presumptive diagnosis of brain tumor, that would constitute a medical emergency. Then, I would have to be admitted and the insurance company would have to pay the bill. It's an enticing idea, but a trifle too devious for our New England consciences.

One thing we know from the preliminary tests: The tumor has grown since the studies just a few weeks earlier. We are not about to wait to get in to see a Portland neurosurgeon, only to have to take the same tests all over again. But wisely, the medical advice is clear: Ted is to come back into the hospital Sunday for readmission.

We continue home, now with one more thing to worry about. This is the first of what will turn out to be a secondary nightmare for us, a long and drawn-out fight over various chunks of insurance coverage.

A couple of hours later, we pull into the driveway. Ted is still extremely unsteady. I ask him if he wants to get out of the car before I pull into the garage, thinking it will be easier for him. He says yes and gets out of the car…slowly.

"Wait there," I tell him, indicating the area where he's getting out of the car, at the bottom of the steps, where he can lean against a stone wall. He agrees. I tell him I will be there in a minute after I park the car. As I approach the steps, he's not there. Why am I not surprised? I hurry, in time to see him tumble forward into the garden, about six or eight feet ahead of me. He's OK, but it's to be the beginning of many circumstances in which he wants to do something for himself—and I really do get that—but, in the process, stumbles or falls.

This fall is also the beginning of what I would recognize, in myself, as a multi-daily event: the heart lurch. There's no Olympic category for that. If there were, I'd get the gold.

The weekend is pretty awful. Although we both have great intentions of making it into something enjoyable and even fun—since we're NOT in the hospital—there's a serious cloud of doom over us. We spend part of the weekend crying together, holding each other, loving each other, and being scared to death—and repeating the basics of all that's going on with our beloved friends and family, via numerous calls and emails.

Ted and I talk and cry—of our love for each other, how awful and unfair this all seems—so incongruous after just being together for a relatively short time and having expected that we would certainly have many more years together. I tell him I will stay with him through whatever path it takes. I will take care of him. We both know that it might entail getting more help, but I will not abandon him. He says that if he dies, he wants me to find someone else. I tell him I will never remarry or be with another man if he goes first. We have no way of knowing what fate lies ahead for either of us, but right now, his illness is our frame of reference. Promises, heart-felt, are important. But they are not easy.

In the recesses of my mind, and vaguely, I begin to think of what it might be like to take care of him if he becomes infirm. It is already taking its toll on me physically. I'll work something out. Then I begin to think through the part about not being with anyone else, ever. Emotionally, I cannot go there. The thought of being without Ted is so crushing that I cannot conceive of any other relationship, even though I am much younger, by thirteen years. If I stay healthy and he does not, long-term, it could be many, many years of being alone. That scares me on a very deep level. It's easy enough to tell yourself platitudes like "Jesus will be by my side" but the realities of living solo, day after day, going to bed alone, night after night, with no one to snuggle, no one for comfort, is beyond what my soul can handle right now. Ted is, probably more realistically, thinking of my future. But all my heart can say is "no."

CHAPTER 8

BACK TO BOSTON

Although good to be home for a couple of days, to unpack, do laundry, and repack with more forethought this time, all we can think about is what is to come, in terms of both the risk of the biopsy procedure and, of course, the results. We feel a depth of sadness and helplessness. The situation is beyond our control. I pray a lot. We talk and talk and talk some more. This is not the way we planned Ted's retirement. I'm terrified he's going to die, and I'll be alone, without him. While I am aching for him and what he is facing, he's worrying about me. At one point, I say that if he doesn't make it, it will be horrible, but that somehow, I know I'll go on. I tell him this even though I am not sure of it, in my gut.

"That's the best thing I've heard from you since this started," he says.

We repack small bags and get into the car to head out of town for hospital readmission. I have no recollection of what we did with the dog, but I guess he ended up back at the kennel. Or maybe they had kept him over the weekend. I know he was cared for and accounted for.

The Holiday Inn across from Mass General knows we're coming back. Sally has arranged to come to Boston again to stay with me, and Randey and Maryellen have also made reservations at the same hotel for our return. They will not let us pay for their room, and arguing with them does no good.

So now, on a Sunday afternoon, we are on our way back to Boston, to the hospital ER, back to the parking garages and the hotel. I am quite aware that not every spouse of a patient can afford a hotel, even at the discount.

On Sunday, driving back to Boston, we receive a phone call from the admitting office at MGH, letting us know that full arrangements have been made for my admission that evening.

"Where are you?" they ask.

We say we're on the way and explain about the insurance snag. They assure us that the non-approval with the insurance company can be worked out. They do not want Ted to go in through the ER, practically beg us not to do that.

"We'll sort it out later," we are told. "The room is waiting for you."

Imagine that—putting the patient first. And once again, we are grateful.

So, on Sunday evening, May 22nd, I am readmitted to Massachusetts General Hospital and prepared for a brain biopsy on the following day, the day before my 71st birthday.

We're back in Boston, and this time I figure out the logistics in advance so I can accomplish a safe entry for Ted into the hospital and me into the hotel, and not wreck my neck and back with bags. Don't ask me how I do it. But it's something like that old brain teaser, the one where there's a fox, a chicken, and a bag of feed on one side of the river and only two of those items at a time can cross in the boat.

> **QUARTERS AND DIMES**
>
> When Ted and I were getting to know each other, we discussed how the expression "a penny for your thoughts"—in today's finances—would be "a dime for your thoughts." Soon after, we started leaving various coins on each other's car driver's side window when we were parked outside our workplace in Portland. Every couple of hours, we'd have to move our cars to a different street, a ridiculous routine due to an annoying parking setup, but having to do that was softened by the humorous sight of a few coins on the driver's side window.

- A man has to get a fox, a chicken, and a sack of corn across a river.
  - He has a rowboat, and it can only carry him and one other thing.
  - If the fox and the chicken are left together, the fox will eat the chicken.

- If the chicken and the corn are left together, the chicken will eat the corn.
- How does the man do it?

- The man and the chicken cross the river, (the fox and corn are safe together); he leaves the chicken on the other side and goes back across.
  - The man then takes the fox across the river, and since he can't leave the fox and chicken together, he brings the chicken back.
  - Again, since the chicken and corn can't be left together, he leaves the chicken and takes the corn across and leaves it with the fox.
  - He then returns to pick up the chicken and heads across the river one last time.

I did it. Ted, the chicken, the fox, the corn, and I all got to where we needed to go.

Sally shows up sometime after Ted's admission, having navigated Boston like the seasoned traveler she is, and meets up with me that first night, his pre-op night.

This time, Ted is in the new Neurology unit in a different building. One thing that stays the same is the excellent staff and, to Ted's delight, he's surrounded by nurses who are not only skillful and capable, but they are also very attractive. His comments about this actually reassure me that he is doing OK. Normally I would have been tempted to smack him. I'm kidding. Maybe. I tease him about the nurses, and it gives him a laugh. I tell him that I think at least one of them really likes him (wink). During those very intense days, this moment breaks up the gloom.

Of course, the impressive thing about them is the way they integrate warmth with expert nursing care. Nurses don't get a lot of recognition. The MGH nurses are simply outstanding.

ALFRED HITCHCOCK'S THE BIRDS—REDUX

On the other side of the street, on that first night, Sally and I hear a noise coming from the window in our hotel room. A flapping noise. At first, we think a bird has flown by the window. But the noise intensifies and becomes more frequent. We both start to freak out. I pick up the room phone and call the front desk about the noise, and I'm on the phone when I hear a loud gasp from Sally. As I'm holding the phone, I look over to the air conditioner to see what she's reacting to—the very large wing of a bird slipping through the slats in the air conditioner!

"Oh, my God!" I shout into the phone, "It's a bird's wing!!!"

Engineering is at our room in moments. Thankfully, we are to be moved to another room. On the way to the new room, I ask if it will be as nice as the room we've had.

"I think you'll like it," is the reply. "It's the Bay View room."

When we get to the room, we can't believe our eyes. It's the most glorious suite I've ever seen. We open the door to find a huge living room area, with various sections for business or pleasure, including a full-size boardroom table, a kitchen area, a lovely, huge bedroom with a ridiculously fancy bathroom beyond anyone's needs, everything in handsome, heavy wood, everything perfectly appointed, marble everywhere.

"Wow!" is all we can say to each other. Sally's big blue eyes are open wide.

For a few blessed minutes, we have relief from the real reason we are there at all. That break from terror is a good one, badly needed, considering what is to come.

BIOPSY DAY

While we are in Boston and things are changing fast, my oldest daughter Cassie in North Carolina does something enormously helpful. At her suggestion, I've given her the email addresses and, in some cases, phone numbers of key people who want to be updated on Ted's condition and in particular, the brain biopsy results. The list includes certain relatives (who can then disseminate information to their branches of the family) and close friends. This way, when the biopsy results are in, I know I have only one call or text to make.

Now, even the most basic daily things are unpredictable. After a year of attending a great weight-loss program, methodically tracking nutrients until I hit my magic 144 and keeping it there another three months, I drop seven pounds in one week—the hell week when Ted is hospitalized—during which I end up grabbing a roll and coffee early in the morning, sometimes a tiny lunch midafternoon, and possibly a few bites of something at night. Literally, a few bites. Often, I don't remember about food until I see Ted's supper tray delivered, and then I feel mildly hungry but too distressed to move. Or afraid if I leave the floor, something will happen to him. It's more important to me to stay with him, this strong, wonderful man, my husband of only a few years, than to go looking for a square meal.

The next morning is the biopsy. My longtime friend Terry lives just outside of Boston. She is a speech therapist, and we'd met decades earlier when we both worked at a school for developmentally delayed children in Maine. Back in our 20s, we'd shared a house rental for three years. My girls were little then, and Terry took the basement apartment, the girls and I on the first floor. We shared common living space, meals, heartbreaks, and joys. We'd remained friends over the years, long after we went our separate ways, she moving out of state, each of us getting married. She has remained part of our family in the best sense of the word. Now, she is in touch with me regarding Ted's medical problem, concerned and offering anything needed. She's been an angel more than once to me. There is no word or phrase in our language that can adequately describe this human being.

She tells me she will be coming by a little later, after work, while Ted is in surgery, to wait with us. Today is May 23rd, the day before Ted's birthday. It's a crappy way to celebrate. I should be out getting him last-minute presents, making plans for a nice dinner somewhere. Anything but this.

Ted is brought to the OR after Randey, Maryellen, Sally, and I say our goodbyes, and we are given instructions on how to find the waiting room. We are also given approximate time frames of how long things might take. The noise level in the large waiting room is low, but the room itself is busy. Groups of families wait, in various configurations of chairs, coffee tables, and standard waiting-room sofas.

Somewhere in the middle of the day, I am transported on a gurney a number of floors down into the bowels of the hospital and into an anesthesia suite. Two young women come by at different times, full of questions about my general health and about my medications. They are very pleasant and obviously very intelligent. I am guessing they are anesthesiologists, but I don't remember. I am left alone for some period of time. Then appears at my bedside a very good-looking, relatively young, light-skinned African American man who introduces himself simply, as "Will Curry." It takes me a moment to realize this is the Dr. Curry who is soon going to drill a hole through my skull and take out a piece of my brain. While we talk, I tell him about my collection of bones and skulls and ask him if he will be able to give me the piece of bone that he removes. He tells me that I am far from the first person to ask that, and no, he will not be able to do so because the procedure that is used does not result in an intact piece of bone. He explains that I will be left with a hole in my skull about the size of a nickel, and it will be permanent. He goes over the procedure with me in detail. I am deeply impressed with his manner, with his gentleness, with his empathy.

Somewhere along the way, possibly from him, I learn how the biopsy is done. It fascinates me. In the operating room, apparently, there is a large-screen video setup. On the screen they superimpose a special kind of CT scan, called a stereotactic CT scan, and an MRI, which contains different information. The surgeon uses these superimposed scans to guide his hands and tools. It seemed to me very much like a surgical Wii machine.

After some while, I am taken into the operating room and put under anesthesia, so I don't remember very much else from the rest of this day.

Every few minutes, "the family of—" is called out to let that patient's family know that a doctor is coming down to talk and report on the surgery. Small children are hopping around here and there, parents reeling them in, some people attempting sleep, or reading, looking impatiently at clocks, milling about to get coffee, use the restrooms, or do anything that stressed people do to pass the time.

I am tense as all get-out. I leave Randey, Maryellen, and Sally and go to a quiet side room. There I pray the Rosary to calm myself and to connect with something more powerful than my emotions. When I come out, Terry has arrived, with bags of muffins and trays of tea from a nearby Dunkin' Donuts. Leave it to her to think of everything. She sits there with us for hours, until finally:

"The family of Edward White?"

We look up, and my heart starts pounding, fast and hard.

A secretary at the waiting-room desk tells us that the surgery has gone well—thank God!—and that the doctor will be down shortly to speak with us. MGH thinks of everything, including updating the anxious family that surgery has gone well, meaning the patient has not died on the table, a rare but potential occurrence that can happen with a brain biopsy. After waiting another half hour or so, the doctor arrives. I have not laid eyes on him prior to this. And he is not at all what I'd expected.

WILL CURRY, AKA DR. MCDREAMY

A gentle male voice says my name. I look up to see a man who, we all later agree, is one of the most beautiful men we have ever seen. Maybe mid- to late-30s (who cares about his age? we are all in love with him, instantly), movie-star looks, and so very sweet and kind, he invites us into a nearby office. There he reviews the surgery. He gives us the bad news that Ted's tumor—actually, three tumors, but two of them are not "hot," meaning not actively growing—is the type called glioblastoma multiforme, sitting on the motor strip in the left side of his brain. He tells us it is inoperable, but possibly treatable. The doctor shares this with us in a most caring, encouraging, lovely way that gives us some hope. His manner is remarkably kind, with an ability to deliver this information in a way that leaves us with a decent level of confidence about the future. He proceeds to tell us as much as he knows about the tumor and the expected time frame for getting final results of the specimen that has been removed and sent to the lab.

At one point, my mind loses focus on the subject. This is one example of why I now never judge anyone going through a hard time. In pain and suffering, we do what we must do to get through. I sneakily try to see if he's wearing a wedding ring. I mean, I'm curious. He is kind, gorgeous, and a doctor. He does wear a ring—and this blip of inner humor and escape from my aching, grieving brain is what I need to do. After all, I have an unmarried daughter to think about.

I'm joking. No, I'm not.

I hope she never reads this. She will not be pleased with me.

Will Curry…paging Dr. Will Curry…

POST-BIOPSY

We catch up with Ted as soon as we are allowed to see him, post-surgery, post-recovery, and back in his room. He looks pretty good, considering someone has drilled a hole in his skull. He talks and smiles. I call Cassie, who in turn does her best to notify others of Ted's status and the "biopsy went well" message.

I learn later that Dr. Curry confirms that I have what appears to be a glioblastoma multiforme, stage four, a perfectly horrible diagnosis, carrying with it, as a median, a life expectancy of only a year and a half at the most.

I think it is important to note that due to the state I am in, I actually don't remember a lot of what happens next, except that we are all happy the biopsy has gone well, and that Ted is alert and coherent. No bleeding in the brain or paralysis, to name some of the worst possibilities. It's our regular Ted. Our wonderful, regular Ted—but wearing a standard hospital gown, with stitches and a gauze-type bandage off-center on the top of his head.

His recovery that day is fairly routine, and he continues to get excellent nursing and medical care. We're relieved it's over. In some way, the doctor and our own mutual support has buoyed us up in a way that "brain tumor" doesn't seem all that insurmountable after all.

Looking back, I think that, once again, my denial was so powerful that I heard what I wanted to hear. And that's OK.

Ted spends the next day—his birthday—recuperating and being a patient. His course is relatively uneventful, although he is still quite unsteady on his feet. There's talk of discharge, which will include an outpatient visit with the neuro-oncologist, Dr. April Eichler, in a nearby building.

I stay with Ted most of the day, while Randey, Maryellen, and Sally take turns visiting with him also. I take a few minutes every so often for essentials. Ted's hospital room this time is also a double, with another man in the next bed, so space tends to be a little scarce. Ted and I will later joke about the man and his wife, who both brag to us about the posh area of Boston where they live, working it into any possible part of a conversation. Truly, where they live is the very least thing we care about now. But maybe they need that focus.

The nursing staff has arranged for a little birthday cake for Ted from Dining Services, which is so kind and at the same time breaks my heart. I have a real thing about birthdays. Ted seems to take it in stride. His family has sent a beautiful potted orchid plant.

I've somehow picked up a couple of books and flowers for him, and I make promises to make it up. Mind you, he cares nothing about his own birthday.

Later that day, Randey and Maryellen head back home. The next day, Sally leaves, and Ted is discharged to our hotel room.

Upon discharge, I'm advised to take Ted in a wheelchair across the street to the hotel and leave the chair outside the hotel. Apparently, it happens that way all the time, and the hospital just collects them routinely. Nice touch. Mass General thinks of everything, except how to make itself a little smaller.

We spend the night in our gorgeous suite and the next day have breakfast in the dining room downstairs in the hotel. Again, the hotel staff is fantastic. Clearly, the right people are working here, and are used to accommodating patients and families from the hospital, and they do a good job. If I weren't in menopause, I'd name my next born after them—*Holiday* Eliscu.

CHAPTER 9

REPRIEVE

I remain in the hospital one more night and am discharged the next day. That night I join Kathy at her hotel room, the suite that she was given after the bird incident. I am given an appointment for a follow-up visit with my oncologist. The oncologist, whom I met during the hospitalization, is a very bright and likable woman, probably somewhat less than 40 years old, who goes by the wonderful name of April Fitzsimmons Eichler, MD. Kathy and I decide that we will take a day to relax and explore Boston a little bit before heading home. Before we are even able to do that, however, I receive a phone call from Dr. Eichler's office, asking if I could keep an appointment with her the next day, on Thursday, May 26. It doesn't seem worth going back to Maine, only to return in two days, so we remain in Boston.

We drive down to the harbor, find a very fine restaurant for lunch. Using my walker, I can make my way around the waterfront for a while. The day is windy, but clear and exquisitely beautiful. We know we have big decisions to make and nowhere near enough information yet with which to make them. I have some understanding that my treatment will include both radiation and chemotherapy, along with medications to control seizures and inflammation and other aspects of the cancer. A big question is whether we should remain in Boston for treatment, whether at MGH or across town at the Dana-Farber Cancer Center, or seek treatment at Sloan Kettering in New York, or go to Houston to the MD Anderson Center, or to Seattle or San Francisco or some other specialty center. We consider taking an apartment in Boston for the two months of initial radiation treatment. Neither of us has any enthusiasm for Houston in the summer, or for New York, for that matter, although obviously we would go anywhere at all if we could be assured of a chance for a better outcome.

And even as we are talking through these choices, we are struggling, both of us, with the reality: brain cancer, incurable brain cancer, which is probably going to end my life and turn Kathy into a widow within the next year, no matter what treatment I receive or where I go to get it. The unreality of it is too much. How can this be happening to me, to us?

TWO DOCTORS, A SOCIAL WORKER, AND STARBUCKS

Let's talk parking lots.

On Thursday, Ted and I and our bags get downstairs to the hotel lobby, with help. Then I get the car from the garage and pay for it. Even the "patient" rates in Boston are high. Then we drive just one street over, until we find the outpatient building and go into that garage. Finding a parking space is dicey, but we finally get one. Then we get lost finding where we are supposed to go from the parking garage. The signs confuse us. At one point, I help Ted to the parking garage elevator, leaning him against the doors so they won't close, and say, "Stand right there. Don't move," because if he moves on his own, he'll probably fall over. He has to wait there because I need to go back to the car to get the paperwork I forgot so we can find out what part of the building we are supposed to go to. Disorganized? I sure am.

We get to the right floor and office eventually, after asking for help. When we get to the right multi-practice office, it is already time for his visit. But we stand in line for what seems like eons. The people in front of us seem to have loads of time before their appointments, and there's a tremendous amount of pleasant chitchat going on. We're cutting it close, and I'm getting frustrated. Finally, I poke my head forward, point to Ted, and say to the receptionist, "Excuse me—he's supposed to be in the doctor's office now, and I just want you to know he's here. *White. Edward White.*"

This is the start of a very long afternoon.

Dr. April Eichler is strikingly beautiful, very bright, and kind, as she lays out the recommended course of treatment, answering our many questions. I feel sick about the whole thing all over again. We learn about the standard treatment—radiation with chemotherapy. There are other treatments outlined, available at MGH and other hospitals, but mostly still in research phases. These are, depending on many factors, available instead of, or later. It's overwhelming, and it all sounds dire.

One thing I notice with almost all the doctors and specialists we've met with is that when we ask a question, the answer generally starts with a slow "So…" I realize this may be a strange thing to comment on, but it happens so often that I begin to see a correlation between a question of a serious or complex nature and the delivery of bad news. If you go into a café and ask, "Are you still serving breakfast?" you'll get "You've got ten more minutes to order." But ask a physician what the long-term prognosis is for brain cancer, and I guarantee you he or she will say, "So…in studies, some of the people who…" This is not at all a put-down of these experts. Implicit in the situation is that there are few definitive answers. There is some research, but maybe not as much compared to some other illnesses.

And yes, the news is often horrible, so it becomes difficult information to pass along in a way that doesn't have patients and families jumping out the window of said clinic.

So…

The meetings with both Dr. Eichler and the radiation oncologist are especially difficult because although they offer treatment options, we still feel discouraged. We ask the hard questions. How long might we expect Ted to be in functioning health? How successful are the treatments? What if the treatments do not work? We're given statistics and some secondary options if the first line of treatment fails. We're told that with the radiation and chemotherapy, which is the standard care, only five to ten percent of patients with this kind of brain tumor make it "for years and years." The others? Dr. Eichler gives an estimate of about twelve to eighteen months, although that's an average.

"Will I be around a year from now?" Ted finally asks her.

She nods, a serious look on her face.

"Oh, yes," she says. We know that averages in statistics are merely averages, and that there is no reasonable way to predict this for any individual. But

Dr. Eichler mentions that some people have what's called a "methylating" factor in their tumor cells, and we won't have results of this test for a couple of months. If Ted has this factor, his cancer will likely respond better to the chemotherapy that is used, with a somewhat longer life expectancy.

It's during that appointment that I sense a tiny little hopeful part of myself saying, *He will be in that five to ten percent. He's got good genetics. His mother is 96.* Despite being shaken by the gravity of the illness, Dr. Eichler's kindness and expertise have given us a measure of comfort. But we are exhausted from the past couple of weeks and the enormity of the task ahead. As the afternoon progresses, we're both beginning to feel like train wrecks. We meet with the radiation oncologist, who outlines his part in the radiation treatment and protocol, if Ted chooses to be treated in Boston.

Next, we're brought to an office down the hall where we meet the staff social worker. As Ted later remarks, he has never seen a therapist so in tune with two people she has just met. Every concern we have, every utterance, she just nails what's going on. I cry, Ted and I both talk, saying how difficult treatment decisions will be.

"I just want us to go home and make love," Ted blurts out. We need so badly to have things normal and happy again.

The social worker takes a long time with us, listening, directing, reflecting, letting us know we have some time to decide on treatment. So, although we feel pressured, we actually have a few weeks to decide on treatment options, because nothing can be done until the biopsy site has healed. We have been at the clinic for hours. We're tired, confused, inspired, grateful, distressed…so very tired. After the session, she suggests:

"Go home and make love."

She gives us lots of information to take with us in the event we decide to have treatment in Boston, which would necessitate a temporary move. She also lets us know *that no matter where or what we decide, she will be available to us.*

We head home via a quick take-out from Starbucks around the corner from Mass General. Starbucks feels very good. Normal. And there will be time enough for anguish and decision-making. It won't be that insurmountable. After all, we're medical professionals.

REVISITING MY WONDERFUL CASE OF DENIAL

I know that the correct terms were used by the doctors at the final medical visits before we left Boston, affirming the brain tumor diagnosis. I was sitting right there, listening. I know that somewhere in the ugly fabric of phrases and test results and meanings and clarifications I have been told the nature of his tumor, that it carries a grave prognosis, and yet later—a couple of days later—after final biopsy results show what we all feared, it is during a phone call to my daughter in North Carolina when I begin to piece together the full story. Oh, I had heard it. But my brain had not accepted it.

"Is it a glioblastoma, Mom?" Cassie asks. "Did they say it's that kind of tumor?"

"Well? I think...I don't know," I say, and I mean it.

For at this moment, wheels in my head start to turn in a direction I cannot bear. It's as though the words of encouragement we'd heard overrode the reality of the dire diagnosis.

Cassie has a fair amount of science background, and her husband, Paul, is a physician. She asks me about the type of tumor cells that were found—in part, because she is helping us investigate various experimental treatments being offered around the country to help us uncover options via www.clinicaltrials.gov. She and I go round and round about the type of cells before, in the course of conversation, I realize that the type of cells is, in fact, called glioblastoma. As I am talking to her, reassuring her, I realize inside myself that I have not fully faced the fact about the biopsy result. I know how absurd this sounds, considering I have written about how I was told this information, in these very words, before this point. In my panic, I rush through the next minute of conversation until I can get off the phone.

It is just after that call that I begin to incorporate the full meaning of Ted's medical condition. And I am scared to death all over again.

Acceptance is a huge concept. Perhaps we hear what we want—or need—to hear.

It all feels like a death, right now. That awful pit-of-the-stomach feeling that hits one physically as well as emotionally.

"Yes," I finally say to Cassie, a full day later, "it's a glioblastoma."

I have subconsciously been trying to protect us all. Turns out being a so-called medical professional means little—at least for me—when a bad diagnosis is happening this close by.

With this backdrop, Ted and I continue a journey we did not want or ask for—one without a map—that contains a larger and more ferocious roller-coaster than any amusement park, and one that will prove to us what love and devotion mean—not just between us, but among our family and friends. This is very, very tough stuff to deal with. Sometimes we do it well; often, we do it poorly and with great agony. For me, who likes things spelled out beforehand, it takes every bit of me to just hang on. I never knew how ugly, angry, stubborn, and stressed-out I could be. Nor how strong and accepting.

PART 3

CHAPTER 10

SHOCK

My husband has a brain tumor.

Those are the words that have gone through my head a hundred times, in a hundred different ways, in these last weeks.

It's part of my consciousness, my subconscious, it's in my words, and in my prayers as I ask for healing. It's in the anxiety-ridden acrid taste in my mouth, and my repulsion at food, at times. We are going through emotional turmoil and disturbing images beyond anything we could imagine. I know what my internal world is like. But for Ted, who is sick, well, that's another story. There is no way he could have prepared for this. That is true for nearly all cancer patients and the ones who love them. Really, no one sees it coming. One day you are going along, just like normal. Then suddenly, your world turns upside down.

Once, as a young adult, I was swimming in the Atlantic Ocean off Long Island, New York, and a ferocious wave pulled me off my feet and down under the water for a few moments. It had such power that it took me several seconds to figure out which way was up. This is how it feels to learn that my husband has a life-threatening illness from which there is little hope for recovery or a long future together. It is completely disorienting, in ways big and small.

As I begin to write this, we are on our unplanned "trip." I'd started writing, naively, in hopes of offering practical help to those whose loved ones are going through serious illnesses. Instead, it's become a journey of dealing with the frightening and the unpredictable, and something very personal to us.

For as long as we have known each other, Kathy and I have been talking about writing something together. A newspaper column, maybe an advice column about relationships, or about mental health. Or a piece of fiction. A nurse and writer for years, she has a regular column and many freelance credits. I am a practicing psychiatrist and psychoanalyst. I think Kathy has been frustrated with me because I have agreed with her that it would be damn interesting for us to work together in these ways, but I have not, for the most part, followed through on the promise.

Before these recent events, Ted's and my ideas for writing together, maybe an advice column, are great to imagine, but neither of us really takes that first step. Once, I sent him a writing prompt, but he didn't follow through. Our joint ideas have become more of a "wouldn't it be fun if" game of dreams, at least for now. Meanwhile, I'm working on my own long-term project.

Now, all this has changed. Has been changed by illness. Mine. I have a brain tumor—glioblastoma multiforme. Such tumors are considered to be uniformly incurable and generally fatal within a year or two of diagnosis. Some people, however, live for seven or eight or ten years with this condition. I am hoping to be one of them.

Since April, we have had to find ways to cope with my tumor and the probability that my cancer will end my life in the near future. It is my brain and my tumor, and I have to deal with it as such. Kathy is my wife, friend, and lover, and she must deal with my brain and my tumor from her perspective. We have our separate experiences with this terrible illness, but intertwined lives. I find it very difficult to write what I want to write, to express what is in my mind and heart but is often so hard to put on paper. But now the heat is on. My illness may end my life before this work is done. My story may never be told, at least not in the way I want it to be told. In that case, I will be leaving her alone in more than simply the physical sense. And that possibility leaves me deeply sad and anxious.

Sooner or later, we all have to die. Everybody knows that. We have all, always, known that. When we are young, dying is an intellectual proposition, perhaps accompanied by the occasional friend or schoolmate who dies of some rare illness or is killed accidentally. In our middle years, the truth begins to take on more reality. Somewhat more reality, anyway. One or both of our parents dies, or a grandparent, and we go to the funeral and the burial, and we visit the cemetery from time to time. But when we become old, into our 60s and 70s, or beyond, and we witness our age mates and friends slipping away, developing serious illnesses, some of them dying of those illnesses, that's when things become really real.

My mother will be 98 years old this summer. In general, she is in good health. I have assumed since I was young that I would follow in her path, that I would live to some great age and die, I guess, only when great age had prepared me for it, when age had taught me all I needed to know. Now it seems that this idea has been an exercise in wishful thinking, even hubris. What led me to believe that my life course would be similar to my mother's? Well, I have always been very active and fairly athletic, like her. My father, on the other hand, developed diabetes and heart disease while he was still in his 50s, and he died at the age of 66. I have always been pretty absurdly pleased to recognize how much better I have taken care of myself, physically, than he did. So, for years I have had this idea that my course in life would be much more like hers than like his. Now, it seems more likely that I will die much sooner than I want to. I am sad as hell about this. I am also angry. And I am scared, not so much because I will probably die much sooner than I want to, but more because I fear what I may have to endure along the way, and what Kathy may have to endure with me. Pain. Neurologic losses. Dementia. Memory and speech problems. Fear.

It is so tempting to write with whimsy, to make light of things, as in "so, a funny thing happened the other day" or "you won't believe what's happened," an obvious bit of denial, an avoidance. The truth is this is real and very frightening. And overwhelming, a word I have despised for years. Overwhelming, beyond a doubt.

One of the things that you begin to learn after you receive a diagnosis of cancer is that there is no way to get all the information you really want to have in order to make the most important decisions of your life. There are famous centers for cancer research and treatment around the world. Would it be better for me to find treatment at one of these centers, or would it be just as well for me to get treatment in Portland, Maine?

The advantage of staying in Portland is that I would be close to home, in a familiar environment, and close to my friends.

We have so many friends and people who are just like family to us near home. My cousin Fred and his wife, Meryl, who *are* family and stood up for us at our wedding less than three years earlier, live ten minutes away. We also have our church friends we sing with every Sunday, several of them close buddies, and other close friends nearby.

I find myself thinking that if I am going to die in a short space of time anyway, I would rather die at home, among my friends and familiar circumstances. On the other hand, if it's possible that one of the major world centers of research and treatment might come up with something more effective than I could find in my local area, then I do not want to miss out on that, no matter what it might require in the way of travel or expense. No one seems ready or willing to answer questions about things like that. And if my life expectancy is going to be limited to a matter of months, it seems to me there is an argument to be made about what difference does it make, anyway. I mean, what difference does it make if I live for eight months or nine? We search and search the Internet for answers to our questions. We read medical journals. We discuss these questions with our friends and family and with each other, endlessly. For a long while, we do not seem to be getting any closer to a decision. We research condominiums and other residences in Boston where we might live for the six weeks of my initial treatment. At times I find myself thinking that a couple of months of living in Boston could be a kind of vacation. Hell, if I'm only going to live a few more months, might as well make the best of it and have a good time for as long as possible, right?

Another thing you learn, and rather quickly, after you receive a diagnosis of cancer is how many other people you know who have the disease or who know people who have the disease or have family members who have the disease, and how many of these people have knowledge and opinions about how you should be treated and where. Most of these people are well-intentioned and some are, in fact, quite knowledgeable, but some also have motives that might be questioned. I hear from an old friend, himself a doctor, that he has an old friend whose wife is afflicted with a tumor similar to mine. He puts me in touch with his friend, who lives in Los Angeles, and I have a conversation with him that is quite fruitful. A friend of my family members has a close friend who has suffered a tumor somewhat like mine and has been treated, apparently successfully. I find a conversation with her to be helpful and educational and supportive.

Cancer is not a neutral word. Everyone has feelings about it. The news media and especially the Internet are alive with bits of advice. Most of this information is worthless or even misleading, although some of it is genuine and helpful, and it is sometimes difficult to sort out which is which. We've known from the start that within my head is something that will kill me within a year or so if I don't do something about it. We also have advice that the tumor is likely to kill me even if I do something about it, but I might prolong the process by six months or year. No one in these early months is talking about "cure."

Dr. Eichler is quite willing to continue as my doctor, but she also makes it plain that she holds no particular magic and that I might do just as well if I am treated in another center. In an odd way, that's reassuring. It's reassuring because it's some indication that it doesn't matter where I go for treatment, the outcome is likely to be the same, so this supports the arguments in favor of staying home and getting treatment in the local area.

By talking with Dr. Eichler, our primary care physician Dr. Emery, and others, we eventually become educated that the treatment for glioblastoma, after an initial diagnosis, has been standardized around the world. That treatment consists of six weeks of daily radiation, five days a week, in addition to a drug called temozolomide, the trade name of which is Temodar. The radiation is administered in very finely tuned doses that are aimed specifically at the tumors. The Temodar is administered seven days a week at the start, at a moderate dose. After the initial six weeks of radiation treatment plus Temodar, the radiation is discontinued and the Temodar is then given on a different schedule. From then on, Temodar is given for five days out of each month and the dose is progressively increased. The primary side effects of the radiation and chemo treatment, we are told, are likely to consist of fatigue, nausea, and perhaps headaches. I will also continue to take Keppra to prevent seizures. I am given other medications to counteract nausea, constipation, diarrhea, and pain. I have not had any pain associated with the tumor, and the other side effects present themselves as minor, if sometimes messy, inconveniences. Another medicine I am recommended to take is dexamethasone, to decrease the swelling (edema) around the tumor. I continue also to take medicines I have been taking for years for high blood pressure and high cholesterol. Additional testing shows I have a thyroid disorder, leading to a recommendation for taking a drug called methimazole. The issue regarding place of treatment for the brain cancer is, as yet, unanswered.

CHAPTER 11

BETH

Ted has owned a silver flute since before I knew him. He is self-taught to some extent, and, being musical, took to it nicely, just as he's picked up other instruments.

A couple of years prior to Ted's diagnosis, I'd come to know a warm, outgoing young woman named Beth, who worked at our local Starbucks. We'd chatted often. She was just finishing her music education degree at the nearby state university, with a concentration in flute, and was looking for a regular teaching job.

One day, as Christmas was approaching, I asked her if she taught private flute lessons.

"Yes," she told me enthusiastically. I explained the situation, that my husband would be an older student. She seemed happy to take him on as a student. I told her I wanted to give him lessons as a Christmas gift, and that I wasn't even sure he'd like it or would want to continue, that I was taking a chance on doing this. She was quite agreeable.

"How much do you charge?" I asked. She was a dark-haired but quite fair-skinned girl. With her ready smile, she blushed slightly and looked a little uncomfortable.

"A half hour lesson? Would fifteen dollars be OK?" she asked.

"No," I said. "That's *way* too low. Don't ever charge so little for your time," I quickly added.

We both giggled and agreed on a more reasonable price, which I still felt was a bargain.

That Christmas, one of the gifts I gave Ted was a 9" x 11" printout, rolled up with a ribbon around it, announcing "flute lessons."

Soon thereafter, he and Beth were in touch, and they decided on a start date. At first, before he began, he told me he was skeptical because she was so young. But very soon, after each lesson he would say, "You know? She's a really good teacher." She was a taskmaster of sorts, gently done, of course. But he remarked over and over about how much he was learning. It was the only instrument for which he'd ever taken lessons, and he had played several instruments over the years.

He practiced between lessons and began to talk about getting a better flute. At the end of some lessons, I would joke to Beth, "Do you want my little boy to fill out a practice card?" I was remembering the clarinet and violin lessons of my youth, when I agonized over a mere twenty minutes of practice per day. But here, Ted was clearly enjoying his progress. Even early on, they played duets. It was impressive.

Over time, we came to know and love Beth. In the summertime, when we had a bounty of vegetables from our garden, she happily received the overflow. The flute, the lessons, and Beth were becoming a happy part of Ted's and my life. Would things like flute playing remain a part of Ted's life, now that he was sick?

And would life ever be so simple again? So many things to deal with. And then...Butterfly Corner.

BUTTERFLY CORNER

A little history.

For many years, we were boyfriend and girlfriend, having fun and very much in love. We grew close, met each other's families, developed friendships with other couples—the stuff most couples experience as their lives merge. For us, part of that included helping my aging parents, who lived nearby. They took an immediate liking to Ted, and were very happy we were together, as were our grown children. My youngest, William, was a teen at the time.

My mother died in 2006, after a long illness. My father, at that time, was becoming quite demented, and eventually, we had to move him from their condo, where family and hired helpers took turns taking care of him, to an assisted living place near us. When he became too ill and needed more care, we placed him in a nursing home close by, where we could visit him often. It worked out well, though we could clearly see he was in his last months, weeks, then days. That was in 2008. We'd been engaged, by then, for over a year, and had planned for our small wedding to be held at one of our favorite restaurants, down the street from the nursing home where Dad was being cared for, so he could more easily attend the wedding. I had arranged for my brother and a nurse's aide to help get him there and stay with him through the ceremony and reception. Dad had been looking forward to our marriage for some time.

Then, one week before our wedding, Dad died. We spent the next week going from funeral home to preacher to plan both the funeral and the wedding. We decided to go ahead with the small wedding. We'd planned to stay nearby in Portland that weekend anyway, instead of taking a honeymoon further away, since at the time of planning, we did not know what my father's condition would be. And family already had travel plans in place.

The wedding came off without a hitch, which would have pleased my father very much. Although we were very sad to lose him, we knew he and my mom were watching us from a spot high above. In my family, my dad had always been known as the "cheap" one. In truth, he was generous in many ways, but extremely frugal with himself. It was a joke in the family, and he laughed the hardest. So, after the wedding, I kidded that he was able to watch the wedding, but saved us the price of a plate at the reception.

That weekend, Ted and I checked into a beautiful new luxury hotel on the waterfront in Portland. Though only a few miles from our home, we giggled that we were tourists. We took a boat ride, had lovely meals together, and were as delighted with each other as any young newlyweds could be.

On the day after our wedding, we were walking around the Old Port, which is a funky, wonderful area of Portland near the waterfront, with great shops and restaurants. We were headed to Starbucks, at the corner of Exchange Street and Middle Street, crossing the street, when the biggest butterfly either of us had ever seen started hovering about us. It was remarkable in its size, bright orange, and simply would not leave us alone. Once we had crossed to the other side of the street, it crossed over and circled around me, then landed on Ted's leg. Finally, it left us long enough for us to go into Starbucks. Ten or fifteen minutes later, we emerged. There was the butterfly, as if waiting for us. I couldn't help myself.

"Hi, Dad!" I said.

Once again, the butterfly did his little hover-dance, and finally took off. I felt like this was a sign that my dad was finally free of the physical impairments on earth that had been caused by his dementia.

After that, we called this intersection "Butterfly Corner."

Fast forward now to the spring of 2011, as we face the big decisions about where to go for treatment for Ted's brain tumor.

It's now been several weeks since the work-up at MGH. Ted is still investigating factors to help with the decision regarding whether to get treatment here in Maine or go to Boston. It's a tough call and time is closing in.

I suggest to Ted that we talk to local medical people, and that makes good sense to him. The folks at Mass General, although understandably confident in their own level of expertise, have said from the start that the treatment can be given almost anywhere, and we know our nearby Maine Medical Center is no slouch.

We just aren't expecting anything magical.

Wait for it...

GATHERING INFORMATION

I call and leave a message for Dr. Rodger Pryzant, a radiation oncologist we have come to know and admire for his excellent and compassionate care when my mother was ill years earlier. He is part of Maine Medical Center's Radiation Oncology Department. He phones us back promptly and listens to our story. We get in to see him just a couple of days later.

He looks over all the material, test results, and medical records, examines Ted, and makes recommendations that make sense to us. He sets Ted up for an appointment with a neuro-oncologist, Dr. Devon Evans, at the Maine

Center for Cancer Medicine (now called New England Cancer Specialists). Dr. Pryzant is well aware that we are looking into all possibilities. Part of our dilemma is that a decision should be made reasonably quickly at this point, because whichever treatment center we choose, it will take the better part of a week for the team of physicists to calculate and set up the complicated radiation details. The tumor is growing. We have to catch it as soon as possible. It makes sense to meet with Dr. Evans while we make our final decisions about the "what and where" of treatment, knowing that there are no perfect answers. The standard care seems to be a good idea, considering all factors, including Ted's age. Despite near-insistent recommendations of out-of-state places from some of our loved ones, the decision is Ted's. We are fine with other people recommending various treatments and therapies and programs. But just once. After a bunch of times, it seems like less an issue of them trying to be helpful and more of some kind of issue within themselves. Ted must pilot his own ship, in Boston or Maine or wherever he chooses.

"I trained at MD Anderson. I *choose* to live in Maine," says Dr. Pryzant in his sincere and direct way. We get the message, and I am forced to look at my own prejudice in thinking that a big-name hospital means superior treatment. What is emerging is a trust that Ted and I are finding in our own Portland-based medical community, impressive in its own right.

Despite this, as one can easily imagine, our heads are spinning. It would be easier if there were a road map, but none exists.

EVERYONE'S GOT AN OPINION

"He should go to my chiropractor, Dr. Backbone. He really helps with neurological things." OK, but I'm pretty sure he can't fix a malignant brain tumor.

"Did he try taking extra Vitamin Blah-blah-blah? It really strengthens the immune system."

Please.

Treatment is very personal. I haven't heard so much input since the 1970s, when Lamaze was hitting mainstream America, and I'd joined in, pregnant with my first child.

Later, Ted would add acupuncture and massage therapy to his regimen, mostly for me, I think, because I nagged him. But for now, we just need to make headway around the first part of treatment.

We calculate that it will cost us about $8,000 to $10,000 to live in Boston for six or eight weeks—in the hot summer—if Ted gets his treatment in Boston. I find a hotel in Boston that offers suites to MGH patients at a reduced rate, and the woman with whom I speak and tentatively book a reservation is very accommodating, assuring me on all counts, including the fact that I can cancel the reservation at any time with no problem. We can even bring our doggy with us.

With just a few days left to agonize over it, we need to decide, as there will be preliminary procedures for Ted to go through in preparation for the radiology component, in particular.

We go back and forth. And forth and back.

We are completely lost, not knowing what to do. One moment, Ted says he wants to go back to Boston.

"Fine," I say. "Done. We can do it."

A few minutes later, he says, "Maybe staying here is best. They seem to know what they're doing."

Back and forth.

We are in a tailspin. Around the time we need to decide, we're having a particularly tough go. It's around ten p.m. when our anxiety peaks to crisis level. Then I remember that the social worker at Dr. Eichler's office had said to call her any time we needed to. I find her card and make the call to her office. We know she is not there at that hour, but I leave a message outlining the problem, and leave our phone number.

My voice must have sounded desperate.

The next morning at nine the phone rings, and it's our social worker. Ted and I both get on the phone. She tells us that many people get great care in their hometowns, that it sounds like we'd be in good hands in Portland, and she gives us enough sound information to make a decision. We will stay in Portland. We breathe again and we feel good. Ted, in the way we processed this, feels very comfortable with staying in Portland for the coming phase of treatment, and we know we have MGH as a backup should we need it. We realize we'll get the same quality of care right here.

We make the necessary calls, and Dr. Pryzant presses to line up the preliminary visits for the physicists to do the calculations necessary for the intricate and precise radiation treatments. We're relieved. About 98% relieved.

I think that any time people have a choice, in a serious medical situation, there is always a tiny bit of doubt.

But then, I promised a story about a little bit of magic.

CHAPTER 12

BUTTERFLY CORNER REVISITED

A few days later, Ted and I are downtown in Portland. In fact, once again we are at (big surprise) Starbucks, at one of the branches we haven't been to since, I don't know, maybe our honeymoon in the Old Port area. We live several miles away and aren't in this part of town very often. My niece Kathy is visiting us from NYC, and we've parked the car, the three of us going in somewhat different directions, with Starbucks being the meet-up point.

As Ted and I are coming out of Starbucks, cold drinks in hand, a car pulls up beside us and stops. Bear in mind, this Starbucks is right at a very busy corner in the touristy part of downtown Portland.

"Ted!" we hear a female voice call from the car.

We look, and in the driver's seat is my old boss and a colleague of both of ours, Leah. I've known Leah for a long time, and Ted has also known her for the ten years he's been working at the hospital. She's a nurse practitioner in the department in which we worked.

She pulls over enough to be out of direct traffic. We go over to the passenger-side window.

"How are you, Ted? I heard you were sick," she says.

It sounds funny to say this. She is so sincere, but at the same time has a big smile on her face, indicating how genuinely happy she is to see him, even though she has acknowledged his distressing news. We stand there, hovering at the car window, and chat for a minute, and Ted immediately mentions he is still deciding whether to have his treatment here in the Portland area. You know—that leftover doubt.

Ted says he will be seeing "a Dr. Evans" in a few days.

Now we get a really HUGE smile.

"He's *fantastic*!" she says. I know Leah is a cancer survivor herself, many years out and doing perfectly well.

"You'll love him. He's great!" she adds.

We tell her how happy that makes us feel, as we've been leaning toward staying here in Portland for treatment, and how great it is to run into her like this. I mean, what are the chances? Pretty slim, we say. Pretty slim that we would run into this particular person at the time we're struggling with our big decision, and that it would be someone we seldom see anymore but for whom we have much trust and respect. And that it just happens so spontaneously during a mundane activity such as getting a cup of coffee.

And then she says:

"You know, the funny thing is that whenever I come here to this Starbucks, I get my coffee and paper and get back into the car and go somewhere else to read the paper. I *never* just sit here. But today, for some reason, I did."

She points across the intersection where she had previously been parked.

"And after sitting here for a while," she says, "I saw you coming out of Starbucks."

Leah's personal and professional "two thumbs-up" about the doctor is what we need, to know we have made a sane, sound decision.

And it isn't long before we realize it happened…at Butterfly Corner.

Several days later, we meet with Dr. Evans at his office in Scarborough, just minutes from Portland, at a large cancer and treatment facility. Years ago, this renovated building was a K-Mart. Ted may not find sales in aisle three, but we know this place has a solid reputation for good care.

We meet a new oncology doctor today who looks to be about 12 years old, as all doctors look to be nowadays, but who is terrific: positive, optimistic, *fantastically* knowledgeable and up on all the latest stuff, enjoyable to talk with, a real boost. He really made the day for us.

Dr. Evans is very open to using our Boston doctors as consultants as needed, although we later learn that he is expert, despite Ted's cancer being one in which there are frequently few answers.

My niece Kathy stays with us for a few more days, providing me with an endless supply of laughs, nearly to the point of asthma. She instinctively knows and understands that Ted and I also need to process things privately. It continues to be quite an emotional time for us, preparing now for treatment, knowing there will be trials ahead.

A bare six weeks earlier, we left our home, headed west, looking forward with joy and enthusiasm to a reunion with dear friends, expecting a week of warmth, love and laughter, good food and drink, and music. We expected to return home to my last two months before retirement. We had begun to lay plans for travel, for visiting friends and family, for relaxation. Now I am facing a death sentence.

Ted's email:

And what a long, strange trip it's been...

After doing myself a mini-fellowship in neuro-oncology, I'm convinced for a bunch of reasons that the best treatment option for my ailing brain is right here in Portland, at least for the basics. So that will begin next week, midweek... Radiation treatments will happen five days a week until the end of July. Seven days a week, I take an oral chemo drug, along with maybe a couple of other drugs to counteract some of its side effects. I'm told it ain't too bad for most people, but I can expect to be rather less than my usually bouncy level of boyishness for the summer. After that, I continue the chemo drug on a reduced schedule for the next year or so, depending on a number of factors which are so far indecipherable. Then, we see where we've gotten. One option for the future is to have special electrodes implanted under my scalp, attached to a battery pack I wear all day long, with my head shaved twice a week, to generate alternating current impulses into the tumor bed to make it behave. Sounds very science fiction-y, and kinda cool. They've had some remarkably good results with this thing. FDA approved and all. I'm thinking I'll need some tattoos and a single dangly earring.

Maybe a Harley.

If we let ourselves slip into the downside of this thing, it can be quite horrible, and Kathy and I both, separately and together, have had and will have some terrible moments of grief and sadness. We have found ways, though, to truncate that quickly, and to get back into fighting mode, which seems the only reasonable way to go. So, we cry, hold each other, talk a lot about all the things you would imagine we talk about, and then we find ways to laugh, hang out with friends, go for walks, eat eat eat (I'm taking some steroids that do great things for Ben & Jerry's), and get on with it.

I have still some right-side weaknesses, mostly my leg, but I walk OK. Yesterday we did a pretty fast walk for a couple of miles around a small island that sits out in Casco Bay here. It was tiring but wonderful. I'm going up and down stairs almost perfectly. Prediction is that I may get back some more functionality, although probably not all the way. Still, I bet my kayak gets wet in Casco Bay before fall. Thankfully, there's been no effect on my speech, thinking, seeing, hearing, feeling, etc. I only wish it could've happened to my left side instead of my right. My left has never done me much good, ever.

And meanwhile, it's Maine and it's summer. Can't go wrong with that.

THE DAY BEFORE THE FIRST RADIATION TREATMENT
LETTER TO KATHY

Afternoon, by myself at Home, June 14, 2011
I want to be able to capture something in words that can't be captured in words by anyone else. You told me once that if I really wanted to appreciate and comprehend your late brother Bob's music, in a group called "Between," that I should get stoned. At the time, I was kind of taken aback, because I've always assumed you disapprove of pot use. But I've always loved smoking the stuff, so I've been careful to do it in secret around you. Mostly. I just haven't smoked much since you and I have been together. Until today.

Funny, the standing joke about potheads is that they are kind of valueless, that if you ask one to make a decision, it'll come out "Whatever" in an easygoing way. Except it's not a joke, it's part of what I'm talking about, the peacefulness. Like, let go, let's see where the road goes, wherever it goes.

So, this afternoon what I did was, I did get some stuff from a friend, and I smoked just a tiny bit, one drag, carefully, and put it out. And then I thought what do I do now? And habit led me first to the computer and then to music and then to earphones, loud, and Between, and your brother's incredible piece called "Listen to the Light." And I put on iTunes video display, full screen, while the music ran loud in my ears. And the video, which I did nothing to change or choose, it just happened, turned out to be a moving, graceful, lovely worm-like thing, with a white interior and then a coat that changed colors from time to time between blue and green and bright yellow. It didn't so much move as it flowed from one place to another. Sometimes it elongated into a snake or a straight line. Other times, it would turn a corner and slide downward, and then its mirror image would show up in the lower part of the scene, perfectly matching its movements, except backward and in high heels. All of this was in slow motion. The background of the top of the screen is very black, but the bottom third or so is a kind of musty gray-brown, makes it kind of seem like the surface of a pond with the night sky above, and the wormy thing is moving through the air and watching its image reflected in the water.

And all the while, there's Bob playing both oboe and oboe d'amore, overdubbed, doing this sinuous, ethereal dance with each other. Sometimes it almost sounds erotic, but then it isn't again, a kind of tease, and then another, and it just goes on and on that way, first one oboe and then the other picking up and releasing each other's notes, dancing with each other in slow motion, playing, in the very best sense of that word.

And Jesus! And I don't mean that lightly: Jesus! And I ended up in tears because my biggest thought was that this man, your late older brother whom I never knew except through your family lore and through some of his classical work, this man has created out there in the world exactly the music I have carried around inside myself all my life, but I have never had the gift of expression that he did. And I had the sensation of being taken up into something, somewhere I'd never been before. You'd probably call it a manifestation of Heaven, and that's good enough for me, although I'd put it in other terms. I'd say there was something eternal, mystical, forever, in there. And it brought with it an intense kind of peacefulness.

You have said many times that I seem a lot like him. Once or twice you even suggested some kind of reincarnation, I think.

So twice in a row I listened, loud, stoned, encased in earphones to shut out all the rest of the world. With the iTunes worm, full screen. And I let it take me wherever it wanted to go, and where it wanted to go was exactly back there: Heaven, something eternal, mystical, forever. And peaceful, so peaceful. You are a baby in the universe. You are a child of God, if that's your pleasure. You are a passenger on a never-ending train, or maybe a wanderer on an endless trail that is also endlessly fascinating and beautiful. And it doesn't matter how fast or how slowly you walk, because there is no destination, there is only now.

Kathy, you have brought me there. It isn't your brother or his music or the pot or, God forbid, the iTunes program. It's your soul, it's who you are all the way down inside, that leads me into the eternal, peaceful place, that then can reach deep down inside of me to my soul, if I have one somewhere. There must be one.

I was going to say I wish you could/would join me in that place, but as soon as I started to write that I realized how dumb it is: You go there yourself, when you can let go enough of your daily struggles and worries and pain. I hope you can let go more often and more deeply in time. I want you there with me, when you can. Forever, mystical, eternal. Peaceful. At peace. Whatever.

At peace even in the face of a terminal illness.

I love you so much.

CHAPTER 13

CANCER

Cancer.

What comes to your mind when you see or hear that word?

My hunch is that the concept that comes to your mind, if you have not yourself had cancer or loved and lived with someone who did, doesn't begin to take in the subtlety and complexity of the real thing.

How does one approach such questions, e.g., Will it be OK if someday I find someone else to marry? Or, more subtly, "If you go before I do, I will never want to be with anyone else in the future." I want to believe that such a promise of eternal fidelity, born out of eternal love, is a realistic hope. But what I've experienced of human life and living does not lead me in that way.

Another thing nobody much talks about is role shifting. A bit more than a year ago, if there was any significant physical work to be done in or around my home, it would automatically have been my job. This would include gardening, minor carpentry or electrical repair, and most jobs that require tools. If I couldn't do it, I'd get someone else to do it. Now all that has changed. I am now dependent, to a greater or lesser extent, on others to do some things that used to be "mine." We are still working on the details of what it all means. I did not know until recently how central is Kathy's desire to have a strong male in the house and in her life, particularly since she's been impaired physically and in pain since her car accident. I never in a million years would spontaneously have thought of us in those terms, but it makes good sense. I am always happy to learn there is someone who thinks I'm good at that role.

There are aspects of this, however, that puzzle me still. Last evening, she was making supper. Actually, I thought we were going to put together a light supper, both contributing to the effort. But when I went into the kitchen and attempted to do anything, she batted me away like a moth, and then she said something about there only being room for one cook, and so I left and went to watch the Olympics.

Going through the cancer experience with someone you love more than life, and who you know loves *you* more than life, leaves not an atom of your earthly existence unchanged. From the moment of diagnosis, you move abruptly from one universe to another. In every one of your relationships, the balances shift along axes having to do with power, authority, spontaneity, and activity level. People who know you look at you differently. You look at each other differently. You look at yourself differently.

Yes, we've all known that death is the natural and inevitable end of us all, but I suspect that most of us, very much including myself, expect there to be a gradual slowing down over years of time. In my situation, though, the transition from vibrantly healthy to profoundly sick takes place within a matter of days, sometimes only hours.

Most kinds of cancer announce themselves in fairly definitive ways. There is a lump, or there is an odd pain, or you can't catch your breath, or you cough and there is red stuff on your tissue. Brain cancer is different. In the first place, the way it announces itself depends on what part of the brain is affected. Brains are very, very complicated organs, serving, as they do, to control memory, emotionality, cognition, movement, speech, and all the varieties of the sensory systems. The part of the brain that controls vision is in the back of the head, the occipital lobe, which seems odd, given that the primary organs of vision are the eyes, in the front. If a brain tumor grows in the occipital visual cortex, it will announce itself by causing some degree of blindness or other visual disturbance. Perhaps you wake up one day and find that you can't see things that are low down and to the right side of you. There may well be no pain, or any other symptoms, and the change in vision may even be so subtle that you are tempted to ignore it at first. If you go to your doctor, he or she may test your visual fields and discover that there is a deficit in the lower right. There are several possible causes for such deficits, and further testing will be necessary to determine the culprit and to determine what needs to be done about it.

In my case, the tumor took up residence in the top of my brain, near the middle on the left side. The area is called the precentral gyrus but is commonly referred to by doctors as the motor strip because it contains the nerves that cause muscles to move. The muscles of the different parts of the body are controlled by nerve cells in correspondingly different parts of the motor strip, so that an injury or illness in that part of the brain will show itself by causing weakness or seizures or paralysis or some other disturbance in the muscles that correspond to the affected nerves. And because the right side of the brain commands the left side of the body, and vice versa, my tumor, in the left side of my brain, caused me to develop seizures and weakness in my right side, especially in my right leg and foot.

TREATMENT

We are told that as the initial six weeks of treatment progress, Ted will be tired. Somewhere around the third week it will start and get progressively worse.

Radiation treatment for this kind of cancer needs to be extremely precise, that is, the beam of radiation requires exquisitely careful aim and dosing. With that in mind, I am fitted with a mask that will hold my head and shoulders in a set position while the radiation machinery moves around me. On the day before my first radiation treatment, I go to the radiation center for the mask to be created. I lie down on my back on a table surrounded by large beige-colored machinery. The technicians bring in a flat white sheet of plastic mesh. The sheet is approximately three feet square. The technicians immerse the plastic mesh in warm water to soften it. Then it's placed over my head and face and the upper part of my shoulders while the technicians very securely and tightly press it over my face, head, and shoulders. This weird plastic mask of my head will later pin me down on the table like a Chilean miner in a cave-in, immobilizing me so the killer beams can be directed at precisely the right spots. The process of setting the mesh takes about fifteen or twenty minutes. When they are satisfied, the technicians chill the mesh to harden it. In the end, they have created a mask that consists of a stiff piece of white plastic mesh that exactly conforms to the features of my head and face and the upper part of my shoulders. Furthermore, the final mask includes a series of clips around the outside with which the mask can be secured to the radiation table.

Each day for the next six weeks, except for weekends and holidays, I go to the radiation center, where I remove my shirt and don an examination gown. Then I climb up on the table and lie down on my back. The technicians, usually working in pairs, place the mask they have created over my head and shoulders and secure the clamps. The holes in the mesh are large enough for me to have some limited vision of the room, but the mask is so tight that my eyes are squeezed shut, so my sight is not very clear. Of course, I also do not have my glasses on. It's absolutely impossible for me to move at all with the mask in place and secured to the table. The technicians make minor adjustments to the equipment, and then they all leave the room. I am left by myself, pinned to this table like a frog in a high school biology class. It always seems pretty creepy. Before they leave, each day someone asks if I want to have music played during the treatment and I always say no. My way of enduring treatments like this, including CT scans and MRIs, has generally been to put myself into a sort of trance state, and music interferes with that.

Each treatment lasts for just a couple of minutes. During that time, I hear humming noises from the space around me, but I have virtually no idea what's going on. After that, the technicians come back into the room and release me by opening the clamps on the mask. I discover that the skin on my face and head has taken on the configuration of the meshwork in the mask, so that I look a bit as if I've been in a waffle iron. The entire process is not as uncomfortable as it sounds, or at least as uncomfortable as it sounds to some of the people I have told about this. I am not subject to claustrophobia, in the first place, so that's not a worry. There are a few times when the pressure on my skin and especially on my nose becomes so severe that I begin to wonder if I will be able to breathe. Those times, however, are unusual. Most of the time, while the treatment is taking place, I simply fall asleep.

CHAPTER 14

WHAT HELPS

I go with Ted to his treatments and other appointments.

"Do you need help with an appointment next week? I have Tuesday and Thursday off," asks a friend who wants to give me a break.

Friends frequently offer to help. Many say that don't know how to help, and possibly they can't or are not able to help (*which is OK*), but they feel badly about our situation. The fact is that *we* don't know what would be useful at any one time.

Our friends David and Theresa give us love and support in so many ways. David takes Ted to a treatment and then out to lunch one day. I need a little free time and it removes any sadness I have from not being able to take him. Ted, at this point, can drive, but he doesn't feel very peppy, so this is a chance for just a couple of guys to have lunch together. For all I know, they talk about something dreadful, like the upcoming Monday Night Football.

These friends nudge us regularly to find out what we need. They really want to help. Theresa phones me. She wants to do something for us.

"I don't know," I say. She asks again.

"Paper towels?" I finally say, my mind nearly blank.

She shows up the next day with a small vase of flowers from their garden and a grocery bag full of paper towels, paper plates and cups, napkins—a dream bag of stuff.

Meryl and Fred become our go-to people when we spontaneously want company, or to go to dinner or a movie. A bonus is that if Ted needs to use a public restroom, Fred can take him. When Ted and I are out alone, I'm that person who helps him, and I've been inside a lot of men's rooms. One day during the summer, Meryl and Fred call us to invite us to dinner at their place—lobster, salad, homemade bread, blueberry pie. It's wonderful. They have no expectations of us. It's also a meal completely devoid of cancer talk. Delightful. Did I mention that by now I am no longer following my weight-loss plan? Eh. Maybe later.

People offer prayers and good vibes, bring practical things like food, or send a simple note or email: "We're thinking of you." Every little, simple thing makes a difference. Then again, some blow me away. A friend stops by with a basket of homemade muffins she's made, with a jar of jam from her husband's delicious recent summer batch. That...is amazing. Promises to do something, when kept, make all the difference. I realize that good intentions are good enough, too. God knows I've fallen short of promises to do something. We get busy, we get tired, all human stuff. We do what we can. One friend of mine insists on buying my coffee when we get together. Another friend hugs me every time I run into her. And a couple of other friends? I can call them at any hour if I am having a crying jag, which usually happens in the middle of a public place. And one of those friends...is my older daughter, grown up and with a family of her own to care for.

GOOD BILL HUNTING

I call the billing office at Mass General. On two separate occasions, I speak with billing reps who are kind and wonderful, as opposed to the "customer care (as if) representatives" or whatever duplicitous name they're called at our insurance company, the company I'll call "Big Insurance," so I don't get sued. The woman at MGH says she will put his account on hold.

"Don't worry, honey. Just let us know after you get a decision and we'll go from there," she says. No pressure, no deadlines. Later, in a subsequent conversation, a second woman in billing tells me she will pray for us, after I disclose what we are going through.

Although there are moments when I feel completely alone, I realize I am not. There are God's angels all around me (except at Big Insurance). But virtually everywhere else I look, I can find a few.

I begin praying every night. I pray often throughout the day in brief little blips. When God looks down on a hospital, or the home of a sick person, He must hear a veritable roar of prayer. I pray and pray and pray. I believe all prayers are heard. Mine are not eloquent. But I feel the love. I feel it, over and over. It was—and is—there.

Lying in bed next to my very worn-out, energy-sapped husband, I say prayers to God and the saints, rereading written prayers. I am not alone. Ted sometimes asks me to say or read them aloud so he can hear them. *We* are not alone.

BEGINNING OF ANNULMENT

Meanwhile, some things in life seem to go in a different direction altogether. That is, something that has nothing directly to do with cancer. Ted and I begin to pursue the annulment process, first talking with our parish priest, Father Jim, about it, then setting up appointments with the canon lawyer at the local diocese. It's going to be a long process, but the people involved are extremely kind, and all things point to it being ultimately successful. They understand Ted is anxious to get it going, and initial appointments are set up. One aspect of this that is important to me is talking with my son, who is the child of the marriage I am seeking to annul. I talk to Will, who seems to take it in stride, realizing that it in no way invalidates the joy or meaning of his birth. After that, I have a brief conversation with my ex-husband, who is understanding as well. Ted contacts the women on his side of things, too, and is met with some sarcasm and bursts of laughter, but a nod to go ahead. There is also compassion around the news of his brain cancer. During the process, which takes many months—mostly because we've dragged our feet and/or were just very busy with appointments, plus Ted is busy being sick and exhausted—there are times when I question if it is worth the hassle.

"Look, Ted. We're already married," I say more than once, "and any God who is truly loving will not care about a piece of paper."

Each time I watch Ted slowly make his way into the diocese offices to discuss something, it makes me very sad. I worry it's too much for him.

But he plunges onward. I tease him that he will become Catholic if he isn't careful.

"No," he says, "I just want to make sure we're together after this life."

RADIATION ONCOLOGY APPOINTMENT

A pretty good day. Beautiful weather, high 70s, sunny and bright, light winds. Will is here. Kathy had a psychotherapy session in the early morning. Midday I go for my radiation. They tell me I'll be meeting with the doctor and the nurse, so Kathy comes along, too, because we have several questions about medication schedules, etc. Treatment is, as usual, uneventful, although the mask is really uncomfortable. Kathy suggests it's getting worse because I eat so much and have gotten fatter. I have gained about twenty pounds since all this began, partly because of the steroid medication I take, the dexamethasone. I swear that stuff was invented by the ice cream industry. The doctor we see today is Dr. McGinn; really seems like a good guy, takes some time, is good-natured, answers all questions. He says that after several weeks of radiation, I may start to have headaches and other symptoms, mostly fatigue, from the radiation alone, let alone the drugs. Dr. McGinn also asks me if I typically wear a hat when I'm out in the summer sunshine. I tell him that I have always disliked wearing hats and very often do not do so. With a slight smile, he looks me straight in the eye and says, "You don't need to get any more radiation up there. Wear a hat."

THE SOCIAL LADDER—FILLED WITH LOVE AND FOOD

Haagen Dazs, anyone? Ted and I have developed something of a party brain. We'd spent weeks crying, hugging, pledging and re-pledging our eternal love for each other. Now we've begun to think of our days together differently. One day it hits me: What if he has only eight months to live? Would we want to look back and remember eight months of crying and agonizing over not having much time together? Or would we want to say that we blew the roof off? Though a little tricky to pull off, we go full speed ahead, going to movies, sometimes three times a week, eating popcorn some nights for supper, sometimes bringing fruit along, or red licorice and chocolate. We skip a movie called *50/50* even though it's gotten good reviews, as we don't want to think about cancer, the subject of this film. We see good movies and bad ones—a great diversion—and the seats at our favorite movie house are very comfy. I pop a couple of Tylenols for my back, and Ted brings his medicine along to take at the scheduled times.

Oh, we eat well, overall. We go to restaurants. I figure we can blow through a little bit of our savings if it means good quality of life. And if it turns out that Ted is a longer-term survivor, then we'll just eat peanut butter sandwiches later when our savings are gone. We are fortunate to be able to afford this as a temporary salve.

But there is a different kind of food, the food that fills our souls, an outpouring of love and support from family and friends, as they hear what's going on. Because Ted's managers in the workplace have kept his information confidential, there's only vague knowledge that Ted is out sick and will be out indefinitely. So, after careful thought, Ted constructs a memo revealing his illness and emails it to his manager, asking that it be distributed amongst the staff. Following this, people from his workplace stop over with hugs and casseroles, baskets and dishes of healthy snacks, offers to help, plans to bring meals once a week. One coworker brings the heaviest, most fabulous sausage and veggie lasagna we have ever had. We joke that it almost makes having a deadly illness worthwhile. It's accompanied by a dark, dense chocolate cake that must weigh ten pounds. Those ten pounds, incidentally, makes its way to my abdomen in short order. In a gift basket we receive from his workplace, someone has added in a $20 Starbucks gift card. Incredibly thoughtful. I use it. Caring for the caregiver and all that.

"I'm thinking of you. You are strong. That cancer doesn't stand a chance against you!" one friend writes in a card.

One of the sentiments Ted likes best is from a friend who writes, "This bites."

Being forgotten, especially when sick, hurts. Even worse is to hear a voicemail that says, in a low, depressed voice, "Oh, I'm so sorry this is happening to you. I feel so terrible about this…" and on and on, clearly implying that the recipient is sure to croak at any minute. It's in the tone of voice, and not helpful to either of us.

One friend emails me every few weeks for months, usually a simple one-liner: "Hi. Thinking of you, hoping things are improving. Here's my new number ——, and of course, you can call me at any hour. No need to answer this email. Just letting you know you are in my heart." This woman has recently lost her husband after a long battle with illness and knows what it's like to walk in my shoes. These emails from her are perfect, requiring no response from me unless I feel like it and have the time and energy to do so.

A friend of ours from our former workplace at the hospital, Bill, who is known for his wonderful workplace cartoons, sends copies of these to us regularly, with simple and sincere notes to us, wishing us well, reminiscing about old times via cartoons. What a treasure it is to receive these.

When an old friend of mine from Nova Scotia plans to pass through town over the summer, I explain to her that I might not be able to see her or put her up overnight as we have done previously when she's traveled through Maine. It's clear she understands. I ask her to email me when passing through town, both coming and going. On her way through the first time, I don't even respond to her email, a reflection of what's going on with us. On her way back a week later, she emails me, and I try calling her. I figure we might chat for a few minutes on the phone.

"Where are you right now?" I ask her.

It turns out she's at a hotel just a few miles away. I suggest we meet at the nearby Panera for a cup of tea. Ten minutes later, we are sitting at a booth. For an hour. The world continues to slowly spin, and my husband is safe at home. It turns out to be one of the highlights of my summer. She shows me pictures of her home in Nova Scotia, of her pup, and pictures of her late husband who died of cancer just a couple of years earlier. She knows I need friendship. There are no lectures about treatments, nothing like that. Just sitting with a friend and looking at doggy pictures. After I get home, she calls me. She has something she'd picked up for me and forgot to give me. Two days later, I open the packet she has sent, which contains a colorful summer tank top she had picked up for me on her trip.

Another day, a package arrives for me from Ruth, the wife of Ted's friend Bob. It contains a lovely note from her and a bunch of sweet and practical little gifts, including a rubber ducky tea strainer, which becomes a permanent fixture on my stove next to the tea bag container, salt and pepper. It moves me to know she cares so much.

Ted is tolerating the radiation and chemotherapy overall, but the radiation treatments fatigue him progressively. The chemotherapy carries several uncomfortable side effects. There are times when he feels like total crap. I suffer with him, in a different way. Sometimes he's too weak to get his shoes on without help. He is deeply discouraged.

At times, I wonder if it's worth it, and I'm tempted to quit treatment.

Ted's a physician by trade, but a runner by joy. He also kayaks, hikes, and skis. In the past, when we would go outdoors to get some exercise, I'd walk and he'd go off running, and come back to check with me every ten minutes or so. He'd be dripping wet, and he loved that part, too. He'd raced in the San Francisco Bay to Breakers many times, and in Maine, in his 60s when we met, he was still running up a storm. Now, some days when he gets up from the sofa in the living room and walks into the kitchen, he announces, "That's all I can do for now."

There are so many ways in which this illness has changed our lives. His emotional health normally finds buoying through physical activity, and that's no longer possible.

Thank God he still has his curious mind.

After about the first month of this treatment, I decide I want to have a recording of the radiation treatment itself. I show up for my treatment one day with a video camera and a tripod. The technicians are very surprised and ask me what I have in mind. I tell them I want to make a movie of my radiation treatment and ask if that is all right with them. Apparently, no one has ever asked that before, and they are hesitant at first. While they discuss it, I just go about setting up my own equipment off in a corner where it will be out of the way. I arrange the camera and tripod in such a way that my head and shoulders will be central to the view. Then, having gotten the agreement of the technicians, I turn on the camera, climb on the table as usual, and we proceed. The short film that comes out of this is pretty interesting to me. This is the first time I really discover that the radiation machinery, which is quite blocky and heavy-looking, actually moves smoothly and with great precision around my head as I lie pinned to the table. For some reason, I have envisioned that the radiation only moved internally inside the equipment. I guess I was thinking of the way things work when you get a dental X-ray or a chest X-ray. In that case you, the patient, hold still and the machinery is also still and stable and they take a picture of you. Now, however, these fairly massive bits of beige machinery are in motion as I lie still. The whirring and humming noises that I hear are the sounds of the various gears and wheels inside the machinery as it positions itself to irradiate the next section of my brain.

CHAPTER 15

THE INN AT HOME

I am quickly learning the art of compromise regarding daily activities, including, to some degree, self-care. That is, self-care of a superficial nature. What's going on with Ted—with us—puts so much in perspective. Some days I don't shower. I wash my hair less often. Not to say I totally let myself go. I just don't see my former routine as so important.

I learn the benefit of wearing less makeup, most days, especially mascara. It's aggravating to be crying and then have the added annoyance of stinging eyeballs from mascara. I cry thinking about what the doctors say. I cry in between Ted's appointments, imagining the possibilities, and I must work hard at reminding myself that there is some treatment, even if it isn't a cure. I feel myself welling up in the supermarket when I pass by his favorite snacks—Fritos corn chips—or hummus—or when we take rides together, suddenly wondering if this is the last time he will see this view or the last time we'll see it together.

Crying proves to be a good release. In some way, it keeps me strong and at the same time helps our distress seem less powerful, which is good because angst is so much a part of everyday life. I'd been seeing a psychotherapist prior to this for the injury that cost me my career as a nurse. At around the time of Ted's diagnosis, I had begun to see her less frequently, maybe every two to three weeks. After we are told he has a brain tumor, I resign myself to the fact that I will see her weekly for as long as needed. She will prove to be a comrade in my mental health, survival, and a mentor, in a sense, to my approach to life in its ever-changing formation. She will always be a personal hero of mine.

However, before long, something starts to happen. One by one, or a dozen or a hundred—I don't know, it all blends together—people start coming for overnight visits. Relatives, out-of-town close friends, all people we cherish, call to say they are coming for a few days to see us. They're worried and need to see Ted. This is in addition to our *expected* visitors. Some ask first if it's convenient to stay with us. We only have so many beds. We've moved through the late spring and early summer haze from Ted's horrific diagnosis, are in the middle of his radiation and chemotherapy, and there's less time to do normal routine activities. We're eating out a lot, which seems easier at first, and now treating many of our guests to the restaurant meals, as well. Finally, we figure out a way to say "No, not now" without hurting people's feelings. It isn't easy. If we say no, we feel like we're insulting people. Neither Ted nor I have the energy for the work involved with having visitors. The irony of this is that sometimes we think we need a quiet week, but a few days later, we wish like heck we could see *that person*. We never know from one day to the next whether Ted will feel up to having a guest or not. I'm so stressed-out that I put my foot down long before Ted does. Frankly, I'm doing much more of the work, so it doesn't have as much of an impact on him. He isn't the one getting the groceries, cooking, washing clothes, and doing the important stuff—like tracking how much toilet paper is left in the house. We are emotionally spent. And now I'm running a B&B.

The question of how to ease back on visitors is tricky. But we have a precedent. A couple of months earlier, a dear friend of ours had a stroke. During his recovery, his wife put a stop to all visits for a while by sending out an email that said, "We have hit a wall...exhausted," and explained they needed time apart from everyone. It was well stated and understandable, so now we borrow it as needed.

At one point, I tell my sister Laurie the beds are taken, and she generously says she'll stay nearby at a hotel. She brings her theater work with her, and even gets together with a good friend of ours from our church song group, and they connect on music and theater interests. My sister wins a prize, in my book. She makes no demands and is actually the person I initially feel guiltiest about, until we have a frank discussion. She has no expectations, but really is "there" for me. Same with my daughter Cassie and her family, who have previously planned a vacation in Maine. They voluntarily stay at a hotel. Others seem to catch on.

For the company we don't turn away, one thing that works well is to remind people prior to visits that if they aren't feeling well *for any reason*, please let us know and reschedule. "He's on chemo," I say, "and his immune system is compromised." Ted cares less about this than I do.

I eventually cut my obligatory activities roughly in half. It's just too easy to go full swing into the old, normal schedule only to find out that someone nearby is frustrated and cursing very loudly, and that person turns out to be, um, me.

Ted's illness and treatment are our daily reality. Certain practical things make a difference. For example, I try to keep our car gas tank full. I don't want to have to stop at a gas station when we're en route to a spontaneous medical appointment or the ER. In the past, I was famous for being the one whose gas tank light went on, often when we were nowhere near a gas station.

"Should I fill it up now, or can we wait till after we go to dinner?" I'd ask.

"Whatever you want. But I'm not walking to a gas station if you run out," Ted would say. That was usually enough to get me to stop, and we'd fill it up. Now it's more important to be on top of that.

I start keeping a small nonperishable snack and a decaf teabag in my purse for times when we get stuck at a long appointment. I find myself getting pretty good at throwing together things like peanut butter on crackers, or quick mixes of nuts and pretzel pieces. Pretty much anything I have on hand works, especially wrapped bite-sized pieces of Dove dark chocolate candy.

I keep the basic food and house supplies on hand, keeping a running list of what we need for when I'm near the store. I'm learning to keep an extra carton of milk, a loaf of bread, surplus toilet paper, those basics that we really don't want to run out of. This whole cancer business is so unpredictable that I've started to treat the essentials as though we are having a winter "storm watch" here in Maine. What do we *not* want to be without? Extra paper towels are amazingly handy for all kinds of unexpected things that I won't go into. I am environmentally concerned, believe me. But there are times when an extra roll or two of paper towels are crucial when taking care of someone who is ill. Some other year I'll be more environmentally conscious.

JUST ANOTHER DAY

After my treatment, we drive to Skillin's nursery and buy some garden plants, tomatoes, beans, cucumber, basil, etc., which I will plant tomorrow. We also have been talking about buying me a used BMW sedan, maybe 5-series, auto shift, which would make driving to NYC and other places a lot more comfortable, I think. Both of my cars, the old BMW and the 4Runner, are now out of action because of too much rust to pass state inspection. Not sure what exactly I'll do with my wonderful old 4Runner, but the BMW is going out front by the street tomorrow, with a for-sale sign on it.

I need to add that both these vehicles are pieces of shit. Especially the BMW, which Ted bought for about $1500 from a swindler at a meeting point who, at the time, kept telling us he was "a perfectionist" in reference to taking care of the car. The thing, we later discovered, was *literally* duct-taped together in places. Lesson: Do not buy an old car from a sleazy guy at the side of the road even if the car reminds you of the first car you owned decades earlier.

I play some flute this afternoon, a series of minuets that are part of the Bach flute sonatas. Sounds really pretty good. I worry that I may have lost a small bit of dexterity in my right hand, and my right arm tends to slide lower than it used to, so I have to work at keeping the right side of the flute high enough. But, overall, I really sound good, and it feels good to be playing.

July 4, 2011

Today is our wedding anniversary, number 3. And we spend most of the day trying to figure out what to do about it.

At loose ends until midafternoon, we both recognize we're sitting here wondering if there's going to be a fourth anniversary, and we start crying and holding each other. After that, we go for a walk, rest, make love, sleep, and cook up some burgers and hot dogs and corn on the grill. Then we go for a drive in the "new" used older BMW, a great deal purchased from a reputable dealership a few towns away (yay!). And we end up along Baxter Boulevard watching the fireworks with arms around each other. Sweet, wonderful, sad. We love, and we're deeply happy in our love, and the future is now unknown and unknowable. And, yes, it's all well and good to say that, well, isn't that true for everyone, but it is not the same when you face a known and real threat. Yes, you could get hit by a bus tomorrow, but there are no buses currently in sight, while my body tells me every minute that something is very wrong.

LIVING WITH CANCER

July 11, 2011
Today marks the halfway point for my radiation treatments. Fifteen down, fifteen to go. The mask is really uncomfortable, sometimes almost bringing me to the point of mild panic.

I realize today, on the way home from the treatment, what people mean when they say, "living with cancer." When you first get the diagnosis, the terrible news, there is an enormous amount of furor and anxiety and new things one has to learn in very little time, and there's fear and grief and terror. But after a while, things just settle down. It helps that our steady river of house guests has dwindled off. Will is here now, Randey was here for one night over the weekend, both wonderful to have around. My sisters were planning to come up in a couple of weeks, together, but now Mom has fallen and sustained a cracked pelvis and may need them to stay with her. Aside from that, it's mostly back to Kathy and me, us, which is good.

It's just us, living with cancer.

CHAPTER 16

GASPS

I am currently living my life with near-constant gasping, like what happens when a baby is just learning to walk. Ted will sometimes take my hand or arm when he is unsteady, but more often does not want to and does not find it helpful. He has not one, but two walkers in the house, parting gifts from MGH. Except for one very shaky night after a seizure, he refuses to use them. His reasoning is that unless it is a dire need, he's better off navigating and practicing balance on his own. True, maybe. But witnessing his poor coordination daily is not fun. I can practically feel the adrenaline pumping through my system a couple of times a day.

THE IMMORTAL BRAIN OF TED WHITE

July 19, 2011
Have found myself thinking about modern astrophysics, in an unquiet way. It occurred to me yesterday that the approach being taken by physicists, mostly, is to employ ever more huge energies in order to smash things to bits in order to study the bits. There has even been speculation, and not just from crazy folks, that it might be possible to create our very own black hole. A black hole in a laboratory. Wow!

One way of looking at this is: If you enter a black hole, you move "backward" through space-time in such a way that eventually you arrive at the beginning of the universe. There is also an argument between some of the deeper thinkers in this realm about what exactly happens to you if you decide to go into a black hole. It's something like this: The edge of a black hole is known in physics as the "event horizon." If you or I watched someone walk over the event horizon, we would see that person obliterated, ripped apart into tinier and tinier bits and pieces until there was no sign that he/she had ever existed. However, at the same time, that individual would not be noticing anything out of the ordinary, just out for a summer walk in the country.

I'm not trying to explain how this happens. Although my undergraduate studies were in engineering physics and mathematics, and although I've attempted to keep up with the field in some degree, I don't have nearly the knowledge or sophistication to account for the amazing weirdness of subatomic physics.

Seems to me, however, that we are approaching a teaching about something like immortality. I hope my more un- and anti-religious friends will pardon me or let me off the hook with the consideration that perhaps my cancer has eaten up my thinking. But I have been thinking a lot about immortality for some months now, and I find that it is easy for me to accept that at some level of reality we are immortal. The connection back to astrophysics is to my belief that the physicists are stuck. They keep trying to do more and more of the same thing, and they get impressive results as they go along, but I can't help but feel that they're not looking at something that is right there in front of us, but unperceived, and it has something to do with those arguments about the nature of black holes.

I mean, suppose the center of a black hole is the origin of the universe. The origin of the universe! The mass becomes so great that even light itself is stopped, time stops or even moves backward, everything folds in on itself, everything becomes one. One moment, one place, one experience.

But here's the thing: There are tens of thousands of black holes. So, are there tens of thousands of ways to get to the beginnings of the universe? Or asked another way, does the universe have tens of thousands of beginnings?

And then, of course, comes the worst question of all: What was going on before the universe began? Was there another universe, maybe one that was a mirror opposite of the one we know? Are there infinite numbers of universes "out there"? And just what does "out there" really mean?

And how does all this relate to human consciousness? I mean, consciousness in the sense that we humans may be able to make some small dent in comprehending just what this "universe" thing really is.

Here is for me another, related question: We seem to exist in a world of solidity: trees, people, cars, tables, dogs, have substance. When we bump into them, we take notice. They and we have weight: We know how to measure that. But the physicists tell us that if you represented the nucleus of an atom by a pencil point, then the nearest electron would be about two miles away, and in between would be nothing but empty space. In other words, almost all of everything is actually "empty" space. What saves the day is that those incredibly remote objects whirling about in that empty space are held tightly to each other by several forces of unimaginable strength. So that when you pound on a table, the hardness you experience as your fist hits the wood is the resultant forces working to hold the wood molecules together. But really...REALLY, really...all that is there is almost all empty space.

And the same could be said of you and me. You and I are almost all empty space.

So there. How does that make you feel?

How does this relate to the questions about black holes and immortality and all that? I don't really know. But if you and I are almost all empty space, would it be possible someday to find a way to merge into each other, or exchange parts—or the opposite, become so estranged and weird that we would no longer even see/recognize each other?

Kathy and I have a belief system. There is no other term for it. We believe, both of us, that we have been together since the origins of time and that we always will be together. OK, make of it what you will, but we believe it quite solidly. This is not a concept I have ever had with previous women in my life, or men, either. I guess the idea started to creep in some years ago. One of us might be telling the other a story about something that had occurred years ago, before we met, something that maybe involved other family, or people we never have known together. And partway through telling the story, the listening one would say,

"Well, of course, you remember, I was there, too." And we started to become characters in each other's stories. So, Kathy might say, "Hey, remember when you and I and your friends went camping?" And this was a way of getting to know each other in deeper ways. And it has led to this idea that in some way we not only are intimate parts of each other's lives, but always have been, always will be.

CHAPTER 17

A CLEAN HOUSE, PRAYERS, AND FINAL RADIATION

> **LOVE CALLING**
>
> He calls me "Sweetie dear." He calls out "I love you" from another room, for no other reason at all other than that he loves me and wants to tell me.

July 2011

The summer takes a hit on us financially. And it disrupts our (OK, *my*) sense of order. If you want to have control over your life, don't get cancer, and don't let a family member get cancer. Now, somewhere out there in reader-land, I hear someone saying philosophically, "Maybe this is your lesson—to learn to give up control." OK. I've thought of that, too, although I don't have any rationale for that kind of thinking. And fuck lessons.

Stress, exhaustion, meals out due to company...necessary purchases, like the shower chair we bought but used only for a short time because thankfully, Ted's balance improved enough to safely stand and wash during a shower, with use of shower socks. For now, that chair becomes another table in the bathroom to pile things on. We eventually turn it into a bathroom plant stand, which also works nicely.

I can barely keep up with the laundry. I'm not even close with the housework. I'm still working ten to fifteen hours a week and writing very part-time, both a regular near-monthly column, and some feature stories locally that I have lined up. I stop taking on extra stories for one of my favorite publications. It saddens me, but I have to be realistic. It's still relatively early in Ted's illness and treatment, and I don't want to be responsible for a story with a deadline I can't make. We're in a serious learning curve with his illness. There are frequent unexpected events. "Any day without a visit to the Emergency Room is a good day" becomes my motto. My own medical needs also take time—physical therapy at home, visits to my back doctor and various therapists, picking up medicines, making phone calls, and so on. Offers to help sometimes seem to make things more complicated than to simply do it myself.

Midsummer, a bunch of Ted's coworkers arrange for two women to come to the house to clean. Naturally, I go around the house in a mad frenzy, straightening up as best as I can. Isn't that what anyone would do? I mean, I have to at least get some surfaces clear of stuff so they *can* clean.

They are amazing. They're not housecleaners by profession but do this once in a while as a semi-volunteer effort. In about three hours, the house, which is a big 200-year-old farmhouse, looks remarkable. I don't know how they do it. Apparently, they have been paid by Ted's coworkers, but we try to give them a tip. They refuse.

"What we'd like," one says, "is to pray with you."

So here we are, outside in the front yard, a coworker coming up the driveway with food, and we all just stop, join hands, and one of the women says a few words of prayer for Ted's healing. It's lovely. Even Ted, no fan of any particular doctrine or belief, is moved by this.

Some weeks later, I pick up the phone and call a man whom I'd interviewed for a story a year earlier. He runs a local franchise of a national cleaning company, and the story I did about him and his wife and family focused on a program he offers in which his company does a thorough, one-time cleaning for a person or family that is experiencing a serious illness or event. I call and tell him what is going on, and that I want to set up regular cleaning services, but no, I do not need a free clean. He argues that point, but in a few days, his wife shows up at the house, takes inventory, and we set up an every-other-week cleaning schedule. It's the start of my every-other-week rants, running around the house screaming "It's such a mess!" and "We'll never get this junk cleared out!" and other shouts of despair, in preparation for the maids coming the next day. But it's worth it. They are fabulous.

My husband and I have different views of certain things in the house. Although I fully take responsibility for my part of the clutter, he is not bothered by any of it—his or mine—and doesn't understand why we need to straighten up for the maids. He doesn't care if the house is clean or not. Why do I bother to do all the preparation? he asks.

"So they have some surfaces to clean!" I yell. Yeah. I'm a living doll.

It's a point we never agree on, other than to agree we both have a lot of sorting and throwing out to do. Sometimes it gets better, and the piles of junk get sorted, put away, thrown away, or donated. Then real life happens, and it all goes to crap.

When we aren't watching our credit card bills rise directly related to the circumstances of Ted's illness, we worry about the medical bills our insurance company is rejecting.

July 28, 2011
My final radiation treatment! In a way, it seems uneventful. I go in and lie down on the table, as usual, and the technicians pin down my mask, as usual, and the radiation equipment circles around my head, as usual, and then I am done. The technicians wish me well, and I wish them well in return. They ask if I want to keep the mask that has been used to focus the radiation and, of course, I say yes. That mask now sits atop an old woodstove in our bedroom and stares at us every night as we retire. Who knows, maybe it keeps watch over us as we sleep.

A strange irony: This same date is the date I chose for my final retirement from my workplace. So I am unemployed—retired, if you will, although not in the way I hoped it would come about. I no longer have to go to work unless I choose to. I probably will not choose to. The simple truth is that, even though I have usually profoundly enjoyed and been moved by, not to say challenged by my work as a psychiatrist, psychotherapist, and psychoanalyst, in recent years I would have to say it has worn me down. That is especially true of the work at the hospital, which has been enormously draining for me. So, for the most part, I am overjoyed that I don't have to work anymore. At the same time, there is also a kind of melancholy feeling.

METHYLATING FACTOR

Around two months after the biopsy in Boston, the test results come back which measure the tumor's "methylating factor." Ted does, in fact, have this factor present in his tumor cells, which puts him into a potentially longer survival category. This is great news within the category of bad news. Although not everyone with a high methylating factor is in that small group of longer survival, everyone in that group does have the methylating factor. This is more hopeful, even though more than one doctor has told us, "Cancer is unpredictable."

"Remember, the doctor says you have a high methylating factor," I remind Ted, when he's feeling discouraged or anxious about his survival chances.

BOB, LUBEC, AND RAILS

Ted's dear friend Bob comes to visit from the "other" Portland (Oregon) for a week. It's a scheduled visit, and a chance to relax my standards. I decide *not* to clean up simply because we have company. Goodness knows he wouldn't expect it. He is here to spend time with Ted. We have a great time, and the three of us even take a mini trip together while he's here.

Driving up to Lubec, almost into Canada in the easternmost coastal area, Ted intermittently naps in the backseat, and Bob and I, in the front, chat and get to know each other a little more, as I drive part of the way. It's not an easy week in some ways because we are all feeling the impact of Ted's illness, but it goes well, and we are so happy the visit is happening. This is especially important to Ted and me in other ways. He and Bob have been the best of friends for decades, although not unlike some friendships, they have had some rocky times. It was not unusual for Ted to mention a "falling out" from a previous time, and how they had managed to rebuild the friendship. Also, I had a minor run-in with Bob some years earlier, which had left me feeling unhappy. Bob was not a friend who glossed over things, and I respect that, even though it can also make me uncomfortable. But what is happening this week is about Ted. In our love and concern for Ted, I think there becomes an unspoken, new respect that we both have for each other. I watch Bob as he patiently helps Ted when needed. I give them time together to talk, which gives me a break, too. Bob has post-polio syndrome, so his walking pace is slowed. For the first time, both men are moving at about the same pace. During one of the last days Bob is visiting, he takes me aside while Ted is busy with something else. His manner is so sweet, and I have a deep understanding of why Ted loves him so much. He points to the front of our house.

"I think now would be a good time to install rails beside that second set of stairs," he says, as he directs my eyes toward the lower three stone steps that lead from the paved driveway to an area of grass below the upper steps (where there is already a rail to hold onto).

"And maybe get an electronic chair for the inside staircase," he suggests.

I agree with him. But sometime later when I suggest it to Ted, he says he doesn't need nor want them. Much, much later, he would agree to the outside stair railing, adding, "But I don't see how we can get one."

ME: BITCH

Summer days blur, with doctors' visits, treatments, naps for Ted, and my own errands. My anxiety is barely manageable, coming out in the form of overprotectiveness, blatant nagging, and overeating. Every now and then, I see Ted trip or fall, which renews a need within me to have him hang onto me, accompanied by my countless utterances of "Be careful." I offer to do things for him that he wants to do for himself. I am overly solicitous. Most of the things I offer are things that, although requiring much effort, Ted *can* do for himself. But then he says things that make me wonder if he has any idea at all how unsteady he appears, like wanting to get up on a ladder to fix something on the roof, making me especially bitchy. I probably ask him this universal question at least once a week:

"Are you crazy?!?"

And here's another thing, as long as I'm confessing. Most of the time, I have a ton of sympathy for my wonderful husband. But being human, especially after working, grocery stops, traffic, and inattentive or rude drivers on the road, I come home to more than my share of chores. The dog is barking his fool head off, I need to fix supper, my back is killing me...then, seeing my (did I say wonderful?) husband lounging in the living room, chuckling at a good book or contemplating astrophysics...is just plain ANNOYING. I'm exhausted, and he's asking me some big philosophical question like what I think happened before the Big Bang.

"Before the Big Bang?" I mutter. "Before the Big Bang? Probably a husband was sitting around eating corn chips while his wife was ready to collapse!"

It's in these moments that he looks at me, puzzled, and asks, "Is there something wrong, sweetie dear?"

For better, for worse, in sickness, and—oh, never mind.

CHAPTER 18

VISIT TO TED'S MOM

September 14–17, 2011
What's been going on between July and September?

We're on a weekend visit to Mom's. I'm deeply depressed. It occurs to me that some things that must be talked about cannot be talked about. One of these is the real possibility of my early death and what it's like for her to face the loss of her firstborn. I can't bring myself to talk with her about this, and I guess she can't, either. We do, both of us, make an effort, make occasional references, but the sorrow goes too deep for tears.

Mom's life seems so limited, sitting in her same chair in the same living room most of every day. She is in the early stages of Alzheimer's disease, which has robbed her of some memory function and concentration, although in most ways she remains alert and attentive. I can't help but think that my cancer may also deprive me of some of the same mental functions. I hope I never end up with a life as empty as hers seems to be.

TAKE CARE OF YOURSELF

This is the phrase I hear most often from people. This is a tough one; even tougher is hearing it from people who are keeping you on the phone asking about your mate's progress, expressing concern, and keeping you from, well, taking care of yourself. I can't tell you how many times I finally have a few minutes to get into the shower, cell phone nearby on the floor in case *Ted* needs me from downstairs, or in the event a doctor or insurance company is calling back, or any number of real or imagined reasons why I'd need to answer a ringing cell phone mid-shampoo—only to answer it and hear, "Hi! How are you? I've been worried about you guys." Drip, drip.

"Can I call you back? Can't really talk right now."

"Sure. I was just so worried about you. I hope you are taking care of yourself."

Deep breath. Drip.

So, you might be thinking, *why do you take your cell phone into the bathroom with you?* and I think I can explain it this way: I don't know.

The truth is that when a normally high-functioning adult is faced with a disaster, all bets are off. The mind, at times, turns to putty. The mind and body are both fatigued. Although I hate the overuse of this word, there is a tremendous amount of *stress* from areas you've never even imagined, physical and mental. Body, mind, and soul take a huge hit. So, taking a phone into the bathroom—and knowing intellectually that there is little basis for doing that—does not seem so crazy after all.

Nevertheless, I know it's crucial to find a way to cope and take care of myself—and Ted—in the process.

One day, I catch my reflection in the bathroom mirror in a way I haven't for a while. To say it's not pretty is being kind. My regular self-care has fallen to crap. I picture a trash can somewhere housing all my previously used cosmetics, lotions, all the things that, at least in my mind, I felt made a difference in my appearance and to some extent, how I feel about myself. But now, my hair is dry and out of control, my eyes look tired, with darkened bags under them...in short, I look like a hag. Funny. That's how I feel.

Letting it all hang out has gotten old. I begin to extend my shower by a few extra minutes (oh, joy!) just to feel the warm water flow over me and take a couple of extra minutes to properly condition my hair when I wash it. Some days, I put on my makeup, figuring that the worst-case scenario will be a mascara-streaked face from a spontaneous cry.

Here I am in the late afternoon on a beautiful and brilliant early fall Maine kind of day, and all day long I have been fighting really hard to convince myself I am not failing, that my leg is not giving out, that my

balance is not much worse, that my memory is still good. Lots of tears this morning. But, as I try to view myself as from the outside, it seems that my walking is fairly steady, my leg is pretty steady. I have a physical therapy session this afternoon which I almost call and cancel, because I don't think I can do it, but I do go and it goes fine, which is to say there is a lot of muscle fatigue, which limits some things I might otherwise have done, but the basics are there. The therapist and I agree to cut the session a little short.

There are times when I tell family and friends to email rather than call. I can give a group email update in five minutes instead of repeating the same thing ten times on the phone. Some calls I want to take. I instruct my loved ones that if they want to call me on my cell phone, to please *not* leave a message, because I'll certainly see that they've called and can return the call when I'm able. Most understand this. Some still don't. Then I must go through the longer process of hearing a voicemail in case it's something important. Some send texts with a nice supportive message. That works well until I have trouble if I'm in-process of placing a call and suddenly a text is coming in. Maybe if I had a "smarter" phone it wouldn't be a problem. But I have successfully resisted that. A smart-enough phone is all I can handle right now. [Note: At the editing of this, I have an iPhone. Finally.]

Writing about this experience helps, and I continue some of my freelance work. Unless there's something emergent, Ted waits until after my fingers are done typing and I am done cursing—two activities intricately linked in my life. Writing—accomplished with large doses of swearing—is a great outlet.

In the midst of the confusion and emotional turmoil, I begin to have a greater appreciation of the smaller things in life, the small things of normal life that are now immensely comforting...a cup of tea with a biscuit; watching a silly TV show, feet up, hand cream nearby, massaging it into my own hands and feet; a walk with a friend; a walk alone; taking in good scents at the grocery store; stretching; getting into bed early with a good book.

I begin to free myself from certain discussions. I choose to go to most of Ted's appointments. I attend them because I love him and want to be supportive throughout this ordeal and, in part, because Ted and I hear things very differently. During each visit, he gets his lab work done, followed by the nurse visit, the doctor's exam, discussion, and off to the car we go.

"Well, that was encouraging!" I say.

"Not at all. I didn't hear encouragement at all," Ted replies.

"Are you kidding me?" I say. "The doctor had a huge smile! He almost *never* smiles like that!"

I soon realize that in the presence of the doctor, we need to clarify things. I feel like an idiot at times, like I'm trying to be Ted's mom.

"So—you are encouraged?" I ask the doctor. "Things are going well right now? The chemo seems to be helping?"

The doctor agrees, turning to Ted to reinforce that. It isn't that Ted isn't smart. He is one of the most brilliant people I know, and the tumor has not affected him intellectually so far. He runs circles around me in the brain category. But there is something—probably fear—that doesn't allow him to hear encouragement. Even a year after diagnosis, after months and months of treatment, when things are certainly stable, he will remark about his downhill path. I think these comments are made more often when he's just coming off his monthly chemo treatments, when he's feeling at his physical worst—very low energy and, sometimes, intestinal symptoms. He has medication to help with the latter. But there seems to be nothing but time to help with the profound lack of energy from the chemo, which is helping to shrink the tumor.

MORE BOUNDARIES

Visits from old friends often call for long, repetitive information and updates. I'm learning it's OK to leave the room if Ted is telling friends about his illness and I've not only heard it twenty times but am living it every day.

"How are you, Ted?" asks an old friend, visiting us.

Cue. I smile at Ted and get up.

"I'm going to make us some tea—back in a bit," I say.

Ted completely gets it.

"Kathy's heard me talk about this so many times—and it's difficult—so I'll fill you in. Go ahead, sweetie—I'll get them up to speed," he says.

Sometimes we tell people, "Come visit. We want to see you. But we don't want to talk about cancer." One night, we meet with good friends for dinner at a restaurant. Beforehand, I tell them we have a no-cancer-talk rule for that night. They're surprised, I think, but it works for everyone. And it feels like a real night out, not a medical update. What a relief. Cancer takes up a tremendous amount of time and space and energy. In our opinion, that can be better spent *living*.

We get better at saying no. Cancer battles aren't called battles for nothing. Cancer saps the energy of people with cancer and their mates. We say no to company, to events that sound boring or tiring, and to people who irritate us (not many, and not often). We free ourselves to drop out of any groups for a while. Things change, and maybe later or even tomorrow we'll feel differently. The fine line between dropping out of things and becoming isolated is not lost on me.

It's tricky to explain to people why we're not participating in something if they don't know about Ted's illness, and at least early on he doesn't want many to know.

I don't know how to balance commitments. Me, who likes things to be predictable, who doesn't like offending anyone...but Ted is more laid-back and takes these kinds of plan disruptions more casually.

Cancer being what it is, it seems incongruous that one day we're in a very difficult predicament due to Ted's symptoms, making calls or seeing one doctor or another, yet the next day things improve, and we plan a day trip to a state park. That's the nature of cancer. It's just as important to enjoy the good days as it is necessary to face the bad days.

"Don't let anyone tell you how to spend your time," said a wise doctor who took care of my late mother years ago.

That is taking care of oneself, one of the biggest challenges.

CHAPTER 19

NOVOCURE

*S*eptember 2011

When Ted finishes the initial six weeks of treatment, he's offered participation in a research study.

An oncology company called Novocure is developing a new cancer therapy called Tumor Treating Fields (TTFields). We happen to live in one of the areas where patients can be enrolled in a clinical trial evaluating the efficacy and safety of TTFields therapy when used along with the standard treatment of care for glioblastoma. The idea behind TTFields therapy is that low-intensity electric fields at a range of 100 kHz to 500 kHz may selectively disrupt multiple cancer processes while sparing healthy cells, stopping the growth and division of the cancer cells. TTFields therapy is delivered right into the area of your brain where the cancer is located, using four adhesive patches called transducer arrays. They resemble a soft, cap-like helmet.

After reading about it, Ted goes through the preliminary enrollment process. We are very, very hopeful that he will be randomized into the experimental group—meaning that he will receive TTFields therapy. He meets with the study nurse, a lovely woman named Debbie whom we come to know well, as she will thereafter be at all his medical appointments and other helpful aspects of his care for quite some time to come, possibly two years, depending on how Ted's health holds up. In this study, two out of three people receive TTFields therapy; one of three will be randomized into the control group. It's done by computerized randomization. All patients will continue with both the standard chemotherapy, with or without TTFields therapy, and periodic mental status exams.

The day Ted meets with Debbie to do the randomization, I'm at my part-time job. We are both hoping and praying he'll get in, which will mean wearing this apparatus—essentially soft headgear with wires attached to a six-pound electrical battery worn at his waist or on his back for carrying—nearly 24/7. He'll have to get his head shaved and the battery changed on an every-two-week schedule. With this research going on all around the world, it will not necessarily limit any travel plans. And it might give him an edge on a better prognosis. There are virtually no side effects, other than possible skin irritation and walking around looking like a bionic man. Other experimental treatments carry significant and possibly life-threatening adverse reactions in some people, but this one is extremely safe. Ted plans to call me at work after he meets with Debbie, who, after all the signing of paperwork, will go to her computer to discover his treatment assignment.

I get the call late in the morning. Unfortunately, he has been randomized into the control group. I think we both want to cry. It feels cruel to have the possibility of something that could really help him, but not be able to get it. Debbie is genuinely disappointed for us, too. And this is how clinical trials work: Some people in a group of participants receive treatment for a particular illness while some do not, and there are phases to check for side effects, whether the treatment works, dosing, and so on. Now, the only way Ted can make use of this treatment is if his tumor grows, and of course, neither of us wants that. In time, we are told, TTFields therapy might well be released for use in stable tumor patients, and then he can get it. For now, he is in the study, requiring monthly participation but not getting to use the therapy.

But I can be ferocious when I want to be. I start our own routine. Every night, I lean over his head, put my face close to the little dent in his scalp where the biopsy was done, and yell, in a gruff voice, "GET! OUT!" which later morphs into "GET THE FUCK OUT!" It makes Ted laugh. He is doing pretty well, overall, between that and the chemotherapy.

INSURANCE BLUES

So far, our medical insurance has not approved either Ted's initial visit at the Mass General Epilepsy Clinic (even though they approved the week's emergency stay immediately following that appointment), nor have they approved the biopsy and accompanying hospitalization during part of that second week. Seems we are embarking upon a long battle with Big Insurance.

In the ensuing weeks and beyond, Big Insurance changes its mind several times about paying for the biopsy and subsequent hospitalization. Their stance is that it could have been done locally—for the biopsy, the operating room, and subsequent hospital days post-op. They go so far, in one letter, as to state that they consider a brain biopsy to be "an outpatient procedure."

Have a neurosurgeon stick a needle into one of the most fragile/easily damaged parts of your brain, and go home a few hours later? We are not talking about a mani-pedi here. This is beyond belief, and we can only wonder at who is in charge there. We have visions of setting up a table at Starbucks and doing brain biopsies, shouting:

"Special today: Brain Biopsies!

In at 10, out by noon!

Sign up today and get a complimentary latte.

All major insurances accepted! Run along now. Next!"

This fantasy dances in our heads and conversation as a way of dealing with the outright stupidity and evil nature of their decision. Mass General has sent more than 50 pages of medical documentation on our behalf, showing clear medical necessity. Ironically, if they'd had to redo all the initial tests locally, it would have greatly increased costs at that point.

My husband is terminally ill.

Three times, the insurance company decides differently on the charge: denial, approval, denial. (*Before the rooster crows twice, you will deny me three times…*)

One day, when I am out, Ted is at his home office desk, which is about six feet from my desk and our landline, and he hears someone leaving a voicemail. It's a woman from Big Insurance saying the biopsy/hospitalization has been approved after all. He hobbles over, grabs the phone, talks with her, and insists she put it in writing and email it immediately. Reluctantly, she agrees, but not before he must argue the point with her. That's a huge relief, as it was an enormous expense.

We never get approval for the initial Epilepsy Clinic appointment at Mass General, so we appeal it in person. That's right. I bring my husband, limping from damage from his brain tumor, into the fat-ass local offices of Big Insurance in our area, where we are led to a conference room. We are both angry at the system and are on a mission, and not just for us. We sit with the insurance claims worker, a Big Insurance lawyer, and a small black box about the size of a dessert plate which contains the live voice of a physician-reviewer who is, apparently, somewhere on the planet.

They turn down our appeal.

I later pursue it with the Bureau of Insurance in our state, only to find out from the good people there that our policy is written by the workplace where we had both been employed and through whom the insurance is offered, so any complaints must go through them, and if wanted, the federal Department of Labor. By the time I investigate that, the time period has lapsed so we can no longer appeal it through our employer, which also blows the next level of appeal out of the water: a complaint to the Department of Labor. That is something I hadn't realized—that if we wanted to appeal something, we'd need to go to our employer because their medical insurance policy is considered self-insured. We end up paying that bill, which, thankfully and kindly, is reduced by Mass General, and comes to just under $600 for that single but crucial consultation. It's not that big of a deal to us financially. But it feels mean, and for many, that would be a payment they could not afford. (It's also a lesson to read those big thick informational packets that are given to employees. Not every insurance path or appeal process is the same.)

People with illness, and their loved ones, are in a poor position to fight with insurance. What happens to those who are too ill or unable in any other way to fight for themselves? People who aren't as knowledgeable or persistent as we are. It's a question we ask ourselves repeatedly. We realize the relative advantage Ted and I have, as a physician and a nurse, in navigating this system even though we have much to learn, and we do have some backup funds. But what about people in a situation in which they can't advocate/afford/connect with good help? And all we can come up with is this: Sometimes, they can't navigate treatment easily at all. Sometimes they die.

Insurance companies have their own bottom line, which normally includes huge profits. It can wear people down at a time when folks are too sick, too stressed, too undereducated about the "system" to cope.

Fuck you, Big Insurance.

CHAPTER 20

KEEPING MY BIG MOUTH SHUT

*F*all 2011

Family and friends ask me how Ted is getting along. He sometimes hears me talking to someone on the phone and gets angry that I'm sharing something personal, things that I don't think of as intimate, like test results. Certain people close to us who know he's having an important test and are praying for him are waiting for test results. They phone or text me, and I don't always realize he doesn't want me to release good news, like "The tumor is a tiny bit smaller."

"I want to let people know when I'm ready," he tells me one day.

OK. Got it. But it leaves me with relatives or close buddies who wonder and worry more because we aren't saying anything. Still, it's his head and his tumor, and he gets to call the shots. I tread carefully after that, balancing my need to have support and his desire to have privacy. We talk about this at length. I have no intention of betraying confidences. It's ironic to me that he has told the entire mental health staff at our workplace what's going on. So it's no secret. Portland, Maine, is a small city with a small-town feeling, and people's paths cross often. Occasionally, he even tells a complete stranger about his illness. Recently, in a coffee shop, someone said to him, "Hurt your leg?" when they saw him walking unsteadily.

"Actually, no. I have a brain tumor," he answered.

So this is a topic I've learned to be more careful about. Is he embarrassed by it? Thinking it will go away if we don't talk about it? Wanting control in a situation where there is little control at hand? I get it. And I need to be careful.

FRIENDS

Friends from California come to see us in Maine. They're visiting family in Boston and come up to see us for an afternoon. They come to the house, and after an hour or so, we all go out for a late lunch, catching up on each other's lives. They are determined to pay for lunch. We let them. We walk around the Old Port shops, and in a specialty cooking store, my friend insists on buying me a lovely bottle of gourmet olive oil. Continuing our expedition in this part of Portland, Ted can't continue. He's too weak, quite suddenly. We get a chair from a storekeeper, and our friends sit with Ted while I get the car and bring it the six blocks to where they are watching out the store window for me. I pull over as best as I can, considering there are no parking spaces available in front of the store, and they help Ted into the car. All this happens during what has turned into torrential rain.

Back at the house, we have tea, more conversation, then they head out. They should win an award for that visit, treating us like kings (or to be accurate, a king and a queen), and never making more inquiries about Ted's illness than he wants, so we don't have to relive the whole horror show again. They leave while we all still have that "good visit" feeling. It costs us nothing financially to enjoy the afternoon, demonstrating a level of giving from visitors that is quite graceful.

FEAR

Initially, people had come out of the woodwork (a creepy idea, at best) to offer to help, bring food, and so on—amazing and welcome. Now, the attention and visits have fallen off, though not entirely, of course. Neither of us is working in our chosen profession. Ted, though he'd been very close to his original retirement date, had planned on doing part-time or consulting work, and now that is out of the question. The robust activities of leisure he'd have enjoyed are no longer an option. It leaves us in a very weird space of not quite knowing what to do with ourselves, schedule-wise.

I suggest several times that maybe we can ask a friend to help get his kayak into the water and help him into the kayak. He resists this idea.

Photography is still left, which necessitates, at times, use of a tripod. He needs help getting that out of the house and getting set up. The equipment is not heavy, but it's bulky. His motivation to do photography tapers off for a time, as the effort seems too great, even with my offers of help. He's still invested in the singing group we are a part of at church, and when he's up to it, he sings. We put a chair nearby, so when he doesn't need to be standing, he sits.

"I don't think I can go to church today. I just don't feel up to it," he says one Sunday.

On this day, when he really feels terrible, I am unable to make it to the rehearsal, which is always held the hour before we all sing, with this group of eight or so. Ted and I hug, and I head out. I arrive just before mass, and am on the verge of tears, I'm so worried about him. I go to sit near the front, on the right side of the church, so I can sit with my friends from the song group. They immediately ask me to join them, not caring that I haven't rehearsed. This group is called "On a Wing and a Prayer"—and not for nothing. We are very flexible, and usually sound decent for the amount of time we prepare for mass. I turn down the offer, feeling too raw inside. It's one of those times when it wouldn't take much to start crying, which is not something I want to do standing up in front of the congregation. Mass starts, and at some point, my mind goes to Ted, alone at home. I miss him so much. I can feel that swollen, aching feeling in my throat. What will it be like coming to mass week after week without him? My mind goes to a very dark place. And with no ability to shut it off, the tears start rolling down. Where is that darned tissue? I am quietly reaching around in my purse. For the next ten or fifteen minutes, I'm sniffling, dabbing, sniffling some more, trying to pretend I have a cold (what difference does it make? It's church, after all—if I can't cry there, then where?). But still, I am embarrassed. Feeling out of control. Self-conscious and self-pitying. The thought of being alone without Ted, pushed well to the back of my mind and heart so much these days, has made an unexpected and uninvited appearance. Like a bratty child, I try to put it in the corner, unsuccessfully. If I really let it rip, in a different setting, it would probably be a good thing, and I would get past it more quickly.

Just before receiving Holy Communion, there is an exchange of the sign of peace. I am hoping that no one comes over to me. No such luck. A woman nearby whom I see now and then but don't personally know well comes over to me and puts her arms around me, whispering a kindness. I mutter something about having a cold. A lie. Then one of my friends comes over and gently strokes my head for a moment, as I am trying to hold it together, head down.

Anticipatory grief and loneliness are tough things. They are, in a way, unnecessary, because only God knows when we will leave this earth. I often tell Ted that he might be around for a long time, and I might go first. Regardless of one's beliefs, it is normally not up to us to regulate such things. My faith says one thing: that this life is not the end. But inside, there is a battle. I really want God to win this one for us. I'm coming to a crisis of faith, and I desperately want to put the control into hands other than my own, to be able to truly believe in something larger, in something beyond our silly world of things and "stuff." It's not easy to be so often in a place of fear, not faith.

BETH AND THE MAGIC FLUTE

Despite everything going on, Ted continues his flute lessons, except when he feels sick from chemo. The lessons are relaxed, and Beth enthusiastically tells us about her new part-time school teaching jobs. Ted's illness does not deter her from continuing to teach him in our home. Through all Ted's ups and downs, she respects those times with ease when he calls or emails her to reschedule. As an added challenge, there are physical obstacles for Ted's difficulty with the flute now. His balance is off a little, and his right leg and arm are somewhat impaired. Standing in the typical flute-holding pose is becoming more difficult; fingering and holding up the flute with his right hand is more challenging.

Yet Beth still regularly comes over for lessons, chats with Ted for a while beforehand, and with both of us afterwards. I listen to the music from upstairs, if I'm home. If I've been out doing an errand, I come home to hover at the doorway of the living room. Sometimes I'm in the kitchen making supper preparations, where I can hear them in the background. A duet they are playing is coming along beautifully, occasionally interrupted by Ted if he's frustrated by a rough patch, or if he needs to stop for a moment. I'm sure Beth has no idea how often he picks up the flute to practice during the week, only to curse and yell at his fate.

"My fingers just aren't working! I can't do this!" Then he tries again.

One day, I can't keep it in.

"It's a *lesson*. It doesn't have to be perfect. You are not performing," I remind him, certain he is completely dismissing what I think of as encouragement. He expects perfection from himself and is extremely angry when his fingers don't work. He finds this happens now when typing, as well.

As each lesson rolls around, he gets anxious. Yet during his lessons, he seems to relax and enjoy the process. When I hear Beth and Ted finish playing a duet, I can't keep myself from entering the room, clapping my hands and grinning. It gives them both a chuckle.

"So good!" I say, and I mean it—beautiful music, and Ted still trying. Beyond that, it's lovely to see young Beth's gentle and casual attitude, so important during this period in our lives when underlying emotions are strained. And always, every single time, after a lesson, he remarks on his progress with surprise.

"You know," he tells me, "I really think the practicing and lessons are helping."

"Duh!" I say back.

CHAPTER 21

CALIFORNIA AND THE SHERWOODS

Ted and I hear from his Cornell buddies about a fall Sherwood reunion in California. We'd missed the California gathering a couple of years earlier, and very much want to go to this one now. On good days, Ted's at a point where we think that *maybe* we can make the trip. We dream aloud about it. The host is a wonderful guy whom we're anxious to see again. Ted and I talk about taking a train across the country—rolling hills, the open plains, small towns—well, it's the kind of trip we have talked about and dreamed of taking for years. And now we are aware there might not be too many chances to take this kind of trip. After weeks of talking about it, we decide to take the plunge—kind of. We make hotel reservations, knowing we can cancel. We talk with Ted's oncologist and the study nurse Debbie about how to do the medical piece. We go down to the local Amtrak station and practically hold the nice Amtrak woman hostage with our questions and negotiations on berths, contingencies, and backup plans, including how to easily cancel the trip if needed.

We are doing it. We have everything in place. Over the next many weeks, Ted begins to have several spontaneous doctors' and urgent-care visits, and various tests are done. Most are directly related to the cancer; others are for the side effects of treatment and a couple of other situations including thyroid issues. Although that is a lower priority than his brain tumor, he now sees an endocrinologist. We've been told that the thyroid nodules are, thank God, benign. He starts medications for that, which need monitoring.

And then there's this reality, in the middle of our plan:

November 16, 2011

It is almost impossible for me to believe how drained I get from this chemotherapy drug, temozolomide. I take this medicine five days out of every month. The dose is 420 mg, once a day. For the first several days, I don't notice much of any effect from it. It has now been three or four days since my last dose, however, and I am so drained that I can hardly move. Climbing a flight of stairs is about the most I can muster, especially if I try to carry our little dog up and down stairs, and he only weighs 12 pounds. I have to be exceptionally careful to hold onto railings and especially careful where I put my feet. Much of the time, I wear slippers that have sticky soles, and those can be hazardous because it's so easy to trip on things. Some of the times, like today, I'm just wearing socks, but that can be hazardous also because socks can be slippery on stairways. For the most part what I do is read and sleep. I know from experience that within a week or so, I will begin to regain my energy and will be able to do more things, but for now it just feels awful.

One day, we start discussing and envisioning the reality of the trip to California. It involves several different train rides, all with adequate handicapped accessible sleeper cars. We can get ourselves to Boston, then take a train from Boston to Chicago, then Chicago to Portland, Oregon, then a train from Oregon to Oakland, California. There, we would rent a car to drive down the Big Sur to Cambria, the destination of the Sherwood gathering. The return trip back would vary slightly. We would take the car back to Oakland, then the train (Amtrak's California Zephyr) to Reno, then Chicago to Boston, then bus home from there. The California Zephyr, which Ted has taken in the past, is a trip across Gold Rush country that is described as quite beautiful.

Soon we realize that in a perfectly healthy world, it might be slightly challenging, though fun. But—what if we are halfway between Chicago and Oregon and Ted has a seizure? Or if new symptoms arise, or he has a medication reaction? There are hundreds and hundreds of miles on each leg of the trip. It begins to feel overwhelming. The thought of flying instead, with its connections and waiting in long lines, does nothing to make us feel any better about going.

Ted's email to the Sherwoods:

For those not so biologically inclined, mitochondria are tiny beings which live inside our cells, accomplishing the task of converting oxygen and various biochemicals into the energy that drives our daily lives. Sadly, mine have unionized and gone on strike. It's one of those situations in which the treatment is causing more difficulty than the underlying disease. As far as can be told, my tumor is under good control and my doctors are uniformly optimistic. However, I take fairly large doses of seizure medications every day. These work nicely for what they are intended to do, but side effects include a definite sapping of energy. Worse, for five days each month I take a chemotherapy agent, which leaves me almost unable to do anything at all, physically, for more than ten minutes at a time, without stopping to rest for a half hour or more. When I complete the five-day cycle, the lethargy will get worse for another three to five days, then will lighten, and I'll be back to my usual (reduced) activity level until the next round of chemo. So, out of each month, I have a couple of weeks of reasonably "normal" life and a couple of weeks of real wipe-out. I'm in the middle of one of those wipe-outs right now. Today was an utterly beautiful New England fall day, when normally I would have been hiking or kayaking, but instead I dozed a lot and watched the Patriots whup the Jets. Yeah!

All things considered, it's not going to be possible for Kathy and me to come to Cambria. We have had the trip all planned out, as many of you know, but the more I get into this treatment regimen, the more it becomes obvious that I simply cannot do it, neither the traveling nor the singing. If my cancer is responding as well as my doctors believe it is, I'll see you all next time around, wherever.

Cancelling the trip is terribly disappointing and utterly relieving at the same time. It would have been too much. We don't have the sign of a butterfly this time, but we know we've made a smart decision.

Sometime later, we receive news that Kendall's wife Ellen, who has also been in treatment for cancer, is having a hard time, and we are heartbroken.

Even with all that is going on with Ted, it would be so nice to hear encouraging words about Ellen.

GOOD, BAD, UGLY

This has been a really tough day. Yesterday I was able to walk almost without a hitch, and my energy was fairly good. It's been just a week since I completed my most recent round of chemotherapy, and I had reason to think that the worst was over in terms of the side effects. But today has been terrible. I have felt weak and unstable all day. I have also felt like crying all day, as has Kathy. Yesterday, also, we had a terrible fight. We yelled at each other and said some awful things. For a while, we were not speaking at all. Somehow, we got past that, at least temporarily. She is in pain beyond words at the thought of losing me. I am in pain beyond words at the thought of losing her. This being Sunday, ordinarily we would be singing in the group at church. As the time approaches, however, I realize that my weakness and tiredness are too extreme for me to do that. Last week I was able to sing, for the first time in a number of weeks. It felt pretty good. This week she has to go by herself, with tears in her eyes. Well, both of us have tears in our eyes. I have not showered or shaved or changed my clothes today, and I realize that for me to do so would take every last iota of energy in my body, and I would still not be able to get to the church for the singing. It's quite possible that tomorrow I will be more energetic and more physically active. These things seem to come in waves, unpredictably. Yesterday was a good day, tomorrow may be a good day, today is a terrible day. I just want to curl up in a ball and cry. I don't want to have this tumor, I don't want to have all of these awful side effects from my medications, I don't want to see the pain in Kathy's eyes, and I don't want to know about the pain in her heart. It's too much.

PANCAKES WITH THE CATHOLICS

Nearly a week later, I am having breakfast at the local IHOP with a few friends from the church song group. Saturday morning breakfast had become something of a ritual with us over the previous few months, and it's a brief but important hour or two for me. Occasionally Ted joins us, but usually he's content to stay home with his bowl of bran flakes and the newspaper. I choose pancakes and prayers and friendship, and afterwards I swing by the nearby mall and briskly walk for about twenty minutes, then a quick stop at the grocery store to pick up those few items we always seem to run short on.

On this Saturday, I sit with three women, chatting and giggling. This fun completely erases the memory of the previous night, a night Ted had gone to sleep early. I'd been doing various "busy" things around the house, the dog was in our bed, and I was getting ready to go to bed myself when suddenly, out of nowhere, I had this thought: *I can't live without him.*

Pow. Right in the gut.

I don't want to live without him. How will I ever be able to stand it?

A rush of thoughts swept through me, and in seconds, I was heaving with sobs, trying to keep quiet so I didn't wake Ted, who was sleeping fifteen feet away in the bedroom. All the reassurances I'd managed to give myself before did not work. The "I'll be OK after a while" didn't cut it—the realization that without this person in my daily life, nearby, to be with, to soothe and be soothed, to laugh, to share a meal with, to snuggle up to at night, to hold hands with—unbearable. I'd cried and cried. Finally, I forced myself to put a halt to it, pick up my prayer booklet next to the bed, read a few prayers, remind myself that God will not leave me completely alone, and I'd gotten into bed.

So, this next morning at breakfast I particularly need to be with friends. At one point, they ask about Ted, and I give an update. I can feel my eyes filling up, and I will the tears to stop. The conversation eventually moves on to other things. At the end of our time together, my friend Marilyn pulls me aside.

"There's something I want to do," she says. She wants to come to the house and weed our gardens, haul off unneeded brush, basically do the after-summer cleanup we haven't been able to do. Ted has long since given up doing yard work—a former passion of his. She goes on to say, against my weak protests, that she's used to doing a lot of farming and really wants to help us in this way.

"Then come do just a little, and I'll run out for bagels," I say.

"I don't want you to do a thing," she answers, and adds, "I'll probably do it when you guys aren't home."

My heart is filled with unspeakable gratitude. Has she read my mind? Had I previously complained we couldn't weed the gardens? It doesn't matter.

"Whether you can or not," I tell her, "the fact that you want to is good enough for me."

A couple of weeks later, she leaves me a message to say she'll be around on the weekend, that it doesn't matter if we're home or not. She shows up a few days later and spends several hours weeding, raking, hauling. She has a thermos of coffee with her and even some type of portable potty in her truck. Completely self-reliant, I don't think she would have even waved at us if I hadn't come out a couple of times to see if she needed anything, and to thank her.

Through this time and beyond, I learn something that is difficult for me: how to accept help.

THE MALL AND THE ER

I am walking at our local mall with my friend Jeri, mentally filing said activity under the category of taking-care-of-myself, when my cell phone rings. It's Ted.

"I don't want to worry you, but I think I'm having a little cardiac thing and I've called 911."

I leave the mall and drive to the nearest ER, where I figure he will be taken. I'm a wreck, and although Jeri offers to drive me there, I want to drive, and really need a few minutes to breathe and be alone to recapture my sanity and keep the panic down. I'm thinking in practical terms, as well. If my friend drives me to the hospital, she'll either need to stay with me or come back for us, as I have no way of knowing how long he or we will be there. All I know is that he is going to the hospital via ambulance.

Ted has occasionally experienced a rapid heart rate over the past several years, which has been checked; it's possibly his thyroid or a medicine that might be causing it. I'm upset to think he might have something else besides cancer going on—like a heart attack.

On the way to the ER, I do a lot of praying. I try to push away thoughts that are fatalistic, sad, morbid. (How's that working? Not very well.) But I keep driving.

When I get there, he isn't there. No one knows anything about it.

"He's coming in by ambulance," I tell them. They've had no such notification. Finally, after what seems like forever, someone from an ambulance calls the ER to let them know they're on the way. It's about twenty or thirty minutes after my arrival in the ER before he shows up, which feels like a very long time—a long time to wait if you are worried that your spouse may or may not be alive. At first, I am told he's almost there, so I watch out the window, go outside to look, ask again. "Nothing yet. We'll let you know."

I repeat the whole process every few minutes. By now I'm terribly worried. What's happening? Finally, I'm told he's arrived, but they have brought him "out back." What does that mean? My own heart is now racing.

"They are assessing him. They'll let us know when you can go back there," I'm told.

Bullshit.

I snag a young candy striper, ask her if I can get back to see my husband, and like magic, she says, "Oh, sure" and takes me back to see him in the inner workings of the ER. I guess it's who you ask.

He's alive.

Ted and I spend five hours in the ER while they poke and prod, take blood, run a continuous EKG, do a chest X-ray, and monitor him. He is released with follow-up instructions to get set up with a Holter monitor, to be attached to his chest to wear for a few days.

The next morning, my near-and-dear Fred and Meryl come over. We give them a house key and show them where the dog food, treats, medications, and leash are kept—your basic "Dog 101." See, when I was in the ER being scared to death about my husband's condition, every now and then I thought about the dog. I knew I had walked him before I had left for my walk, hours earlier. That part was probably OK. But Ted couldn't recall if the dog had been gated into the downstairs rooms before he'd been transported to the hospital. And our dog, now older, isn't very good on stairs. I didn't think he would go upstairs if we weren't home, but I didn't want to take a chance. So now, in the ER, I kept saying, "Maybe I should go home and check on the dog" to Ted. Then we'd try to find out how long we might need to stay in the ER. I love my doggy, yet I couldn't leave Ted. In retrospect, I probably could have called our neighbors. If they were home, they could get into the house because they always have a key. But there's that paralysis/anxiety in certain circumstances, and it happened on this day. I could only give full thought to the most critical thing, which was Ted. Long story short, it would have been better to have a system in place beforehand.

The dog was fine. The gate was in place. He was happy to see us when we returned. We were happy to see him, too.

Extra doggy treats.

CHAPTER 22

UNRELIABLE LIFE

Living with cancer brings an intrinsic unpredictability.

Just a few days after the ER visit, we have a Japanese dinner out at our favorite place with Fred and Meryl, now our assigned primary emergency dog-sitters. The next day, we take a short walk, drive to the countryside to pick out pumpkins for Halloween décor, make love, and go to the movies. A big day. It kind of makes up for the days when Ted can't get off the sofa without feeling every ounce of energy drained from his entire being.

I try to push past fear, but my brain doesn't necessarily cooperate.

I feel unprepared to be the mate of someone who is so ill. There's no handbook for this. Here is when my fellow Christians might say "Trust in the Lord." Indeed, when I can remember that and "give it up," as they say, it's helpful. But my brain, in its reality, is not hard-wired that way. Heartbreak, fear, grief—these and other emotions present themselves and must be dealt with. I cannot erase them. Even the most faith-filled people feel deep personal sorrow, fear pain for their loved one, feel helpless, worry, and watch their long-term dreams threatened.

Our days are like a lottery. Sometimes we win a good day, sometimes not, often connected to our mental health du jour. When I look back over this first year, sometimes it's such a blur that all I can think of is "I don't know." My brain has become mushy, my emotions unpredictable, unplanned, unreliable.

DOLLS

Ted and I procured, over the years, a couple of small Fisher Price dolls, probably left at the house by grandchildren, each of whom we called Blue Man because of the painted-on blue pants. It became a running gag, as we'd leave them for each other to discover in surprising places. I might open a drawer in the bathroom and find one of them staring at me. Or holding a card or love note. Once, I came to bed, only to find them both together on my pillow in a compromising position. Good times, indeed.

IF WE'RE NOT IN THE ER, IT MUST BE A GOOD DAY

Our baseline has changed.

The first time Ted trips over his right foot, which doesn't work well, it's awful to witness and obviously distressing for him. The twentieth time, neither one of us panics. Well, I still do, briefly. It's instinctive. For Ted, this stumbling happens because the connection between his brain and the nerve impulse to his right foot is interrupted. Most of the time, with deliberate thought, he manages his walking well enough. But now and then, he trips over his own feet. A startling realization of how things have changed is that one night, he trips on the curb while we're heading into a movie theater.

I kneel next to him. He says he's OK and makes it clear to me he does not want any of the well-meaning passersby to help him up. He just needs a minute to get his bearings. Then he gets up.

"Do you want to go home?" I whisper, thinking he'd be relieved to leave the scene.

"No," he says. "We're here. We're going to the movies."

He's not physically hurt. We go in, and I help him to a seat in the lobby. I get the tickets and we go into the theater and find seats. I go back to get the snacks. I'm heartbroken, having seen him fall and manage to get himself up, pull himself together—this man who could, quite literally, run circles around most adults half his age just months before.

We recapture the night and it's a good movie. We're learning to roll with the punches—and falls—and be flexible. If he had felt like going home instead, we would have changed the initial plan. We'd have read books, or we might have played cards.

But you know what?

A day without an ER visit is a good day.

WHO IS IT WITH THE CHEMO BRAIN?

Fall/Winter 2011
Memory lapses:

There's this phenomenon called "chemo brain." Every day, something comes up that points to a slippage in my memory. Seems like a lot of these have to do with whether I've taken my medication. And I'm a psychoanalyst. Yesterday afternoon we were at Lowe's, at a checkout line, and I was fishing around in my pants pocket for loose change. What I came up with, in addition to an assortment of quarters and nickels, was two tablets of Keppra. Well, when we go out in the evening, for dinner or a movie, I will often take along my 8 p.m. dose. If I forget, which I often do, Kathy keeps one dose in her purse, which she gives me. When we get back home, if I have taken the medication in her purse, she refreshes her supply from my pill caddy with the dose I left behind. So, either I have my evening Keppra in my pocket or she has it in her purse. There is absolutely no reason, however, why I would have two tablets of Keppra in my pocket in the middle of a Thursday afternoon. I cannot remember going out for an evening recently and taking along some Keppra in my pocket. I cannot imagine why, if I had done that, I would have taken Kathy's Keppra instead of my own. The pants I was wearing, with the Keppra in the pocket, I had only been wearing for a couple of days, so however this happened, it must have been very recent. And it's clear that I have not skipped a dose of Keppra, because then I would have had a seizure within a few hours. I learned that the hard way, several months ago.

So, we have a mystery. At the center of the mystery is the failure of my memory. I have no idea in the world how this happened. None.

This is not an isolated incident. Things like this happen almost every day. Usually, it'll be Kathy asking me "Do you remember...?" and I don't. Even after she reminds me, I still don't. In most of these situations, there is simply nothing there at all. Just a large black hole.

I'm not around small children, so I don't worry about keeping Ted's extra dose of medicine in my purse. My pocketbook is never far from me, a trait I inherited from my mom. I think my mom may have actually slept with her purse.

Since Ted got cancer, we tend to be disorganized. Statistically, cancer occurs when people are a bit older, although tragically, this isn't always the case. But as an older couple, we notice that we're a little more forgetful than, say, 20 years ago. Dealing with illness presents disrupted daily routines, with treatments and appointments. There's fatigue, so there's napping. Some medicines require rigid schedules. It doesn't matter if certain regular medicines aren't taken at precisely the same time every day. Ted is famous for running out of his blood pressure medicine. Days later, he'll drop a casual remark about needing to pick it up at the pharmacy. Then a couple of days later, I'll hear the auto-voice over the answering machine, "This is Blah-Blah Pharmacy calling..." But with cancer medicines and anti-seizure medicines, there is a rigid schedule, and it really, really needs to be followed as closely as possible. And aside from the schedule, we never want him to run out of a critical pill.

Me: "Honey? Did you call Dr. Evans for your next prescription refill?"
He: "For what?"
Hmmmm...didn't we just discuss this last night?
Me: "For your medicine."
He: "Oh, yeah. That's right. What's his number?"
Silence.
Me: "Don't you have it?"
He: "No. Don't you?"
Me: "Somewhere."
He: "Where?"
Me: "How should I know?"
Multiply this type of conversation by 10. Daily.

Reverse the above "Me" and "He" and the whole thing will still be close to reality.

Or:

He: "Oh, no. Did I forget my physical therapy appointment?"

Me: "I don't know. Where's the appointment card?"

You can guess the answer: nowhere.

I write down all his appointments on our kitchen calendar and in my own appointment book, and I keep a list of names and phone numbers of doctors, specialists, pharmacies, and therapists of various sorts. At one point, he has two different pharmacies, a primary care doctor, an oncologist, a radiation oncologist, a team of neurologists, an endocrinologist, an acupuncturist, an orthotics place, and a physical therapist—plus his regular dentist. I have my own list of doctors and specialists.

Are we having fun yet?

Mostly.

THE COLD WAR

Now and then, there is great tension between us. I get crabby, and so does he. This takes a while to sort out, with the help of the doctors, that a good part of his irritability is medication related. And while some of the medicine can be modified, others cannot.

So, his medicines are contributing to our cold—or sometimes heated—war. At one point, we see a therapist at the cancer place, helpful after just one session.

But what's my excuse? For that, I talk with my therapist and with myself. It's hard to be a caregiver in a situation in which you are emotionally invested. I'm not a nurse working an eight-hour shift and going home at the end of the day. I'm a caregiver all the time, at least in my mind. And I'm no spring chicken. My injury kicks up a notch regularly. It's taxing to think of ways to help while still protecting my own health and body. Helping him on with shoes and socks is hard. Bending. Pushing. But he really needs the help. I figure out that it's less taxing to sit on the floor to help him, but even then, the simple act of pushing his shoes on hurts me. And forget about most "adaptive devices." They work best on people who don't need them.

What works best for putting on socks and shoes is to have him lie down, face up, *on the bed* so I don't have to bend to help him on with his socks. Then I put the brace for his right foot on, but that isn't too difficult. The brace looks like a big shoehorn that extends partway up the calf. So, if he can get his foot aligned properly with his brace and shoe, he can do the work of pushing his foot into the shoe. Sometimes I move the shoe into position for him.

I'm tired. When Ted gets up during the night, I awaken, too.

"You OK?" I ask.

Sometimes he doesn't need help, so I try to get back to sleep. Sometimes I get up with him, walking next to him, offering a hand, each time, sometimes two or three times a night. The normal routines of the day become major operations of sorts. It's exhausting. What does it remind me of? Oh, yeah. Taking care of my babies. Thirty years ago. When I was young and strong.

CHANGING THE GAME RULES

At times, Ted gets on my nerves, what's left of them. And plenty often, I bug the living crap out of him. He's more than a little tired of my solicitous behavior. I bet I ask him, "Do you need help?" a dozen or more times a day.

I'm so scared he's going to lose his balance. There are times when I'm less anxious about it, and there are times I drive us both crazy, taking this now to a new level of anxiety. For periods of time, I hold my breath when he goes up or down the stairs. If I walk next to him, and his foot is a little hesitant, my internal, reactive sense of terror screams "HE'S FALLING!" and I automatically gasp. Then he gets angry. I can't even count the number of times we've had the same argument over these kinds of things: me, worried/terrified, and he is nonchalant/wanting me to get off his back. When I see or hear him start to trip, even though most of the time he counteracts it with smart, practical things like holding the railing, it's almost impossible for me not to react. And of course, sometimes he does fall, which, like a variable-ration schedule of gambling (think of a Las Vegas-type *occasional* win, which furthers the eagerness to keep playing), reinforces the panic response on a deep level that's difficult to control.

It takes repeated conscious efforts on my part to lessen my response even slightly. When he takes offense at my smothering, overly protective approach, we bicker. Many times over, we decide on a plan: If he needs help, he'll ask me for it. But we are two old dogs learning new tricks. Neither of us adhere to this very well. I try not to overwhelm and (s)mother him, which I know makes him feel weak, and he assures me he'll ask for help when needed. I continue to overdo it. And sometimes when I back off, he'll start to stumble, and if I'm near, I help, pronto—always to his gratitude. But he seldom asks for help.

It's a good day when Ted is clearly able to say he needs me and tells me when to leave him alone, or to let him do something himself, and I listen.

"I hate when you hold onto the back of my pants that way!" he said, some months ago. At that moment, I was holding onto the back loop of his pants, ever so lightly, as we walked along a difficult path. It actually made it harder for him to keep his balance, he told me. I didn't know that. See, early on, when he was very, very unsteady and freshly post-surgery, and getting used to potent seizure medicines, a medical worker had suggested I hold the loop in the back of his pants as we walked. Then, it was helpful. Now, apparently, it's not. But he has to tell me this on a number of occasions before I get the message.

They say it takes a month to break a habit. "They" never met me.

We do the best we can.

AND THEN THERE'S THIS

There are things about cancer that your doctors and nurses don't automatically tell you. I'm not sure why, but most likely it's simply because there is so much to say and it's impossible to say it all. But here's something they often leave out.

Diarrhea. Voluminous. Sudden. Explosive. Very embarrassing. Very unpleasant! Not often, but sometimes it doesn't give me time to make it to the bathroom, or I may make it to the bathroom, but can't get my clothes off in time to avoid making a mess all over the place. I'm not going to go into this any further. Use your imagination.

Did I mention the amazing usefulness of having a large supply of paper towels and cleansers on hand?

CHAPTER 23

ON DYING AND HELPING

Some people think being in denial is a bad thing. I was once one of them. Years ago, when my mother, in her early 80s, was in the last months of living with cancer, we (her loving family) and her doctors tried to talk with her about death and dying. She would have none of it. She fired doctor after doctor who dared to talk with her about the reality of what she was facing. Oh, she understood she had cancer. But she simply refused to discuss it.

"Mom," I said one day, "I expect you're going to be around for a long time. But someday, *some day*, you won't be here. When the time comes, do you have any special wishes?" Now, mom was a bright, accomplished woman who had also drawn up a will, and had appointed me Power of Attorney.

LIGHTS

Early in our relationship, we stopped on North Street in Portland one night when Ted's brother Rob was visiting. This was during that first year Ted and I were dating. We three had been out having dinner and now, in the dark of the evening, we took the long way home. Getting out of Ted's car, looking out over the city of Portland, masses of buildings on the left, Back Bay just to the right, city lights twinkling, Ted asked, "How many lights do you think there are?" Before I could answer, Rob asked, "Lit or unlit?" That would be something we would laugh over for years. And I would remember how very much I was falling in love with Ted that night. How exciting, how young I felt, how drawn to each other we were, how much fun we were having.

But other than that, she had made no arrangements whatsoever for anything else. At the time I asked her this question, she was in final long-term care, hospice in place, and it was obvious to everyone that she wasn't going home. So, when I asked this question, I was hoping for a little direction. I hoped she might name a cemetery, or a preacher, something, anything to get me going in the direction of what she might want. My question "Do you have any special wishes?" was answered this way:

"Yes. I want everyone to be healthy and happy!"

A little further probing to clarify what I had intended to ask proved futile. She was not budging. She understood that she would die. But she didn't want to waste one minute dwelling on it. She wanted to get on with living, right to the end. And she wanted us to do the same.

Some things need to be faced when dealing with a potentially terminal illness. Despite enjoying most days, our sadness is never far away. Ted and I make several trips to a nearby cemetery to look into buying plots. It's like buying real estate, only not fun. First, we quibble over burial versus cremation. He gives in to my strong preference for burial. I might end up burning for eternity, but I don't want to burn here first. We look at plot choices and still can't decide. Eventually we do, but it takes a long time to get there.

Now I understand my mother so much more.

WINTER 2011 APPROACHING

Around six months into Ted's illness, we realize winter is approaching. Winter in Maine is beautiful, if you like a lot of snow and frigid temperatures. It lasts for months and months. The joke in Maine is that we have two seasons: winter and July. We occasionally get a mild Maine winter, but normally, I liken it to three to four months in the "frozen tundra." Throw in a husband with a brain tumor, making walking even in good weather difficult, a steep driveway—our car would sometimes get stuck simply heading up or down in the snow—and you have a formula that says *go south*. However, we are facing a dilemma. The idea of going south and renting a condo or something like that is very appealing, but we also know from experience that Ted's condition changes with some frequency. Example: Two months into treatment with chemotherapy (after the initial six-month blitz of radiation and chemotherapy), his platelets dropped too low to have his monthly chemotherapy. We had to wait an extra week to get his blood retested in order to proceed with the planned treatment.

We're not opposed to spending money on a winter rental in the south, but we don't want to throw it away, either. It soon becomes apparent that it will be difficult to pinpoint start dates for a getaway south. And the question of how long to lease a place becomes a concern. What if he has to return to his doctors in Maine, or the surgeon or oncologists in Boston, and we're locked into a two- or three-month lease? We have to look long and hard to find a flexible plan. Is it better to find a "suite" style hotel to stay at, as we probably would pay more overall, but have the option of cancelling?

We struggle with the decision to go south, where to stay, how to make it work, and to find a place that will allow us to take our dog.

I enlist the help of my daughter Cassie, my oldest. She and Paul have been living in North Carolina for close to fifteen years. They initially moved there because Paul got a great job offer at East Carolina University School of Medicine (now named Brody School of Medicine at East Carolina University) near the end of 1997. Five years and two children later, he opened a private medical practice. They became quite connected to their community, his practice, and the mild weather. The thought of going there is appealing to me on many levels, not the least of which is the opportunity to spend time with them, to get to know my grandchildren better, and to be a part of Cassie's and Paul's lives for a while. Ted and I talk it over. He is willing but doesn't see the urgency to get out of town as acutely as I do.

So, when he balks at the idea of heading south for the winter, my response is warm and caring:

"Too bad. We're going."

FLUTES CAN BE HAZARDOUS TO YOUR HEALTH

One day, during one of Ted's flutes lessons, I'm in the kitchen cooking dinner. Suddenly, CRASH. Then, silence. I wait a second, then rush into the living room where the lesson is held to see Ted on the floor, starting to pick himself up. Beth is sitting on the sofa, taking it in.

Beth and I both ask him if he is ok (he is) and if he's gotten hurt (he hasn't.) Apparently, he had just moved a little while standing, and it threw him off balance. We help him up, take inventory, and the lesson continues.

I marvel at how calm Beth is. I wonder if she'll return for the next lesson or decide to drop him from her student list. I wouldn't blame her if she does. It's difficult dealing with someone ill enough to trip and fall so easily. But the next week, she's back, no problem. She's taken it in stride and clearly is not giving up on him. We're so grateful to her for that.

Around this time, my son—my youngest child, living and working in southern New York state—begins having health problems. I'm starting to wonder what the meaning of all this is. Or if there is any meaning at all. It's beginning to seem like a perpetual crisis, sometimes more gentle and sometimes worse than at other times. There are days I feel like I can hardly make it through, and I cry at least once a day. Then I recoup and go about the business of what needs to be done.

Praying at bedtime, I call upon God and the saints and anyone up there I can think of, reciting novenas and trying to keep my head on straight. Trying to sleep at night, trying to function during the day, and oh yeah—Christmas shopping.

THE HOLIDAY SEASON

It's early December.

Between shopping and useless promises to myself to keep Christmas simple this year, I start making calls about going south for at least part of the winter. I search the Internet, email questions to various places, and Cassie helps, acting as my representative and making more inquiries locally in her area. They live in Greenville, NC, which is a town we know little about, except that it contains our family. We figure that if we're going to spend money, we might as well make it feel like a vacation of sorts and get closer to the coast than Greenville, but still close enough to the kids and medical facilities.

We might even have visitors—friends and family—and we'd like to be on the water, if possible. That little flutter of thought goes through my mind, a variation of a now-familiar quotient when making a decision that involves both quality of living and money. It's simple: What if this is our last getaway? What if this is Ted's last winter? I haven't shared my thoughts about this with him at this point, in such a straightforward way.

What if, what if, what if?

As I write this, I am aware of our privilege earned from years of working in the medical field, saving money, and more—that which comes from White middle-class economic family backgrounds.

We talk to Ted's doctors and to Nurse Debbie. We discuss ways of making sure Ted will get some interim medical help, with a plan to fly back for an appointment in Maine in early March.

Debbie finds an oncologist involved in the same Novocure study in Chapel Hill who is willing to see Ted for the necessary February visit, required for his chemotherapy to continue, and mandated by the study. He will need a checkup and labs done prior to starting chemotherapy for that month.

Cassie helps us look into a couple of cottages in a town called New Bern, about 45 minutes from Greenville. We toss around the pros and cons of New Bern, a town on two rivers, versus a place called Beaufort, a tourist favorite, right on the ocean. Another town we consider is Washington, NC, a town a little closer to Greenville. "Little Washington" has some waterfront, but it seems to be a small, quiet little place. Cassie points out that New Bern has much to offer in the way of cultural events, restaurants, and stores. Its two rivers—the Trent and the Neuse—come together, eventually emptying out into the central coastal region. New Bern is also the birthplace of Pepsi. Pepsi? That's good enough for me. Thinking back, I remember we'd visited New Bern on a day trip when we had stayed with Cassie and Paul a while back, and I remember we liked it.

Cassie and I study a vacation rental website, and correspond with a woman named Missy, who owns several properties with her husband, Nick. Two of her three New Bern properties are right on the river. I read about them, study them, read the reviews, and look at the pictures again and again. Day after day, when I'm at my computer—writing or doing emails and such—I look at the pretty and cheerful pictures of the cottages. I reread the descriptions more times than I can count. I research other properties, both in New Bern and Beaufort, comparing costs, properties, contracts. In my search, I find a place in Beaufort that's significantly cheaper, a suite that looks quite nice. The fellow who manages it seems pleasantly casual. I email him to see what it would cost to rent by the month.

"Haven't done that before in the winter, but I could do it for $800 a month at this time of year," he writes.

That's appealing, and less expensive than the other places we have been looking into. But we have our dog with us, and a small suite-type arrangement might feel cramped over time. Also, Beaufort in the winter is pretty shut down.

In retrospect, I'm very glad we passed on that. Later, when we drive there to visit, it's a charming afternoon trip, but it would have been quite a distance from Cassie and Paul and good medical care. Virtually everything in Beaufort seems to be shut down in the winter, save for maybe a lonely restaurant or two. In the summertime, it's a different story. [Note to reader: Years later, I believe this is not the case.]

Cassie offers to check out the New Bern cottages, despite her crazily busy schedule. A week later, she reports back.

With her help, we find the cottage that looks just right, and on the water, except the price tag is a bit steep for our budget because we'll still be paying a mortgage on our house at the same time.

We agonize over it. Putting down a lot of money in advance seems like a risk, and when we check into a traveler's insurance policy, it doesn't look like it would be much help, just more expense. And Ted is wavering on the whole idea. One day he says, "I can't wait for North Carolina!" and the next day, he wants to stay put in Maine.

I bargain with Missy via emails regarding how long we might want to stay. At this point, she knows nothing of Ted's illness, as I'm being attentive to Ted's need for privacy. I think if we can pay just the one month until we get there, we can see if it will work out well for us and whether we want to stay a second month. She is quite agreeable, saying that she will give us first refusal in case someone else wants to have the cottage the second month. This is quite a relief. I don't know her, other than that Cassie has told me what a lovely person she is and that she thinks I'll like her.

I like her already.

I show the cottage pictures to Ted. The smallest, which would be plenty of room for us, is not overlooking the river. Ted and my innate difficulties with decision-making really come into play here. We have wavered on things many, many times before. For the difference of a few hundred dollars, maybe we should splurge. We'll let it roll around in our brains a little longer.

FAT ENLIGHTENMENT

I continue Christmas shopping in between other things, and soon realize that it doesn't matter that I planned to decrease my gift list. Sure, I've made a few adjustments. But overall? No. It's the same list, very few changes. No big shock there. It almost seems like a bother to give it so much thought. But in the process of shopping, I "up" my walking at the local shopping mall, where I walk in bad weather anyway.

And then one day something hits me. I am feeling fat, as usual. I could lose ten to fifteen pounds and be at my ideal weight, and I would like to be there. That's the weight where people say, "You look great!" and my clothes are a little loose instead of a little tight, especially around the middle. But what I start noticing is the contrast between the extreme effort Ted must make just walking across a room, and the ease with which I can move my body. And what hits me is the expression people say all the time: Love your body. Suddenly, it takes on a new meaning.

To love my body doesn't have to mean I need to love it in the sense of it being a smooth, firm twenty-year-old's body. It means I love my body for how it *works*, for how it *moves*. The very fact that it functions and moves makes me really love this ol' body of mine. Maybe not such a revelation or profound statement to shout from the rooftops, but it does make me want to shout: *People! You have a body that moves and does all sorts of wonderful things? Enjoy it! Feel how wonderful it is to strut along freely, to dance, to bend. Enjoy it!* A completely new concept for me, and one I cherish. Even with the limitations from my previous injury, I can still go for a walk, which helps me feel less achy. It doesn't matter that I can't do a lot I used to be able to. I can walk, get into my car, drive to a beach, walk onto the beach, and feel the sand under my feet. I deeply wish Ted could use his body as he once did. Maybe, at some point, he may be able to work in the garden for brief periods of time. Maybe, if he'll allow it, he can be helped into a kayak, and paddle around near the shore. In my wishful thinking and prayers for him, I find a new gratitude for what I have.

URGENT CARE

About three days before Christmas, Ted starts noticing a lot of puffiness, especially around his ankles. He calls the internist and the oncologist's office, and we're directed to the Urgent Care section of our internist's medical group for an exam and an ultrasound of his legs and abdomen to rule out blood clots. We see a very nice doctor, and an ultrasound is scheduled to be done in the same building. But there will be a wait between the doctor and the ultrasound appointment, and then a wait for results and to see the doctor again. I pick up coffee and sit in the car writing while he naps next to me. Fast forward to six hours later. We're back in the waiting room, now sprinkled with people coughing and showing other signs of illness. He's only five days from his last round of chemotherapy, which suppresses his immune system. I'm worried, and I nod in a subtle way to him, as in *Move away from that lady with the junky cough!*

"Stand over here, with me," I whisper. I'm sure I drive him crazy.

Now, at Urgent Care, I pray as we wait. The doctor is great, kind and reassuring, and the tests come out fine. The swelling is a side effect of some of Ted's medication, not blood clots, so another drug is prescribed to help with that. The drug list is really getting long. That evening, I make cookies but we both have a tough time emotionally in this, our new life in which we are constantly getting surprises, and mostly unwelcome. But tomorrow? We can hope for a calm day.

CHRISTMAS 2011

We take the plunge and send Missy the first month's rent and deposit money for the riverfront cottage in NC. We're doing this! I feel only slightly panicked. After all, how hard can it be to pull ourselves together in about three weeks' time?

Christmas comes. In the bustle of activity, I move beyond the persistent thoughts of wondering if this will be our last Christmas together. It becomes something of a blur, as do most holidays, but it's uneventful, with just enough sweetness and simplicity to satisfy us. Ted and I go to mass, which is my one big wish. And he gives me, among other things, a copy of the movie *Bridesmaids*, which I know will provide me with laughs when I need them most. Sally has come up from New York to be with us, as has William, who has more than a week's vacation time from his job in the New York suburbs. My brother Steve comes up from New Hampshire and we have dinner together, followed by the predictable experience of being stuffed and relaxed. Good stuff.

CHAPTER 24

POST-CHRISTMAS—GETTING READY FOR THE SOUTH

The week before we're scheduled to leave for North Carolina, we face the post-Christmas aftermath of exhaustion and mess. Sally goes back to her life in New York. I bind together the Christmas cards we've received with a rubber band so I can look at them again one more time, later. Like many people, I have so many things going on at any one time that our house is like a museum of unfinished projects and well-intentioned piles on desks, bureaus, and shelves. Periodically, I take a deep breath and just toss out a pile. If I didn't, I'd end up on a reality show. So, in spite of many things needing sorting and cleaning, I plunge into preparation for the trip, and getting people lined up to oversee the house while we're gone, for both routine and emergency possibilities.

Our new handyman, Michael, meets with us regarding plowing, shoveling around the house so the fuel guy and others can navigate the property with a cleared path, and anything else that might come up. Michael is agreeable to all that, helping us feel very secure. Our neighbors Sue and Sam, across the street, true to form, volunteer to help keep an eye on the place, and Ted goes out to the hardware store to buy a special apparatus that attaches to a lamp that will be placed in our front window. Plugged in, it causes the lamp to turn on if the heat in the house drops below 50 degrees. The idea is to set the thermostat at 55 degrees, so any major furnace, heating, or electrical problem involving heat will set off the light. We do not want the heat to drop too low, or the pipes might freeze, and that is disastrous in the frigid Maine winter. Sue and Sam will keep an eye on the lamp for us. They, along with our nearby cousins, take our many house plants to care for. I call the local police department to let them know we'll be gone; arrange for the mail to be forwarded; rearrange the cable and internet service; call doctors and the vet to get prescriptions arranged; notify our bank and most-used credit card companies that we'll be out of state; start packing and figuring out what needs to come with us and what we can do without.

Now I'm emailing Missy more often.

Is there a toaster in the cottage? Coffee pot? Pots and pans? Paper towels, soap, laundry detergent?

Yes, yes, yes, and enough to get started.

Towels, linens, pillows?

Yes to all, but do we want the linens on the bed or do we want to bring our own?

I sift through the questions and answers, and Missy is patient, warm, and casual. She says she'll watch for our mail in case any gets there before we do, as we'll be driving there in small increments. We'll spread out the trip by visiting relatives and allowing for fewer hours in the car on any one day.

One major hurdle Ted and I both feel very anxious about is his upcoming oncology appointment and MRI, pre-trip. This is another two-month mark, and we are both on edge. Worry takes many forms. He tends to close down or get very discouraged. "I expect the worst" is his mantra.

I try to be optimistic, and overall, I am. But there is always a nagging doubt in my mind. Will something show up that will be an ominous sign? My anxiety takes the form of obnoxious cheery encouragement. "I see no difference in how you have been for months. It'll be fine," I say, praying my words are true and accurate. After all, I can't see into his brain. I have no real way of knowing if his tumor is the same or changed in some way. But overall, he doesn't seem to be any worse off. His walking is unsteady, but that's no different since the beginning of treatment. But that damned what-if plagues us both.

I feel like a raging bitch as I get stuff ready for our trip. Countering Ted's attitude of "There's not that much to do," my obsessive craziness is focused on the need to get everything in place *yesterday*. I have always been like this when something is coming up. I can't stand to wait until the last minute, because everything always takes longer than one would think—at least for me. So I counter with "There's SO much left to do," and we inevitably grumble at each other. I'm already starting to feel like it's more trouble than it might be worth, heading south for a month or two, spending the money, when all the plans could go haywire if next week we get a bad MRI report, although, in truth, even that might not prevent at least a shortened version of the trip.

Maybe things will settle down.

THEN CAME THE FLOOD

On New Year's Eve morning, Ted awakens, goes downstairs for coffee, and finds a small stream of water on the carpet in the laundry room, which doubles as the room where we lay out our dog Rebel's food and water. Ted comes upstairs, just as I'm waking up.

"I think the dog peed," he says.

Our dog, now 12, is a small Cairn terrier who occasionally has an accident.

It's possible Rebel peed, although the size of the wet streak makes that assumption ridiculous. I use the toilet in the bathroom next to the laundry room, and when I flush it, the water comes gushing up out of the toilet and out of the sink in that room and all over the floor.

Oh, boy. We have a serious problem.

This, on New Year's Eve, as we're preparing to go to North Carolina for a couple of months.

The temperatures outside are quite cold, and at first I suspect we might have frozen pipes. I call a plumber, who argues with me over the phone that what we have is not a plumbing problem, but a septic tank problem. I tell him we had the septic tank pumped out only a bit over a year previously, but he persists in telling me that this is not going to be a plumbing problem and says that if he comes out to my house, he will have to charge me. A lot.

"Two hundred and fifty dollars for me to walk in the door on a Saturday. Save your money. It's the septic tank," he says.

He is loath to do that for something that he knows is not a plumbing problem in the first place. Kathy and I consult by phone with our new handyman, Michael.

The day warms up a little more, and I pour buckets of hot water into the bowl. After an hour or so, we try an experimental flush. All goes well. Fixed. We leave the door open to keep this small bathroom warm, thinking the pipes had simply been frozen. We have soaked up all the excess water with nearly every towel we have.

By this time, William is up and the three of us are sitting at the kitchen table, eating a late breakfast and drinking coffee, when I scoot into the laundry room to start the laundry, which includes the wet towels we've used to mop the bathroom floor. The washer is going, I'm sipping my fabulous mix of decaf with southern pecan caffeinated coffee, milk and fat-free half-and-half, feeling pretty good. Feeling more settled. Proud that the yucky towels are getting washed so efficiently. I'm starting to feel like we are headed in the right direction. I'm looking forward to New Year's Eve—maybe we'll go to a movie, or get some good take-out food, and I'm enjoying having my son here for a few more days of his vacation…until the geyser blows.

The minute the washing machine hits the spin cycle, the toilet in the small bathroom literally erupts with water, a violent volcanic waterfall pumps out huge quantities of water, over and over and over again, into the bathroom, and overflowing into the entryway and toward the kitchen and laundry room.

"MORE TOWELS!" I scream to Will, who takes off for the upstairs linen closet in a flash.

"TED! TED!" I yell to Ted, who, right next to me, is also in disbelief.

"Can you turn that thing off?!?" I ask, indicating the toilet. I know somewhere there must be a shutoff valve, but I have no clue where, or what to do.

I run to the laundry room, now wading through a flood, and shut off the dial on the washer, stopping the spin cycle, never thinking that it might not be a good idea to touch a running appliance while I'm standing in water [I lived, but kids, do not try this at home], and Ted hobbles into the bathroom and shuts off the toilet water at its source.

You can only imagine that at this point, I'm thinking maybe someone up there is telling us it's not a good time to go away.

Michael comes over to the house and suggests that we get a septic tank service, which we do. So, the septic tank gets pumped out again,

but unfortunately this does not cure the problem. It turns out that there are blockages in the sewer lines underneath the house, upstream from the septic tank itself. Michael and a couple of other men go to work on it, discovering the blockages and locating a couple of cracks in the sewage pipes. Apparently, one of the major problems is that the sewer pipes which run underneath our house and lead to the septic tank have almost no slope to them, that is, they are almost perfectly horizontal, and because of that, sewage in the pipes is likely to clot and create blockages such as these.

Later, calls to our homeowner's insurance company are reassuring; they will pay for a good part of it.

Michael calls Servpro, who comes over to assess the damage, sets up industrial-size dehumidifiers, and blocks off the area. I call my friends to hear what they think I can do to sanitize the area when it comes time to get back into the room. I can't believe this is happening while we're getting ready to go away.

Discovering these difficulties is, unfortunately, not enough to solve all the problems. It is simple enough, in a way, for Michael and his crew to fix the issue. However, that leaves the problem of the flooring in the laundry room. Clearly, the carpet will have to be replaced. When it comes to removing that carpet, however, we discover that there is a thick pad underneath the carpet and that there is another carpet underneath the pad. That carpet is a lurid red color, really striking. When that carpet is lifted it turns out that there is a layer of asbestos tile over the subflooring. So, the asbestos tile will also have to be replaced, raising concerns about asbestos contamination, although we are assured that this kind of asbestos is unlikely to be terribly hazardous, as long as it is not damaged or shredded in the process of removal.

HAPPY NEW YEAR

The layers of carpet have been here far longer than Ted has owned the house.

Katrina, the project manager of the local Servpro franchise, continues her assessment to help us figure out how to proceed. There's no way to get everything dried and taken care of effectively. The carpet, both layers and the pad, will have to be removed.

"Are you serious?" I ask, not for the first time.

While asking this, what I'm really thinking about is, *I only have ten days to get ready to leave and I have LAUNDRY to do*. That seems more disturbing than anything else at this point. Then comes more bad news.

"You have asbestos tiles under the bottom layer of carpet," she says.

Holy. God.

Understand, I am a total nutcase when it comes to anything related to germs or any other health hazard. Lysol is no stranger to me. I've always kept masks on hand, and disposable gloves. The thought of asbestos adds a new layer of crazy to my already overloaded brain.

"ARE YOU (very bad expletive deleted) KIDDING ME?!?!?!?!?!?"

As I hold my breath, literally (!), she shows me a corner of the tile from underneath the radiator. Never mind that just looking at asbestos tiles isn't a particular hazard, from several feet away. I cover my nose and mouth anyway.

The nightmare fantasies that go through my head are stunning. Have we been breathing in asbestos all this time—for years?

As I start to freak out, she reassures me that there is no danger unless and until the tile is pulled up, and that it's a procedure that, professionally done, is extremely safe. A special company from a nearby town that specializes in asbestos removal will be called. She will take care of the arrangements. I have no choice here. But letting go of control—once again—is not going to be easy.

HELLO, GOD? IT'S ME—LUNATIC WOMAN

I continue to freak out.

Now I definitely think we should not be leaving the house to go south.

Everyone else disagrees with me.

"Are you kidding? All signs say LEAVE. NOW!" a friend says. Yes, there's a part of what she says that really makes sense, despite the preparations being so unfinished.

I have already sent a check to Missy; all but the security deposit is hers. But instead of swimming through that worry, I have bigger fish to fry.

Katrina and Michael are a great team. While I freak out, they make the necessary calls. Ted and I call the insurance company back—and in a rare piece of insurance humanity, the representative from our aptly named insurance company, Amica, tells me to take our laundry to the cleaners for whatever I need cleaned, and to send him the bills. This is one of the biggest shocks I get the entire year—an insurance company that is cooperative, fair, and—dare I say?—truly understanding and generous. Unreal. "Amica" stands for Automobile Mutual Insurance Company of America, but to me, it means "loved friend," as in Latin. There is a special place in Heaven for the people who run and work for Amica. Seriously.

Thoughts of my laundry being done someplace and maybe picking up something gross like bedbugs appear on my internal movie track. As I said, I really am freaking out. Everything swimming in my head seems to end with worry, ambivalence about leaving coloring all my hours of the day and night.

But there is laundry to be done, and packing...so I call the local dry cleaners and find out they do regular laundering, not just dry cleaning. An angel of a woman tells me about how careful they are to keep people's laundry unto itself, and about all their precautions.

"One of our workers here—a young man—has all his clothes done here," she says. Testimonial enough for me.

I gather everything I can find in the various piles of laundry around the house, now disheveled even more than usual because so much stuff has been taken out of the affected areas and put into boxes and bags, tossed into other rooms. I shove everything launder-able into pillowcases, carry each one carefully into the car so I won't aggravate my darned neck, and drive to the drop-off with their promise that I can get it the next day. I set aside my worries long enough to trust in their laundering capabilities. Boy, am I relieved. Maybe things are taking a turn for the better.

The next day, I go out to do a few errands, and when I come home, things have changed. I've become used to having various "company" trucks parked in our driveway. I am beginning to trust the people who are setting up the machinery, and they are wonderful about answering my questions, again and again. Katrina is so patient. I must drive her crazy, yet she seems to get it, the fact that this is all throwing me into a tailspin. I repeatedly ask about the asbestos. She repeatedly answers my questions. She gives me her personal cell phone number. I use it.

When I get home, a plastic, sealed "zip" door greets me when I walk in the front door. Every time we want to go in or out of the house, we'll need to unzip it from the bottom, and step over a small horizontal area of about a foot or so high. It's apparently a preparatory step in the asbestos removal, which will take place after we leave for the south.

We end up using a door on the far end of the house as much as possible, but I have trouble remembering, habit being what it is. So, there are many times when I go to the front door, groceries in arm, open the door, and curse the plastic in front of me, turn around and go in the other way. "Crap!" becomes the word of the day. Turns out the plastic barrier is a small inconvenience. In the greater scheme of things, it's unimportant. But the idea of a germy couple of layers of old, wet carpet, soaked by yucky backup pipe water and asbestos tile beyond the cordoned off area? That has me going.

I count my blessings, in between grumbling.

I'm starting to get good at that. The blessings and the grumbling.

BETH

On January 3rd, Beth comes over to give Ted a flute lesson, probably the last he'll have until we return from NC. After the lesson is over, I bring out a ribbon-y and girly bag of Christmas gifts. She loves it.

"You shouldn't have! Too much!" she says, smiling broadly. She comments on all the little gifts inside the bag, including a bonus check. Watching her open things is so much fun. She is like a child, eyes wide, enjoying every minute of it. I'll never forget it—she is so sweet, and she looks so beautiful. What we have put together for her is not extravagant. But her enjoyment level is high. I'm sure she has no idea how much her presence means to us, this little Mary Poppins coming into our home just when we need boosts of joy.

ALMOST THERE, PRE-TRIP

Will heads back to NY. We make plans to take him to his appointment for a scheduled colonoscopy, related to his medical issues, when we reach New York.

I continue to bring in groceries, aware that I am bringing more food into the house than we'll use in the remaining days. It doesn't make sense, but then again, not much does. At some point, I plan to cut off cooking and just bring in take-out, throw out much of what is already getting old in the fridge, plus crystallized food from the freezer, and bring the remaining good stuff to our neighbors before we leave. I'm not sticking to the plan very well.

The next day, one of my coworkers calls me to say she's made us a loaf of her special homemade rye bread to take on our trip. She has taken the loaf, sliced it, frozen it, and put it in several Ziploc bags. I always take a cooler with us on road trips, so I'm excited at the thought of having the bread, some good cheddar, and maybe some fruit. Call it my inner psyche or hormones or sense of God within, but getting a loaf of homemade bread from her, a very faith-filled woman, still moves me when I reflect upon this simple act of generosity. Our daily bread, indeed.

The remaining hours zoom by. I finish making and checking hotel reservations at pet-friendly hotels, tending to all our special medical needs, and devising contingency plans. My anxieties about going away loom large, but we are stuck with who we are. Intermittently, there's blind faith.

My to-do list seems unending. The buying of more unneeded groceries continues. I bring groceries to take with us to the south. It's ridiculous. We are not going to a third-world nation. Ted, again, is much more laid-back about everything. I can only imagine what I must look like. Maybe he gets a laugh out of it. In my mind, though, I find nearly everything worrisome and infuriating.

I am unraveling.

Seems like every time I'm about at the end of my rope, something wonderful, though small, happens to change things—more human angels come our way. Our neighbors bring us a container of homemade soup. Just prior to leaving for North Carolina, I go to the vet to pick up the special dog food our pup requires. The veterinary assistant hoists the 17-pound bag of food on her back unasked and brings it out to the car for me, along with the five-pound bag of his dental treats. The kindness of others is a welcome reprieve from the larger issues: Ted's upcoming MRI, and Will's medical test.

TED'S MRI

Ted has his MRI and oncology appointment. The tumor is stable. No progression, and maybe "slightly less dense," the doctor tells us. This is great news, which later, Ted—once again—does not seem to take in. His platelets are low again, so we arrange to have his blood drawn once we get to North Carolina. Dr. Evans gives him a prescription for the chemo so we can pick it up before we leave and take it with us. Other medical arrangements are in place.

Despite tons of things left to do, we drive a couple of miles down the road to a flooring place to pick out a few linoleum samples.

And I fall down as we're leaving the place...

He gets up and seems OK.

At home, we place the samples around the area near the laundry room without stepping in. We decide on one that, we hope, will work OK with color and design, then call and order it. We arrange for it to be installed after the asbestos is taken care of.

Dog food, check.

Dog medicine, check.

Our medicine, check.

Clothes, shoes, personal products, check.

Books, computer components, food, snacks, check.

The night before we're set to leave, my friend Denise comes over to help us lug the heavier things out to the car—all five foot two, one hundred pounds of her. She's tiny but strong, and I don't know how we'd do it without her...or without Sue or Sam...or Fred and Meryl, who help us, prior to what is starting to look like either the Pilgrims heading to the New World or the Joad family from *The Grapes of Wrath*.

I don't want to leave, at this point. Have I mentioned that? I desperately want the time in North Carolina with my daughter, but I'm scared to death. Each person who helps us get ready makes parting even harder. How will we survive without these people in our daily lives? Again and again, the phone rings and a voice at the other end asks, "Is there anything we can do to help you?" *Yes*, I think to myself, *come with us, or tell us we can't leave.*

"No," I say. "Thanks. I think we're all set."

Box of writing notes, last year's published stories for columnists' contest entry, check.

Extra socks and underwear, check.

Prayer list, novena cheat-sheets, daily prayer book, mini-Bible with frayed cover, check.

CHAPTER 25

GOING, GOING, GONE!

On January 10th, we leave for New York.

I still don't want to go. Leaving seems like a crazy idea. Going to a place where we will not be near Ted's medical care, leaving the house in disarray with major problems needing to be fixed—is this not a sign to stay?

We are on the road just before noon. The car is packed to the hilt, the dog is in his soft crate in the backseat, enticed by the doggy treats I put in the crate for him. He makes not a peep about it. He doesn't need to. My soul is making enough peeps for everyone.

The first night, we arrive at the hotel in the suburbs of New York, just a few miles from Will's apartment. The hotel is packed. I approach the front desk. There's a fuss (mine, not theirs) because the room has double beds and we'd requested a queen or a king. The area of the hotel designated as pet-friendly, with easy access to the outside, has only double beds. We did not know that. And like a spoiled baby, I fuss about it. Ted does not. Also, although it's technically the first floor, it feels more like a basement, as in, *You are here with a pet so you must stay down below.* It's totally irrational on my part. We decide to stay in the double room, although the desk clerk is really trying hard to find something else that works for us, and she throws in a free breakfast. The room is fine, very clean, and actually, it's kind of fun to walk our dog down the hallway only to hear successive barks as we pass by other rooms, as the other "best friends" hear, smell, or sense a doggy walking by, the dogs saying hello to each other from behind closed doors. We take Rebel with us almost everywhere when we need to be out of the room, and like a true miracle, it works flawlessly the entire time. He's the best dog ever.

We see Will the next morning. We wait nervously throughout his procedure and meet with his doctor afterwards. The test results are not as good as we'd hoped, and I have a strong aversion for the doctor, whose waiting room wall is plastered with framed newspaper clippings of how well regarded he is. To be sure, it may be the simple fact that we want a clean bill of health for Will, and the doctor's opinion is that there is a chronic problem. I just can't hear that my formerly robust, healthy baby boy now has a lifelong health issue.

We talk with Will about getting a second opinion. So, the first leg of the trip is stressful, though the procedure itself has gone well, without complication. Our son seems OK overall, and ready to start some medication to get his medical problem under reasonable control.

I'm heartbroken. Worried. Anxious. Scared. Hopeful that the doctor is wrong.

Two days later, we leave for the Philadelphia area, where we park ourselves in a nice suite for another couple of days, giving us a chance to see Randey and Maryellen. We're able to get together with them several times, and it's great fun in spite of some medical sequelae Randey has from a recent accident.

At a gas pump in New Jersey, Ted gets out of the car. A man walking past the back of our car takes one look at our Obama bumper sticker and sneers, "Bet you're sorry now!"

Ted chuckles. "Actually, no," he mumbles, and this becomes one of his favorite new stories to tell.

The bond of love has the promise of so much joy. But the other side of it can be intensely painful. It feels like we're getting more than a fair share of that. Ted and I are worried about both of our sons. It's not the first time that I'm feeling as though the men in my life, all dealing with medical issues, are falling apart. I'm falling apart along with them. On this road trip, I begin to pray in earnest, every night. I keep the little packet of prayer papers, from the priest who had given Ted the Anointing of the Sick, accessible in my tote bag. These prayers await me each night whether life is going well or not. Sometimes prayer seems like all I have to keep me from tipping into total crumbling.

The dog does his best to remind us of mundane things—a blessed relief. For example, after bragging to each other and to Randey and Maryellen about how perfect Rebel's behavior is, he taunts us by barking his living head off when we're just a few feet down the hotel hallway one night, on our way out to dinner with them. The hotel where we're staying is very clear in their written agreement that a disruptive dog will not be tolerated. I end up going back to the room, popping him into his kennel in the car, and there he stays, quite happily, while the four of us go into the restaurant.

There's something magical about the soft dog crate, with treats and toys in it. Pavlov might have something to say about that, of course. Rebel loves it and apparently feels very secure in it, thank God. It could have been dreadful—and it isn't. I'm thankful for having thought of dog concerns before we left. In one small duffel bag in the backseat, we have all the medicines he needs for a few months: his medical records; the name and number of a vet in North Carolina my daughter knows; more than enough food and treats for the road trip (the rest are in larger bags packed into the bowels of the car); a plastic lidded container for water; his dog food dish; and bunches of plastic cleanup bags—although we discover that most hotels provide them, as do rest areas. We never drive more than about four hours or so total in any one day. At rest areas, Ted and I take turns feeding/watering and "bathrooming" the dog and ourselves.

ON THE ROAD AGAIN

Despite the worries about my menfolk, I start to see that some things are in control. William is in good, if egotistical, hands with his specialist. Ted is doing what he needs to do—just being alive and waiting for his platelets to go up. Randey is seeing the doctors who will try to help him. And our house with its problems? It's funny. There's nothing I can do about it now, other than an occasional phone call to answer or make, and to follow its progress from afar. So I have a sense of freedom, in a way, because, well, we're on the road.

I'm doing a lot of work during the trip itself (much of the driving, going into hotels to register, helping Ted get in, arranging for a way to get our bags in with minimal risk to my back and without Ted overdoing it). But at night? Ahhhh. At night, I treat myself like a princess, watching reruns of my favorite TV shows on my laptop, with headphones, after Ted falls asleep. I read. I'm an avid Archie Comics reader, rediscovering the "gang" of my teen years. I have a little snack, make a cup of tea in the room, or sneak down to the hotel lobby for a hot drink or a free cookie.

I'm starting to take care of myself. And I don't need anyone telling me to do it. I sense a shift.

Toward the end of our journey south, we start to get more excited and curious about the destination.

Our GPS and an occasional look at a map take us to an overnight in Mechanicsville, Virginia, before continuing on to North Carolina.

Finally, we cross the North Carolina border, with just a few hours left before we reach New Bern.

EN ROUTE TO NEW BERN

They don't call the South the Bible Belt for nothing. There are churches everywhere, from large, imposing newer brick buildings along highways and in cities, to store fronts and older, smaller churches in need of repair. Religious billboards dot the highways, virtually all Christian-based, and posted in front of most churches is a catchy religious saying of some sort.

No God. No peace. Know God. Know peace.

I pass one church that looks like a painted-over gas station. In some areas, there are churches on every block or corner. Turn on the radio and you have your choice of Christian-oriented stations. Christian music, talk shows, it's endless. I'm a little more private about my religious beliefs. But here, on billboards, in mottos on the bottom of ads and on menus in restaurants, God talk is prevalent. I lose count of the number of times I chat with a cashier who says, "God bless you, now" or "Have a blessed day" before I go on my way.

It is sweet but incongruous that in this state, filled with proud Christians of all sorts, I am to learn that you can get behind the wheel of your car and feel like your life is in danger. They drive like hell. "Bless your heart" indeed. I wonder if it's our Obama bumper sticker, although enough time spent in North Carolina tells me it's just how most drive here.

ARRIVING IN NEW BERN

January 15, 2012
We pass from Greenville through the countryside, past old houses and shacks, and some small newer single-levels with aluminum siding. We enter Vanceboro, pass Kite's market, a few small stores, one chain grocery store, a 25-mph sign, and a small police department which, we are warned, is very serious about their speed limits. We also pass Miss Vera's Diner, scanning the countryside after passing through this small town…now a "Craven County Gin and Cotton" sign, broken-down bones of houses and barns, left uncleared. Shells of their former selves, old shanties, possibly once housing for slaves. My heart sinks at that thought. Once through Vanceboro, we continue to New Bern.

As we pull off the main divided highway (Route 43), there's a gas station on the right and a Hardee's and a Hess station on the left. There's a construction site right in the middle of the highway, sporting a large yellow lit arrow pointing left, across the oncoming traffic. Once we figure out that that's where we are supposed to turn, we look for the next thing the GPS tells us.

"Turn left onto…," the female GPS voice continues. We pass the tiny Bridgeton Town Hall, on the edge of Bridgeton, a small town next to New Bern on this side of the Neuse River. Straight ahead is the river, visible now, and on the right is the worn-out Curtis Motel, built in the late 1970s but appearing much more worn. Beyond that is a vacant older building, Mrs. Harvey's Café, closed with little hopes of reopening, from the looks of it. There are many small, old, deserted and dilapidated buildings scattered amongst the larger, more prestigious homes, a stark contrast of wealth and poverty. It's not unlike the scenes on the major roads we've traveled throughout North Carolina so far. Some of the broken-down places have weathered Hurricane Irene of 2011 quite badly. We frequently see rusty tools and machinery, old furnishings and other household items out on the lawn or the side of a house. It's not unusual to pass a house with a sofa or chair, stuffing falling out of it, piles of indoor and outdoor children's toys, bikes, partially broken wood furnishings, piled together, nothing moving, a slice of abstract sculpture depicting the devastation of down-on-luck America. Then we'll see the occasional flowering potted plant mixed in with the clutter and mess, as though someone is attempting to revive and renew...along with a No Trespassing sign.

Maybe much of it is flood damage. It's hard to tell. In short, it's a mess, the aftermath of Irene and its damage, or in some cases, a reflection of impoverished daily life in its basic condition. As we view it and imagine what it was like before the hurricane, we guess that at least some of the homes didn't look terribly different beforehand, simply judging by the small property size and overall condition of the exteriors. Poverty on one street; significant wealth just yards away.

Now we are navigating several tiny streets to find the cottage. Some of them seem to come together in a semi-roundabout. Though still driving, we are "done" emotionally and physically. We just need to be there. When we finally get to the promised road, my entire being celebrates. There is the cottage—neat and clean and inviting—and right on the waterfront.

The driving is over. We have arrived.

CHAPTER 26

OUR COTTAGE

The cottage is easy to recognize from its website photos. All the homes on this stretch of the road are right on the riverfront. I know what the phrase "my heart leaps for joy" means. I am drawn to the water. Maybe I was a fish in a former life. I have the information about the cottage in my tote bag, so we go around to the river side of the building to go up the outdoor staircase that leads to the porch. On the way up, I once again caution Ted to "Be careful!" and then find the key. Soon after, Cassie and Paul and the kids arrive to help us unload and carry almost everything upstairs for us. Then we all head to a nearby restaurant for dinner.

The cottage is everything I'd hoped for and more. Built on stilts, as commonly done on the North Carolina shore because of hurricanes and flooding, it is quite new (built about eight years earlier) and has a very open feeling, with lots of light wood-and-glass cabinetry. The décor is accented by a cheerful shade of blue: sofa, loveseat, countertops, and whimsical fish-stenciled wall highlights and coordinating decorative objects, with occasional light-yellow accents. The walls are white, and everything is very crisp and bright.

I am tremendously affected by my surroundings. I do not mean that I need luxury. But open, clean, colorful ambiance makes me feel happy. I have accepted this about myself for some time now. So, if I have a choice between the look of older, heavier, darker rooms and lighter, airier ones, I always go for the latter. I'd never make it living in an old castle…

Our New Bern cottage is bigger than what we need, but the major living space on the first floor is just right for us. The cottage is smaller and newer than our old farmhouse in Maine, and I love it.

We have three bedrooms (two downstairs, one up) and for the purpose of avoiding more stairs, we decide to use the downstairs bedroom, with a double bed, that overlooks the water, even though the upstairs bedroom has a queen-size bed and a lovely water view as well. The third bedroom, with twin beds, does not look out on the water, but is bright and cheery, with lots of closet space, and is a perfect guest room for the grandkids. There is a large open kitchen/living room and two bathrooms, one upstairs and one down. I'm on board with the two-bathroom idea, especially since the downstairs one is accessible to the bedroom.

So here we are, living in a riverfront cottage in North Carolina, on a quiet road just a few miles outside the city of New Bern. The temperatures are mild during the daytime, usually in the high 50s to 60s, falling a little at night, and the cottage is perfect.

Going from a king-size bed at home to a double bed here, I feel like I might fall out of bed these first few days. Some mornings I awaken without any covers, Ted having pulled them over onto his side of the bed, although I soon fix that by "adjusting" the blankets and honoring my inner selfishness.

I'm kidding, but here's the thing about having a sick spouse: I want him to feel comforted and soothed. Fleeting thoughts of trying to get the landlord to switch the beds for us or using a larger comforter from upstairs on the double bed cross my mind, but it goes no further than that. By now, we've settled into a comfortable nonchalance with our daily lives, some things not worth the energy to pursue.

Then an odd thing happens. About two weeks after arriving, it occurs to me that I like being that physically close to Ted at night. It's something that seems to accommodate itself, all on its own. Bear in mind, we also have the dog with us at night. He generally stays near the bottom of the bed, and I realize that since about two months before Ted's symptoms began, Rebel had been staying much closer to him than to me. So here we are, the three of us, glued to each other on this little double bed, like a couple from the 1950s, before it came into vogue to have larger beds.

Ted agrees that he likes it, too—a coziness unexpected, and very sweet.

NEW BERN—A TOWN WITH HISTORY

It takes several days to get settled, and we spend a lot of time getting to know the area.

Beyond the downtown area, in the north end of New Bern is a winding grid of streets that comprise the bulk of the historic section of town. The streets are lined with large, beautiful, well-kept homes, churches, and public buildings that bear placards posted on the fronts of nearly each home. Most of the placards are 12 x 22 inches, similar in style and framing, announcing the root of the home and its owner in times past. In my wanderings, I pass the John B. Ives house; the Jerkins-Richardson house; the William R. Guion house; the Robert Hancock Carriage House. One after another, they contribute to an old southern charm and extraordinary efforts to keep up the town's historic image. My favorite home, the Bright house, though not one of the largest homes, has a simple charm, white with an off-yellow shade of trim, a hint of gambrel to the shape, the house itself facing slightly away from the street, unlike most of the others. Every time I pass that house, I stop and take note of its understated sweetness.

Some placards on the historic homes simply display the New Bern "bear" logo and state "settled in 1710" or some such date. Ted and I imagine aloud what it must have been like for town councils and historical societies over the many years to get together and heighten its image with colorful statues of bears everywhere, painted fire hydrants, and these house placards. We half expect to see a sign on a temporary facility on the edge of the downtown neighborhood where road construction is in progress, stating "Site of first New Bern Port-A-Potty."

SYRUP ON THAT/COTTAGE LIFE

Most days I make a big breakfast for us, enough to carry us through until midafternoon. The restaurants in New Bern, though varied in style and menu, have decent lunches at very reasonable prices, and lunch is sometimes our main meal. Then for supper, we have the equivalent of a couple of healthy snacks. In the morning, I might make eggs, bacon, and pancakes, often setting aside a glass full of fresh berries and cottage cheese for later. When I make pancakes, I make enough so we can each have a few and there'll be some left over for a day or two later to reheat. Why the focus on food? I'm not a gourmet cook, not even close, but Ted seems to really enjoy having more than his traditional cereal now for breakfast. Back home, I normally only fix big breakfasts on the weekend. But here in North Carolina, we fall into a routine that is fun, laid-back, and easy on the budget. There's one restaurant in town that serves small or large-portion lunch entrees, with a couple of sides, rolls, and a maple syrup–sweetened butter. Our bill, with beverages, comes to just over $20.00. We find comfort in going to the same several places. The servers are always kind, and the southern accent seems to enhance that. Can food be so basic? The fact that Ted is fighting cancer—*we* are fighting cancer—makes us appreciate these small things. Feels like vacation.

Some nights, we order take-out from a tiny Chinese place about a mile from the cottage. It's good food, plentiful for the price, and when we order it there is usually enough left over for at least part of another meal.

"Is it OK to have Chinese food twice in a row?" I ask Ted, as if he's a nutrition guru. I'm thinking of things like sodium content and fat.

"You would if you were Chinese," he says.

I pick up the phone and order more things to supplement what we have in the refrigerator.

Eating, trips to the pharmacy, taking walks, all become familiar and comforting.

We both have good books to read. Ted is plunging into some substantial theology books. I've borrowed *The Namesake* by Jhumpa Lahiri from my daughter, which turns out to be one of my all-time favorite books.

Of amusement is the local paper, a paper so thin it's the size of a supplement to a paper where we come from. It tends to carry the same news stories day after day. Will there be a fee charged for the ferry? Will there be prayer before town meetings? Then there are the local arrests, complete with pictures of those arrested and sometimes retractions, days later, for an occasional mistaken arrest. There are letters to the editor about politics and religion, one that is so incoherent that Ted and I laugh aloud as I read it to him. What exactly is this man saying? He throws around prayer and God, constitutional rights, and demands to include God in government…

says that the Bill of Rights is part of the Declaration of Independence…We admire his tenacity.

Along with the interesting mix of people and places that you might find anywhere, we experience a growing peace with New Bern, although I still experience anything but peacefulness at least part of each day. Where is Ted's illness heading? How long will we be together? What is my role or contribution to him, to me, to others? These thoughts spin through my head.

Sometimes, in the middle of the various go-rounds with our medical insurance company or related mix-ups and obstacles, I think about writing or speaking out on behalf of those who are too weakened by the system or otherwise unable to help themselves enough. For someone who was used to taking care of people through my role as a nurse, I now feel powerless, that I'm not making a difference anymore. Should I speak up more? I know how to haunt myself.

On walks by myself, I sometimes head to a nearby gas station where the billboard advertises "Clean Rest Rooms." Thinking it means "Clean Rest Rooms, fresh coffee, and more," I walk there, affording me two miles of exercise and time to clear my head, to get perspective.

The first time I enter the store, I am overcome by a strong smell of Clorox-type cleanser, combined with tobacco. A few men are standing around talking, and the stench is more than I can handle. I skip the coffee and buy a couple of lottery scratch tickets. Losers, as I recall. The tickets, I mean.

Another time, I have the same experience—the strong smells are awful. After that, I stick with the Hess station, which has surprisingly fresh donuts. It seems funny to think of those being my choices of destinations for a diversionary walk. At home, it might be a walk to Starbucks, or a mall or a nature walk, depending on the weather. But here, unless I want to drive into town, the choice between two gas stations is the big time. No one is forcing me to do this. I can just walk around the back roads, and often do. And yet, damn! There's something appealing about a donut now and then.

Back at the cottage, I do my neck traction next door in the empty lot, where the owners have given me permission to do my inversion traction in my car on their property. The previous year, their big, beautiful riverfront home had been destroyed by fire, leaving an empty lot that happens to have a small area of land with a good incline, the only little hill around here that I can find in this part of the state. Since my injury, I'd found that the standard home traction apparatus was too difficult to gauge, often causing more discomfort than relief. But my little Honda Element has proven to be helpful. Back home in Maine, we have a steep driveway. And in a Honda Element, all seats go completely flat. In fact, the backseat goes a bit beyond that. By releasing the backseat as far as it can go, and parking on an incline, I get a gentle, effective inversion traction twice a week. Here, in this very flat part of North Carolina, I must be more creative. Thus, the use of the next-door neighbor's small hill. I'll take it.

ST. PAUL'S CATHOLIC CHURCH

In outer New Bern, St. Paul's is a large, modern nearly in-the-round church that has beautiful stained-glass windows, placed in a way that enhance the colors and patterns that settle about inside when it is sunny out. As you enter from the back of the congregation, facing the altar, there is a warm-water baptismal font approximately a dozen feet long and four feet wide, geometrically and pleasingly designed. There are a couple of devotional candle-lighting areas. It's a contemporary, esthetically lovely church. Ted and I begin to attend St. Paul's together. There is a smaller, lovely St. Paul's church in downtown New Bern, the oldest Catholic Church in NC, which still has regular masses. But we decide to try the newer one.

The first mass we go to at St. Paul's sets the stage for what becomes an early-morning Sunday ritual for us, as we are completely blown away by the gospel choir. It's not so much that this is a gospel choir of great skill, although they are quite good. But coming from northern New England, we are unaccustomed to a mostly Black choir in a Catholic church, and the hymnal used at this mass is the African American Hymnal. It's filled with a mixture of contemporary hymns and some more southern, old-time hymns. In addition, the choir often uses a soloist, Jack, a beautiful, large man, to sing a soothing, inspired piece during communion. I feel his God-given voice melting in and around us. At the end of mass, the recessional hymn is most always upbeat, including in-time handclapping by the choir and at least some of the congregation.

One morning, at the end of mass, I turn to Ted.

"Are you hearing what I'm hearing?" I ask.

They were singing a gospel/country song called "Can't Nobody Do Me Like Jesus" and totally rocking it. Cool.

Ted and I have been to churches over the years that have had great gospel choirs, but never, ever one like this in a Catholic church. To us, this is unheard of. And great! Getting up in time to get coffee, get dressed, and get the dog fed and walked is a small sacrifice compared to our enjoyment of this mass. I have to say that it really does bring me closer to the Lord. The spirit that moves among these singers and the congregants is evident. The older (and White) Monsignor Lewis is usually the priest at this mass and seems to enjoy it very much. We like him. Once or twice, we miss getting to this mass. The later one, the 11:00 mass, just doesn't hold the same level of spirit for us. Yes, it's still mass. And if you're Catholic, you might be thinking it doesn't or shouldn't matter. But it makes a difference to me. Amid such inspiration in the earlier mass, my internal words, my prayer, are often: "Come to me, Lord. Fill me up with your Presence. Let me be entirely of You. Every cell, every molecule. Let all my being be for Your work."

A total surrender. And that, to me, is being with God.

I find it again and again at St. Paul's.

TOUGH MORNING IN NC

We're about a week into our stay in NC. My phone alarm goes off to signal Ted to take his 7 a.m. meds. I fall back to sleep, reassured that he has taken them. Sometime later, still sleepy and in bed, I hear some noises coming from next to me. The dog is on the bed, but he's still sleeping.

"What's going on?" I ask.

"Just trying...to get...my socks on," Ted says, a struggle in his voice.

Me: "Want some help?"

He: "Not yet."

I'm getting out of bed in the morning. Sitting on the edge of the bed, I'm wearing a T-shirt and pajama pants. On the floor is a pair of socks I wore yesterday. These are long, soft, fleecy socks. It is difficult for me to put socks on now, because the steroids I take have caused my belly to swell to the point that I cannot easily bend down to reach my feet. In addition to that, my right foot has a foot drop and does not coordinate well. Nonetheless, I manage to get the sock on my right foot, bracing my body with my left foot on the floor. The trouble happens when I try to put my left sock on. When I pick up my left foot to try to put the sock on it, my right foot slides immediately out from under me and I come crashing down to the floor, ending up in a very awkward position upside down and squeezed between the bed and a small table. My head crashes very loudly against the baseboard at the bottom of the wall. There is a sudden sting of pain on the crown of my head. Kathy, who has been half asleep, is immediately frightened and comes running around to see if I'm all right. I am not in fact injured in any serious way, but it makes me feel so terribly bad to see the fright on her face when these things happen. Gradually I am able to extricate myself from the awkward position in which I have landed. There's a fair amount of bleeding from my head and she cleans me up and gets the bleeding to stop.

My heart breaks just a little more.

For the rest of the day, I have a mild amount of pain from the site of the injury, but no significant damage is done.

THE AMAZING AMBIVALENCE OF WALKING

Some days, we walk to the end of the dead-end road, to the "point," about a third of a mile each way, where we have a beautiful view of the water and the bridges that go in and out of town. Ted stops to rest when he needs to.

"Go on ahead. I'll be fine," he says. It's not in my nature to leave him in what appears to be a struggle.

So I walk a little ahead or take a longer route for just a few minutes and check back with him. It's hard to walk away. Sometimes he gets so irritated with me and makes a caustic remark that cuts me enough that I do just that—walk away for a little while. My brain works overtime between thoughts of *well, fuck you* and images of him needing me, or having trouble balancing, or me finding him hurt. I have enough insight to realize these contrasting thoughts are all tied up together, but it doesn't make them go away.

Today, around midday, Kathy and I go for a walk in the neighborhood, about two miles. Two weeks ago, I had a great deal of trouble doing the same walk. Had to stop and rest four or five times on the way back home. But not today. The only stop we make is at a gas station, where we want to pick up a local newspaper. A terrible thing happens: The mini mart at the gas station has a supply of Dunkin' Donuts doughnuts, too good to pass up. We each get one and agree that there is sometimes something entirely special about a doughnut. And I make it back home without stopping, although my feet hurt and it is a challenge. But—I do it.

There is a hell of a lightning-and-thunder storm this afternoon, very violent, and the forecast even mentions the possibility of a tornado. Kathy and I make love while the storm rages and screams around us. Rebel hides under the bed.

I'LL BE NICER

On the morning of January 25th, I remember I told Ted the previous night that I would be nice to him "all day" today. That sounds awful. I mean, I love this man with all my heart. But I admit I was damned crabby yesterday.

Here's what happened last night to make me promise him that I would be on my best behavior today: We had gone out for the afternoon. During the past week, I'd suggested he get new running shoes, which he really needed. We ended up at a specialty store, and he tried on a couple of pairs. One pair he found seemed to do the trick, and he was able to walk somewhat better immediately, significant because the slant of the shoe at its toe was pointed enough upward to make a difference with his foot drop, which is a byproduct of the weakening in his right leg. We were unable to try the brace inside the shoe right then because the makeshift padding we'd put between the brace and his calf a few days earlier had slipped down, leaving him with an open, cut area on his shin. Since that took quite a few days to heal, he'd had to go without his brace.

Although the brace normally does help somewhat, the new super-duper pair of running shoes helped even more. It was so good to see him looking happy.

"I'm practically running!" he said. A slight exaggeration, but he did have a better spring in his step, and an improved gait.

After getting the shoes, we went to get a book he wanted at a nearby bookstore. By now, he was getting tired, and when we experienced a problem at the cash register—one of those times when the computer wasn't very user-friendly to the cashier—Ted said he needed to sit down. I waited while the transaction finally went through with the help of the store manager, for whom we'd waited another ten minutes. When we left the store, Ted barely had enough energy to get back to the car, but he insisted on walking, even though I could have pulled the car up to get him.

He waited in the car while I went into Walmart to get a few groceries and a bathroom scale for the cottage. I hadn't been weighing myself regularly and it was important to me. But I was tired, too. In the car, I complained about it, and the fact that my neck hurt.

"Why did you feel you had to go into Walmart?" he asked, an edge to his voice.

It was the straw that broke this camel's back. Or, in this case, my injured neck.

"I just did," I snapped. "Who else is going to do it?"

Once we arrived back at the cottage, I was still grouchy. But I simmered down, we got into the cottage with all our stuff, me carrying the bulk of it. Although it was not heavy, I was feeling sorry for myself. So, when I mentioned we had to bring the bin of recycled stuff in the downstairs carport out to the road, he said he'd do it. I told him I would, but he was on his way, carefully going down the outside stairs.

"Does the whole bin need to go out?" he called up to me, "or can I just take the bagful out to the curb?"

"The whole thing," I called back, "and I can do it!"

No response. The next thing I heard was him picking up the bin and all I could picture was him falling over with it.

"I am not coming to get you if you fall," I muttered.

I don't think he heard that. But what a crappy thing to say to someone you love.

I'm so tired of watching him do things that put my heart in my throat. So tired of seeing him trip over things because he won't take my arm. At the same time, I appreciate his need to be independent.

Tonight is the night for taking out the recyclable trash. There is a single paper shopping bag full of papers and plastic juice containers in the kitchen, as well as several more similar bags downstairs, under the house. I say I will take them out to the street. She says no, she can do it. I say I know she can do it, but so can I, and I will. She argues a bit and insists that I be very careful on the stairs, and carefully tells me where the bags are downstairs that need to go out to the street. I reassure her as best I can, and she has learned, sort of, when to back off. In the end, I do the job, although I will admit here (but not to her) that I incur several frightening moments in the process, several times when I am not at all sure I will not trip and fall. But I make it.

I wonder how many more times I will be able to do that. Maybe for years to come. Maybe just for a few more months.

His stubbornness is really quite admirable, and important. I don't want him to yield to passivity. I *want* him to do for himself. At the same time, it's awful to see him get bumped, bruised, and cut repeatedly; I'm starting to think about buying stock in Johnson & Johnson's bandages. Or wrapping him in extremely large bubble-wrap.

So last night, I pledged aloud to be nicer.

And you know what he said?

Not "Good thing. I'm tired of your bitching."

Not "It's about time."

No.

When I said I'd try to be nicer?

He said, "Me, too."

I love this man.

CHAPTER 27

LEARNING TO HEAR NOTHING

End of January

I am learning to *not* listen. To not listen to grunts and groans as Ted tries to do something for himself. To not listen quite so attentively to his occasional cursing and frustration. When I go up the outside stairs ahead of him, I try hard to NOT LISTEN, because I'm terrified. His right foot frequently catches on the edge of the step. He has not fallen at all for several days, since the time he slipped off the bed putting on his shoes. I'm trying to cut down on the number of times I automatically say, "Be careful" or "Take your time." Learning to shut my ears off. That's important, because if I listen for a potential problem, it doesn't make a difference anyway.

When I see small signs of Ted's improvement, I point it out. He has a hard time seeing the big picture, maybe from the medication, maybe from the tumor itself, maybe because he's generally discouraged. And why wouldn't he be? He and I both see that his memory is not quite as good. His right side is weaker, mostly his leg, but also, to some extent, his right hand.

Here in North Carolina, his walking, overall, seems to improve somewhat. He doesn't see it. Then I remind him of how he was moving with much difficulty on a weekend trip we took to his mother's months earlier. I clearly see he's had some level of improvement. At times, I think he sees it, too. I hope he can.

GREENVILLE

The drive from New Bern to Greenville is 45 miles. The road is narrow, straight here, curved there, and mostly one lane each way. There are only occasional opportunities to pass someone. Though the traffic is normally light, people drive along at quite a fast clip, cars or trucks sometimes passing in no-pass areas. I can't even count how many times I see near-accidents or have someone riding our bumper.

But that 45-mile drive is the key to seeing my daughter and her family, at least once a week. Cassie and Paul live in an upscale area of Greenville, in the somewhat older section of a development. Each home is different in style and character, with trees and mature shrubs. They are on a cul-de-sac, quite private. Cassie and I plan as many visits as possible, between her busy-mom schedule and Ted's and my need to relax together and lay low. Often, we go to Greenville, meet Cassie for lunch, and then see the children for a while. Seeing the kids means a quick frozen yogurt together and then carting them around to dance practice or a violin lesson, or another of their many scheduled activities. Paul joins us for lunch sometimes, if he can coordinate his work schedule with ours, at a little Thai restaurant near his office. Ted especially likes the food there. Many of our visits and outings feel squeezed in, like a whirlwind, but I love our time together. Occasionally, Cassie and I get a little mom–daughter time, accomplished by me riding with her as she goes about part of her busy day. Ted is content to read, and occasionally he skips a trip to Greenville altogether to have a relaxing day at the cottage. I cherish those mother–daughter times. We usually stop for coffee and a treat. We bemoan the need for weight control…as we share a warm chocolate chip cookie. You just can't ignore opportunities for closeness!

One thing I notice is that the children, 10 and 12, are fairly glued to their electronics. I know this is commonplace now. But from the moment Cassie picks them up after school, with a warm hug and kiss, greeting, and brief chat (which usually includes the agenda for the afternoon) until the time they reach their next destination (home, yogurt shop, lesson, whatever), their computers are open. Much of that time, they are getting a jump on their homework. But it's striking to me that their little heads are so busy, busy, busy in their work so much.

One day, after we pull into their garage, I get out of the front passenger seat and look back at them. They are just pulling away from their computers, eyes still glued, even as Cassie's telling them to hurry, that they only have so many minutes to get a snack before the next activity. I turn to David, the younger child.

"David, what did you think of the circus? Weren't those elephants something?" I ask. He looks at me with a blank expression.

"Huh, Grandma?" and he looks around, now looking out the windows, into the garage interior—left, right, forward, and back.

"Elephants?" he asks.

"I'm joking, David," I say, "I just want to make sure you don't miss too much, looking at your computer so often. Look up sometimes. You never know when you might see an elephant in the road."

He giggles, and it becomes a running gag.

A WALK TO REMEMBER AND A PHOTO NOT TO

Ted and I have a leisurely start to the day. He has his usual midmorning nap while I pick up, try to organize things, and make up the upstairs bed for his son and daughter-in-law, who are coming to visit this weekend.

Around the middle of the day, I suggest we go into town and take a walk along the waterfront where there is a lovely walking path. When we get to town, we find a parking place. It's beautiful out, sunny and warm, close to 70 degrees. Ted is wearing his brace, and we've rigged up enough protection around the top of it so that he won't reinjure the area that has been abraded recently. It doesn't occur to either of us for some time that there are socks, though hard to find, that go up to the knee and higher, offering better protection. Looking back, I think it's odd that the people at the brace place back home didn't suggest that. Chafing can't be an unusual problem.

We park and let the windows down enough so the dog will be fine. We get to the end of the walking path, which is basically about two-thirds of a huge circle, taking us 20 to 25 minutes to get there. He is walking fairly well, and I am doing extra steps at times, looping around him. He notices an irritation on the front of his calf now, in a different area than before. He wants to head back to the car and go to lunch. I want to get a longer walk. We discuss it and he's fine with heading back the "shorter way," which we both figure will be two or three blocks. I stick the car door opener in my pocket and hand him the keys, so whoever gets back first can let the dog out.

Twenty minutes later, I'm at the car, and I let the dog out. No sign of Ted.

The dog and I hang outside the car for a while. I give Rebel some water and keep an eye out for Ted, and truthfully, I realize three things at that point which give me pause: 1) I don't know what route he's taking to get back to the car, and the more I look around, the more complicated it seems, and 2) I should have taken the keys and given him the door opener, because chances are that if either one of us calls the other to say "Come get me," it will be Ted calling me. And I do not have the car keys. He does. 3) He does not have a phone on him, either.

After about ten or fifteen minutes, I see him coming down the street, slightly limping, but looking happy. He proudly announces he's walked all the way into the center of town.

I take a picture of him with my phone when he stops next to one of New Bern's big, colorful papier-mâché bears.

We treat ourselves to a fabulous late lunch and go back to the cottage.

When we get back, I ask him if I can send the picture to his mom. It's such a sweet, happy picture. I'm thinking it will reassure her he's doing fine. She worries about him. He gives in to me sending the photo to her. Then I ask if I can send it to others in the family, and he gets angry. I end up not sending it out to the others. I realize, again, that he's more private than I am.

The other lesson for me is to try to think through circumstances beforehand, like the walking scenario, regarding keys, directions, phones. Fortunately, there is no harm done.

The rest of the day, as with most days here, are spent lazily. I do a little writing. Ted continues to immerse himself in all kinds of books about God and humans.

TAKING THE GUILT TRIP

Ted's son and daughter-in-law fly down from Philadelphia to stay with us for the first weekend of February. It's great to see them, and although I'm tired, it's a good kind of tired.

Randey offers to take the trip north back to Maine with Ted for the March doctor's visit. He works for an airline, gets free standby flights, and thinks nothing of flying here and there on a whim.

Reasons why I feel guilty at the thought of him doing this:

1) I really, really don't like to fly. It makes me nervous. Occasionally I enjoy a flight, but I work hard at keeping my anxiety in check. So, the fact that Ted's son could take my place is really good, but I feel guilty because it would get me off the hook. Although…

2) I would be sad to say goodbye, and I worry about not being with him at the doctor's visit, which would include the MRI. Ted is looking pretty good, which is very likely an indication that his tumor is in check. But if it isn't, shouldn't I be there with him? We have become as close as two bear cubs through this, virtually inseparable in daily life. We rely on each other, and…

3) His son had a bad automobile accident last year and still has a lot of pain and problems from the injuries. I hate to put him through a trip, although his wife whispers to me that she thinks he really, really wants to help his dad. Also…

4) I'm very good at feeling guilty, and…

5) I'm an expert at feeling guilty.

    We need to talk about it.
    But at the point that I am thinking about this and want to discuss it, he's talking to his friend Bob from the West Coast. He's happy, and I'm not going to rain on any minor parade he has.
    Instead, I go to check out supper stuff from the fridge. The Super Bowl is tonight.
    Go, Pats!

CHAPTER 28

OUT OF NOWHERE

February 8, 2012
After a few weeks of glorious weather and slightly more relaxed weeks in North Carolina, we have a day of reality that hits us unexpectedly hard.

Nothing horrible happens. No seizures. No falls. Everything is status quo with Ted. But he has a scheduled doctor's appointment a couple of hours away by car, in Chapel Hill. It's a planned, interim appointment with a physician who is participating in the Novocure study, an appointment arranged by our study nurse Debbie. This means Ted can get his monthly visit and the required labs tests.

Hopefully, he will get an OK for his monthly chemotherapy. As a side benefit, it will also fulfill the requirements of the study, which includes being interviewed by a special nurse, as well as seeing a study doctor.

There's no problem with any of that, although this seems as good a place as any to say that after two tries by Ted's PCP, we're still turned down by Big Insurance for this visit. Yes, this doctor is connected to the same insurance company that is a nationwide insurance, and yes, it is an out-of-state appointment—but we *are* out of state!—and YES, it is necessary for Ted to be seen prior to his chemo to avoid serious life-threatening complications as much as possible. But now we must send an appeal to the insurance company. I'd spent hours yesterday making phone calls, getting information, and getting frustrated. I wonder more than once what the CEO is doing while I'm raising my own blood pressure fighting a fight that seems cruel and unnecessary. I know. These things aren't personal. *But they should be.*

We purposely leave a little early for the appointment to scope out where things are located. We find a parking lot downtown and walk around the block in search of food, settling on a frozen yogurt place. Afterwards, I walk back to the car and drive back to pick up Ted, who is not walking well today.

We get to the hospital. I drop him off in front of the medical building and drive around, looking for a parking spot. The handicapped lot is full. I find a spot on the fourth floor of a large parking garage, quite a distance away. I leave our dog in his little crate inside the car with the windows lowered and make my way across a long elevated outdoor walkway to the building where I eventually find Ted. One of the contact people who twice has told him he'd be sent directions (none arrived) has also forgotten to tell him to be there 45 minutes early for lab work. Nevertheless, he gets that done, and then we wait for the doctor. The nurse comes in, very cheerful and chatty (I want whatever she's having), and she goes through all the usual testing and more. Soon, the doctor comes in. She talks with us, then examines Ted. She is thorough, kind, and competent. She reviews lab work, cautions about side effects of medications, the whole bit. Overall, it all goes well. His platelets are low, at 96,000. Normal range is generally 150,000–400,000 per microliter.

But something else happens to us today. We each feel it, and later, in the long car ride back to our cottage, we talk about it. For me, it's like being in the early days of diagnosis all over again. Not as harsh, but there it is: a new medical setting, everything very clinical, sick people in the waiting rooms, the easily cleanable furnishings of a hospital clinic, the cancer-related pamphlet display, the support group posters, the clinic workers in their mix of very-warm to pretty-much-indifferent about their job and patients.

Ted is sick. He has a brain tumor. The medicines might help him, and they might hurt him. The reality of a potentially terminal illness strikes hard once again. The odds of him surviving for more than another year or so are low.

Brain tumor.

Brain tumor.

Fucking brain tumor.

For Ted, it also brings home the seriousness of the situation.

What has happened? Just a visit to a different doctor? She was lovely. Gentle. Even encouraging, I thought.

But…brain tumor.

Here we are, surrounded by *hospital*. Out of our cozy nest—the cottage by the river—and away from the relaxed, somewhat playful lull our souls have experienced in the previous weeks, the harsh reality of this day shocks us. Even being away from Ted's regular oncologist is disturbing. Competent yet laid-back, Dr. Evans always seems to make us feel pretty good about Ted's condition just by his presence and yes, familiarity, and we like him and are comfortable with him, as happens with a longer-term relationship.

This night, hours later, when we approach New Bern, we talk about food. We are both very hungry, and maybe to regain our former state of mind, I suggest Chinese take-out from our favorite place. I tell Ted I love him and can't wait to snuggle him at night. He says it back.

Our order consists of:
- one hot and sour soup
- one wonton soup
- one house special fried rice
- one chicken with broccoli
- one boneless spareribs appetizer
- a current episode of *Modern Family* on the little-screen TV
- checking emails and Facebook
- goodnight kisses followed by me at the computer for a little while to the accompaniment of Ted's gentle snoring
- "pee-pee" outside for doggy
- comfy pajamas for me
- prayers
- lights out

The shake-off is near-complete.

But the emotional difficulty that came before it?

Well, we just never saw it coming.

A couple of days after the appointment in Chapel Hill, we feel like we're closer to normal. Now, we are making calls and plans so that Ted will not have to fly back to Maine early just for a medical test back home. We want to put off another disruption of our time here, if possible. We're able to safely postpone it by a couple of weeks and get labs done in Greenville. We'll get back in time for his MRI and regular visit with Dr. Evans and Debbie. It will be close timing, but we feel we can do it, and the doctor has OK'd it. We're also fighting with the insurance company to cover the necessary recent medical visit, in another of a series of battles that will go on for far too long, adding to the strain of illness.

Today, we plan a long walk together. Maybe that will distract us from our raw emotions. Last night, Ted was particularly down. He saw my mood change, which in turn had an impact on his feelings. I need to put a lid on it. I reassure him that I am not seeing any downward progress—always the fear—and it is true. I am not. But it is a reminder of what we are dealing with. It's our job to get on with the business of today, and deal with life's changes as they come along.

And so—we plan an outing.

EARLY FEBRUARY

Mid-50s to High 60s
Ted had given me a little camera at Christmas, which I've brought with me and have just started using. He, a gifted amateur photographer most of his life, has also brought his camera with all its impressive large lenses, and we frequently make jokes about his big manly…you know, *lens*.

We've begun to take the cameras on some of our outings. Being quite sentimental, I often ask people to take our picture together, at a restaurant or anywhere that has a happy meaning for us. Especially now, I want a tangible record of our trip. We are looking at mortality right in the face.

It's impossible not to.

On an outing to the coast, we stop at a restaurant and notice a couple of very large pelicans outside on the dock, resting atop some tall wooden pilings. One is a big, beautiful, fat bird. After we finish eating, Ted goes to the car to get his camera, then goes out the porch door to shoot some pictures.

My concern—his, too—is that walking on the dock might be difficult, as it has some movement. But he's determined. After my usual "Be careful," he heads out, camera in hand. *Good for him*, I think, and I pay the bill, asking the server for one more cup of decaf. It's getting a little chilly outside at this point of the afternoon. A hot beverage sounds great to me right about now. I resist following him like a doting mama. After a couple of minutes, a couple from a nearby table gets up and goes out to the dock. A few minutes later, they come back in. With a clear view of the dock from our table, I don't see Ted.

"Excuse me," I ask them, "did you see a man out there with a camera?"

"We did, but I think he went inside," the woman says. I walk over to the window area—fast. Nothing.

"There he is," she points, "all the way over at the side of the dock."

I grab my coat and go out. He's just coming up a side ramp. I tell him I didn't see him and was worried.

"Me, too, for a minute," he says, indicating the movement of the ramp. Then we both take more pictures of pelicans and sailboats.

We sit on a nearby bench, looking at the harbor, with its boats and impending sunset, the masts becoming silhouettes. The other couple comes out, walks down the ramp, and we chat for a moment.

"Would you take our picture?" I ask, and the man happily agrees, using Ted's camera.

Later that night, once home, Ted transfers the pictures onto his computer, studying them, and then we look at them together.

Here's what we learn tonight: not that I worried needlessly about him falling off the deck at the restaurant. But for the first time since his cancer treatments began so many months ago, when Ted looks at his snapshots, he sees himself objectively. And he is not one bit happy with it. In fact, he is so shaken by his appearance that he can barely stand it. He goes on and on about his weight, his hair loss, how he looks like a different person.

"I don't recognize myself!" he barks. "I don't look this way in the mirror."

Now, I have watched his appearance change over the many months of treatment. So for me, although initially I have to admit there was a day when I said to myself *He looks like a cancer patient*, I have become used to it. Love does that. I've gotten used to it enough that, when looking back at older pictures of us, it's a shock. But now, really for the first time, he's seeing the physical effects of the disease, or more to the point, of the medication side effects: weight gain with much puffiness around the face and belly, and hair loss. The hair, at this point, is actually looking like it's starting to come back, about which I've gently teased him, as he really didn't have much before.

That same night, he's able to transition beyond the shock to "How do I lose this weight?" This isn't the first time the weight issue has been addressed, because when he went on steroids for the brain inflammation around the tumor, he'd gained weight quickly. What we learned: Steroids (with the likely side effect of fluid retention) plus large and frequent amounts of delicious ice cream = 20+ pounds of unwanted weight. So now he's sincerely asking what to do about his weight.

"Well," I suggest, "you know how you feel after a big meal when you say, 'Ugh. I feel sick. I ate way too much'?"

"Yeah."

"Well, you need to stop and think about how much you are eating. If you're hungry, try taking half of what you normally would put on your plate. You can always go back for more if you're still hungry."

I should talk. The rudimentary elements of weight management that have been a long-term part of my life are a totally new thing to him, as he's been trim and very active all his life.

There is no big lesson here, other than that people with illness can find themselves in the position of not knowing about the effects of a lifestyle change; that some medications that are medically necessary and advisable predispose patients to certain side effects that change their body and body image. When Ted started the nightly ice cream, I did not feel comfortable stopping him, although there were plenty of times I asked if he wanted a bowl instead of holding the entire pint in his hands. He's been ravishingly hungry from the medication, we are glad that thus far he is not having the opposite problem—lack of appetite—and there is the ever-present element of thinking one hasn't much time to live, so live it up! I don't want to be a hall monitor. It's complicated.

CHAPTER 29

VALENTINE'S DAY APPROACHING

Today, Ted says he needs to do a shopping errand.

"Is there a Hallmark store here?" he asks me.

There is, at the little mall, along the road that has a bunch of strip malls and the standard big-box stores. I was there just

> **THE WRITTEN WORD**
>
> Ted always signs the many cards he gives me, "Always and forever." And there are lots of cards and letters, different occasions or no occasion at all, over our years together. I've saved them all.

a few days ago, buying up loads of Valentine's Day cards. During high emotion, I sometimes just go overboard with feelings of love and gratitude, and somehow that translates into buying cards. Hallmark must love me. I'm a Platinum member of their club—at least. I'm pretty sure one day there will be a special designation for my own level of purchasing. I don't think I've ever bought so many individual Valentine cards in my life as I did the other day, and not even in the 99-cent bargain ones. I'm still thinking about people I should send one to and haven't.

We talk about the Hallmark store, get in the car, and decide to go for a walk first. We head into town, park, and get out.

"I was walking much better yesterday," Ted grumbles.

This goes on, and although he clearly is putting forth a lot of effort, he keeps up a good pace and ends up doing a loop of about a mile. His struggle is evident, but not by the way he walks, because it looks roughly the same as usual. It's his level of complaint that's increased. Partway through the walk, he makes a remark indicating it's hard to watch me moving so easily.

I'm afraid I'm not exactly gracious and loving in my response.

"Well maybe I'll have a stroke or a heart attack, and then you won't see me walking so well!"

That wasn't how I wanted to respond.

He apologizes for griping. I'm pretty sure I do, too.

Life is messy. But a few minutes later, we are happier together.

We finish the loop and head back to the car, which we have parked at Union Point Park on the Neuse River. Disrupting the usual gentle cacophony of gulls and small children running around the park, we hear some very loud talking, almost shouting, louder by the minute. When we look around for the source, we see a car slowly rounding the parking area, heading our way around the driveway loop. The driver of the car is holding some kind of old-fashioned-looking megaphone/microphone in his hand, talking nonstop.

"You may have stormy days..." he's saying. "But wait. The Lord will..." and when we turn around, there it is, passing us—the JESUS MOBILE. That's what's painted on it—JESUS MOBILE—along with other written pieces of assurance.

"...take care of you... His sunshine and healing..."

We start to drive away, but I want a picture of it. We try to get one from behind, unsuccessfully, then pull over so we can just experience it. The driver is preaching aloud as he slowly drives along the internal road of the park. This is no prerecorded speech. And although we are amused at the commercialism of it, I appreciate his message of hope and perseverance. It seems appropriate that we should hear that message. And there are to be many times after that day when one of us will turn to the other and quip, "There may be stormy days..."

A half hour later, we are at the Hallmark store on the other side of town. I buy a get-well card for our sister-in-law Ellen, as mentioned previously, who is having her own battle with cancer, and then I walk around the mall while Ted does his thing in the card shop.

Will this be our last Valentine's Day together? I get that all-too-familiar sick feeling in my stomach. But Ted looks good. He might continue this way for a good long while, I remind myself. We've had nearly a full year of holidays and experiences together since he became ill last spring. The "is this the last?" thinking is not very useful, although the intrusiveness of those thoughts does not go away.

We plan for a nice dinner tomorrow night for Valentine's Day. We both have cards to give each other. I got him a "Life is Good" T-shirt, showing a man lying in a hammock, drink nearby, smiling. It's a dark burnt-orange color. He looks good in that color. I buy it, even though I have a good idea he might return it. And if he does, I'll take it as a good sign that he is more his old self, shunning anything that hints of commercialism.

VALENTINE'S DAY 2012

Yeah. He's going to return the shirt.

We have reservations at a lovely nearby hotel restaurant with a reputation for good food. We have a nice day, exchanging cards off and on. Our tradition is to leave cards for each other in odd places, like the bathroom counter, or on the other person's computer, or in the refrigerator. We have a sweet time at the restaurant, a real date. There's a nearby table, elegantly prepared with flowers for a young couple who arrive about a half hour after we do, and the whole restaurant watches as a thirty-something man escorts his date to the table. We watch her self-conscious enjoyment of the surprise he has prepared, rose petals strewn about, wine, and a river-view table. Ted and I feel just as much in love as this couple seems. I refocus on us, then have a twinge, an ache, as I push away the worry thoughts that so frequently emerge with a force of their own.

AT THE COTTAGE

It starts as just another ordinary day, kind of.

Ted's in the backyard with his tripod, taking pictures. I happen to glance out every now and then from whatever tasks I'm doing.

I see him trip and go down.

I race out. His face is bloody.

"I think I may have broken my nose!" he says. I run back into the house and throw together an ice pack.

He'd tripped when he decided to go into the house for something. His right foot hadn't worked. There are small tree roots around the edge of the river, so perhaps his muscles were tired after the long walk we had taken earlier; maybe he'd taken his mind off the intention of walking for a moment.

His nose does not seem broken, but he's got several cuts from his nose to his forehead; clothes dirty; glasses twisted (fortunately he is able to fix them later). His ego and security? Damaged. Hours later he asks me for feedback: What did I think? I tell him the truth of what I think.

"You haven't fallen for a while. You look fine, except for your boo-boos. You're doing fine."

"It stings," he says. This just breaks my heart.

"I am not worried," I tell him, realizing he's really asking me if I think the fall is a sign the tumor is worse.

Truthfully, I'm not concerned that that is what's happening.

As I write this, he's watching TV and holding an ice pack to his nose in case of swelling.

There may be stormy days…

I'll keep an eye on him.

And tonight—reassurance and extra hugs.

TED'S TAKE

February 20, 2012
Went for a walk with Kathy, midafternoon, feeling generally pretty good. After a while, I try some light jogging. At her suggestion, I simply speed up the pace of my walking and keep to little steps. It goes OK, for maybe 100 feet, then I walk a ways and then try it again. Again OK. But when we get down to the intersection, about a half mile from home, something begins to feel weird. At first, I can't tell what's wrong, but over several minutes, a small seizure develops in my right leg, the first seizure of any kind I've had, at least since leaving Maine in January and for some while before, even. Worse, the leg seizure doesn't last long, but is followed by

a seizure of my right shoulder and arm that is more persistent, probably lasted 8–10 minutes. Kathy has me sit on the side of the road until all of it settles down. Then we walk home, slowly, my arm through hers for most of the way. And talk, trying to make sense of it.

Two days ago, I'd smoked some pot, about three tokes, while I was taking photos of the sunset along the water's edge in front of the cabin. I started to feel quite stoned; it has been six or seven weeks since the last time I smoked weed at all. I turned to come upstairs to the cabin, when all of a sudden—and I really mean all of a sudden—I tripped on something and went down hard. My glasses were torn off and twisted all out of shape and scratched. My face had a bunch of scrapes and scratches. There was blood everywhere. I managed to retrieve my cell phone from my pants pocket, to call Kathy. She saw me out the window even before she got my call, and truly managed it all very well, calmly and professionally, got me cleaned up and picked up, including my glasses, which were a couple of feet away from my face. She helped me up to the cabin, and later retrieved the camera and tripod as well. I had no significant injuries, although my face was not pretty.

So, what brought on the seizure this afternoon? Smoking pot two days ago? The episodes of light jogging?

I'd had a lot of anxiety today, because of discovering that, owing to a confusing bunch of issues having to do with timing and insurance changes, my primary insurance carrier is saying I am not covered, and this comes just at the time I am due to begin my latest round of temozolomide. I've had to make a series of phone calls this morning, and Kathy, too, made some, trying to straighten this out. Today is a holiday, Presidents' Day, and some offices are closed. As of now, things are not yet straightened out, although we made some progress and there's a good chance it'll end up OK tomorrow, but through a lot of it this morning I was feeling very stupid and incompetent and anxious.

My monthly dose of temozolomide costs something like $5006, if I must pay out of pocket. And there's the thing, you know. I can't afford *not* to take it.

So: smoking pot? anxiety? attempts at jogging? random chances?

At dinner tonight with some friends who are passing through, I allow myself a glass of Chardonnay. It seems to go OK. I may have been a small bit less steady afterward, and I hang on to Kathy's arm back to the car, but no seizures, and I am actually pretty stable.

CHAPTER 30

MAIL-ORDER MEDICINE

As I write this, we just found out that:

1) Ted did not hear back from the mail-order prescription company that handles his chemotherapy because—well, we just don't know. But when he calls to arrange for shipment (his doctor has already called in the order), a customer service person tries to run it through his insurance, and it doesn't go through. She says she will check into it and call him.

2) Apparently his new insurance has lapsed. We are now on COBRA, and that presents a completely new way of paying. The hospital my husband works for has been contributing to the insurance cost for six months, part of the long-term disability arrangement which will run out soon. But we paid bills last week and used the special coupon book for the medical insurance payments. We'd sent in the check, but it was two weeks late while we were figuring out the transition. That's probably why things are off track. Now he's in a panic. It's Presidents' Day, he's reached the insurance company, but can't reach anyone at the intermediary company that handles COBRA payments.

"We may have to pay for your chemotherapy out of pocket and try to work things out later. You are going to get your medication," I tell him, knowing we might have to do some transferring of funds, yet again wondering how someone with few or no financial resources might deal with this.

I suggest he call the mail-order company back to find out how long it will take to get his chemotherapy drug shipped. He still needs a blood test to see if he can even take the chemo yet, as his platelet counts of the last two weeks have been getting lower. We hope this week's platelet count will at least reach the magic number of over 100,000.

Ted now sees himself as a "fuck-up." Oh, boy. Fighting a brain tumor and feeling so badly about this other stuff.

As I write this account, I've been noticing lately that I have a minor eye problem, an occasional blurry light in my field of vision on one side, just for a second or two. Being far from home, I'm hoping my symptoms will go away. We don't need another problem. Ted's illness, worry about my son's chronic medical problems and my stepson's injuries—all this leaves me feeling, at times, like I could leap over a cliff if just one more thing happens. I am away from my therapist back in Maine, but I use as many techniques as I can, aware she is a phone call away, if needed. But I also take tremendous comfort from my friends back home, by phone. I've developed a close, sisterly relationship with my dear Denise.

"You have a lot on your plate. Don't underestimate that. It's huge," she frequently reminds me.

Those words of reality and reassurance often give me the perspective I need to go on with reasonable mental health. She should charge me.

Wonder if my insurance would pay.

I SEE THE LIGHT AND IT IS GOOD

February 22, 2012
We came to North Carolina to make things easier for Ted and me physically during the winter. I did not expect a life-changing experience myself.

It's Ash Wednesday. I plan to go to mass. This time, Ted declines. He says he'll drop me off and go to the pharmacy to pick up his seizure medicine because they inadvertently shortchanged him a few days earlier. After mass, we will head to Greenville, 45 minutes away, to get his platelets checked. Everything is scheduled tightly, but we've arranged a quick lunch with my daughter and son-in-law.

We're on our way to church for the 8 a.m. mass. It's 7:48 by the time I get into the driver's seat. Always a little late. I am usually the culprit, not leaving enough time for the small things that need to get done before going somewhere—sunglasses, water and snack for the dog, the dog himself needing a quick pee, and me also needing a quick bathroom stop before heading out. But we're finally on our way, and the first clue that this might not be smooth sailing is Ted's insistence that we get off at the first exit.

"No," I say, "this is the one for downtown."

"Yes, but then at the end of the ramp, you take a left," he insists.

Darn it, I know he's wrong. Well, 98% of me knows he's wrong. A scant 2% of my being says *he might be right*. After all, he's always been the one with an excellent sense of direction. Until the six weeks of treatment last summer. Seriously, I think it knocked out his directional sense. Bent his compass or something.

So, what do I do? I get off the exit, then turn left at the end of the ramp. Twenty seconds later:

Ted: "Oh. Maybe this isn't right after all."

Me: "Can you please turn on Phoebe (or whatever I'm calling the GPS voice that day)?"

He does, and we get to church just a few minutes late.

I kiss him goodbye, and he gives me reassurances he can find the pharmacy and that he'll be back to wait for me after mass.

I go into the church.

Sometime during mass, we all receive our ashes.

About ten minutes later, through a glass door, I see Ted coming toward the church, his gait in its usual struggle. Church music is playing. I feel like I'm in the middle of some religious video on TV. Is he coming in to join me? Is he coming to the Lord, as it were?

Recall that this is a large, open-concept church. Lots of big windows. From anywhere, one can see what's going on, due to the design. There are entrance/exit doors behind each of the three main seating sections. I'm seated in the middle, facing the altar directly, but toward the back.

When I see Ted, he is way, way over at the far-right entrance. He manages to open the door. I see him come in and look around. Of course, I can't very well yell "Hey, Ted! Over here!" but I do try to catch his eye. I give a small wave, to no avail. He turns, not seeing where I am, and leaves. I'm heartbroken, thinking he wants to come in and join but can't easily get in by himself.

I move past the man next to me to get out of the pew, leaving my pocketbook (seriously—I never do that), and hurry out the right door where Ted had originally come in. Now I see he's heading around the building to another entrance. I know something is up. I'm just a few feet outside when he sees me.

"I'm bleeding!" he says. "My leg—just started bleeding."

He's had this bleeding problem since this illness and treatment began. The slightest little thing can cut his now paper-thin skin. It's likely a side effect of one of his medicines, and of course his platelets are usually on the low side from the chemotherapy, making bleeding a lot easier.

Now here he is bleeding again, and my pocketbook (where I now routinely stash Band-Aids) is back inside the church. When I left it to go looking for Ted, I wondered if I'd be back in time for communion, but now I am not particularly worried about that. I'm focused on taking care of Ted.

"You go that way," I say to him, pointing toward the main entrance, at the back of the church, "and I'll meet you there."

I go back into the church, mumble an apology to the man who'd been next to me, and move past him to grab my bag. Then I slip past him again to meet Ted in the back of the church, in the lobby.

So, there we are, outside the sanctuary, in the lobby behind the glass doors and wall-to-wall windows, a convenient setup probably for parents with wailing babies, where the mass can be seen and piped in with only glass between. I grab a nearby chair for him and pull up his pant leg to reveal a small area of a previous wound that has become reinjured. I go to the restroom, get some clean paper towels, wet them, and go back to tend to him. There is a fair amount of blood. And of course, all the while, I'm thinking about his already low platelet count. Darn it, I don't want him to lose even a drop. I grab some Band-Aids from my purse and with a couple of them, I patch enough together to cover the scrape. He needs to use the bathroom after that, so I go back into the church for the remainder of mass. He says he'll wait for me in back.

I get back inside in time for communion. Afterwards, I kneel and pray. I watch people lining up, receiving communion. I always love to see that. It makes me feel very connected.

For quite some time, I'd been thinking and wondering what my contribution is at this point of life. I'm no longer working as a nurse, since my injury several years earlier. To say that this has left a significant void in my life would be understating it tremendously. I still experience profound sadness, hurt, and anger over a hospital administration that could not accommodate me in a job I held for 16 years. Now, I am aging. I want to leave a mark, to make a statement, to still do something of meaning. To have a purpose. Not so much to make a name for myself, although like many, I selfishly want to be in some tiny way immortal, but at least make a difference, so that later I can look back and say I contributed. Now I feel that need more strongly. Bluntly put, the end of my nursing career, which had come unexpectedly and painfully, left me with a feeling of unfinished business. It was not how I wanted it to end. With much therapy and soul-searching, my attempts to come to terms with the loss have only been minimally successful. I regularly wondered what might or might not have been, now that my career, as I'd known it, was over.

I'd been looking for something lofty, spiritual. But what? Those are the thoughts floating through my head this day at mass, nearly right from the start. Sure, I try to pay attention to mass. But honestly, sometimes other thoughts override my good intentions, my mind and soul wandering with questions.

Now, kneeling here in church, Ted sitting in a chair just outside the sanctuary where he can still see in and hear what's happening, something hits me in a powerful way. I've been given a chance to do something important. It isn't to be Nurse of the Year. It isn't to write an important paper in my professional life. It isn't to do anything particularly great. *It's simply to love my husband.* To wash his leg and apply a few Band-Aids. I realize, in the moments that follow, that for now, this is all I need to do. Just help someone I love. So simple.

I smile, realizing that, once again, God in some way has infused the answer into my soul and my brain and my heart, and maybe I have finally, finally picked up on it.

If it were a cartoon, there would have been a sketch of me, kneeling in church, hand smacking forehead, saying, "Duh!"

CHAPTER 31

ASH WEDNESDAY—LATER AND BEYOND

Our sweet and sentimental days in North Carolina are often punctuated with funny and sometimes absurd moments. It is the evening of Ash Wednesday and we're having dinner out, seated in a side booth. We've finished our meal and are paying the bill. I still have ashes on my forehead from church this morning. Ash Wednesday is a "fasting" day, and in accordance with Church rules, this was my one meatless meal today.

A young couple walks past us, and though the man keeps walking, the woman following him stops and turns to look at me, and with a surprised look, points at me.

"I know you!" she says.

I instinctively think she saw me at mass that morning, as she is plainly staring at my forehead, which still bears the ash mark. But before I can say anything, she speaks again.

"I saw you today—you came into the shop!" and she moves nearer. "I saw you today," she repeats.

I'm wracking my brain wondering what she's talking about when I realize that in my afternoon walk that day, I had passed an area nearby where there were lots of little shops.

"Oh," I say, "I think I walked by there today."

"No!" she exclaims. "You came in. We talked. You came in to have your hair done."

And she moves into my personal space, now hovering above me, and starts touching my hair with her hand, almost caressing the upper area of my hair on the side. I back up on the bench seat a few inches as I protest.

"No. It wasn't me! I must look like someone else you saw," I say. I'm starting to freak out, as she makes one last attempt to insist she had talked with me and I repeat that it had not been me.

"Oh," she finally says, and looking a little confused, backs off and leaves.

I look at Ted, who is just as startled by this as I am.

"What the hell was *that*?" I ask, and we agree it was completely freaky.

"She didn't take your purse, did she?" he asks.

I reach to the other side and feel it still next to me on the bench of the booth, still zipped up. It hadn't occurred to me to even think about a possible theft.

For a long time to come, we would look at each other and ask, "Remember that woman?"

Mystery unsolved.

But there's more that strikes us as odd—or just very different from our Northeast way of life. Sometimes I'm a fish out of water here.

One day I'm in the Hess station, which has a rather nice mini mart. I'm in line getting a newspaper, trying to get the exact change out of my purse, when a man of about 40 starts talking to me. This is another one of the few times when someone in North Carolina has an accent so strong I can't understand anything that's being said. Not wanting to ignore him or be rude (maybe he's asking me to move aside so he can make his purchase), I'm simultaneously looking at him, attempting to understand what the heck he's saying, and also fumbling for the right change in my little zippered change purse. My fingers just don't want to work. Finally, after what seems like many minutes but probably is only twenty seconds or so, I understand that he wants to buy the paper for me, and that he thinks I don't have enough money.

"Oh, no," I say, "I have the change right here."

He offers again, in his thick dialect, to pay for it, but I decline and thank him. I get out of there as fast as I can. I feel like at any moment I'll have to figure out something else I can't translate. I have my newspaper, all twenty pages or so of it, and I leave as fast as I politely can.

No matter what's going on in your day in North Carolina, our experience is that you can be sure that a trip into a store might involve a waiting time of up to about 10 or 20 minutes more than you expect. There must be some unwritten rule that no matter what checkout line you get into, there will be a problem with the customer in front of you. It will become a problem that cannot be easily resolved. The cashier will try several times to fix the problem, and nothing will come of it. The cashier will then page the front manager, or customer service person. Then the real wait begins. And continues.

It happens so frequently that when we pull into a shopping center so I can pick up a few grocery items, I turn to Ted. "I'll only be a few minutes. Just milk and bananas," I say, adding, "except, of course, for the checkout line."

One day I go into a small "mart" at a gas station outside of town. There is one person in front of me trying to pay for his gas. He has a credit card, and there's some sort of problem at the cash register. Instead of taking his card and trying to run it through, the cashier moves to the next register and starts counting money. This goes on and on. Mind you, there are two registers available, but just one cashier at the time, who is completely ignoring the line. Finally, the line forming longer, another worker comes out from somewhere, and instead of helping the man with his credit card purchase, she begins helping to count money with the other cashier, which has nothing to do with anyone waiting in line. Eventually one of them sees that people are becoming impatient and gets things going in our line. Unreal. I can count on some kind of register problem every time I buy anything, almost without fail. And the weirdest part? Usually no one blinks an eye, no one says anything or even looks particularly disgruntled. Just waitin'...breathin'... but when you leave the parking lot and get onto the highway, it's like being a race car driver in the Daytona 500 all over again.

LOGISTICS

February 24, 2012
I'm now ready to start my new round of temozolomide, which was shipped down from the agency in Portland that manages that stuff. Phone calls and email messages have gone out, and late this morning I get a call from my doctor's nurse. She lets me know that there was a delay because they have not received the faxed lab report, my blood test, from North Carolina. Turns out that the lab here in North Carolina

sent the results to the wrong fax number. So, while I'm on the phone with the nurse, Kathy calls the lab and gives them the corrected fax number, and a while later the nurse calls back to confirm she now has the lab results, and the platelet count is much improved (anything over 100,000 is OK). I ask her to call me again after she has run it past the doctor, at least as a courtesy, and she says she will, because I need to take it at least two hours after my last meal/food and one hour before I eat next.

CHEMOTHERAPY DAY 4

Ted's current five-day chemotherapy round has begun.

He has minor GI disturbance, but not too bad. He has a "funny" feeling in his belly, sometimes feels like he needs to poop again, even though he doesn't. His energy is not too bad, so we decide to go for a walk.

We start out from the cottage to head over to the reliable ol' Hess station. Today, as we near the store, he is looking decidedly weak. Really pushing it, even at a leisurely pace. It's hard work to walk with a tumor sitting on your motor strip. I ask if he needs to stop and rest, or if he wants to take my arm.

He does rest once or twice, briefly. When we get to the store, he says he's had enough. We each get a donut and find him a small ledge to sit on outside. He does not have his phone with him (*crap*) but assures me he'll be fine.

"Want me to let the people running the store know you're going to wait here, behind the store?" I ask.

No, he does not.

"I'll be fine," he says. So I stroll back to the cottage eating my donut, drinking my coffee, and saying a couple of prayers on the way to let go of my worry. Short of calling for a ride, this seems like a reasonable plan. ("Nothing happening here...move along, folks.")

I get to the cottage, get the car keys, say hi and bye to the dog, and go back to pick Ted up in the car. He has gotten up and is waiting for me, thumb out, as though hitchhiking. Sweet guy. Sexy. I love him so much.

I decide next time I'll remind him to take his phone. If nothing else, it could have eased my mind a little while I wound my way back to the cottage to get the car. As I write this, now hours later, he has taken a nap.

> **A SIMPLE PERSPECTIVE**
>
> Ted was much more casual about some things than I was. I lean toward germaphobia. I can be pretty focused on it. He does not have those concerns, generally. I loved how he could gently help me out with a single phrase: "Lighten up, Eliscu."

I'm working on my humor book. Then Ted wakes up and reviews a column I've written that is due soon. Next, he practices his flute on the porch, overlooking the river. I know Beth will be proud of him. I'll have to remember to tell her about it when we get back to Maine.

ROOTS

New Bern is in Craven County, and of all the places in the world, it seems like a parallel universe to Ted's ancestral roots of New England and prior to that, England. Is it merely a matter of initial migration?

Almost everywhere we go in the area, Ted's family names are plastered about, names of a line of early settlers to America from England. Ted's last name is White, his mom's maiden name is Lupton, and Craven is also a prominent family name. One branch of Cravens and Luptons went south, sometime after coming to New England. Ted had expressed an interest in finding out more about this.

Craven Street is a main road in downtown New Bern. In nearby towns, it's almost impossible not to pass businesses with the name Craven or Lupton. I call the historical society in New Bern and am directed to the town library, where they have a robust historical section and a couple of cracker-jack historians on staff. I tell Ted about it, and he seems lukewarm on the idea, which is odd to me, as he'd seemed so enthusiastic about investigating it before we came down. It's almost like the more enthused I get, the less he does. Several times I suggest going to the library, and each time he declines.

I finally let it go, even though I hear him on the phone with his mom, or other friends or family members, talking up the Lupton/Craven link. Maybe that's enough. Maybe he doesn't want to study it. Maybe, maybe, maybe—it doesn't matter. For some reason, I feel very drawn to finding layers of connection. And Ted is finding his own way of connection.

EXPLORING

There is an annual Chinese New Year celebration and wonderful, colorful parade roughly a half hour away from New Bern in a seaside town called Oriental. We drive there and enjoy the colorful festivities. Ted takes a bunch of photos, capturing the upbeat holiday feeling.

Another day we go for a drive, not far from the site of the festival, and find a café where we get lunch and try their specialty dessert, peach pie, pledging to share just one piece. We end up ordering a second piece of what is the best, freshest peach pie either of us has ever had. The buttery crust is amazing. Vanilla ice cream tops it off beautifully. We are just about fighting over it with our two spoons, like a couple of kids. You know, fruit and nutrition and all...

In New Bern, most days are sunny and mild. When I go for a solo walk, I frequently start at the downtown waterside park and continue through the inner streets of New Bern, winding my way through the historic section. I see an occasional human, but mostly it's quiet. Probably most people are at work on weekdays. It feels like I'm getting a secret glimpse into a life few of them see: their homes during the daytime.

Today, I pass a couple of people heading into the nearby library, and keep walking, turning right onto Hancock Street, and heading northerly toward an area I enjoy with brick condos or apartments that are right on the riverfront. As I walk along, I see an older African American man, maybe in his 70s, on a bicycle, on the other side of the street, alternately riding and walking his bike. He's somewhat thin and wears a cloth hat. I eye him briefly, and we smile at each other from across the street. I enjoy smiling at people when I'm walking, and I love seeing their responses. Some, clearly shy or not wanting to connect. Others, not so much. This man quite freely engages.

"Lookin' good there. Lookin' good!" he hollers, waving to me. *Say what?*

"Thank you! You're looking good, too!" I call out, figuring what the heck—maybe I can make his day the way he just made mine. Sweet guy. Are we ever too old to be told we look good?

But then the conversation continues, and honest to God, I understand almost nothing of what he says, his North Carolina accent is so strong.

I think he says something that sounds like "be right there," and it occurs to me that in his calling things over to me and my smiling and nodding and calling out stuff like "Yeah" or "You made my day" or whatever other spontaneous silliness I've said that maybe I have made a date with him. I wave to him and yell, "You take care—have a happy day!" and keep walking. He's looking after me, still saying a couple of things that might mean we're going out on a date sometime, me wondering exactly what has just transpired. And yes, a part of me feels very flattered. It's so easy to forget that upbeat and frivolous things, in their ridiculousness, are important.

God did not make us able to smile and laugh for nothing.

And maybe the universe, through that older man on the bike, is trying to tell me something:

"Lighten up, Eliscu."

WEEKEND COMPANY

March 2012

Our friends Brenda and Joe arrive from Maine on Friday afternoon, March 2nd. They have flown from about a foot of snow to spend a few days with us. We, who have enjoyed almost 100% sunny, gorgeous days, now face a weekend of rain and cooler temperatures. I start to annoy even myself with the number of times I say, "Damn! I can't believe it's raining," to them. We busy ourselves with conversation, good food, and laughing, in between Ted's naps and the realities of daily life—bathroom, showers, laundry.

On that drizzly Saturday, Brenda and I go into the little town and shop around. We don't buy anything (that's smart shopping), and in the evening we go into Greenville for a youth orchestra performance. My ten-year-old grandson David is playing violin in the youngest group. We get there in what is now pouring rain, and after finding a handicapped space close to an entrance, everyone gets out of the car. But instead of going into the nearby entrance, Ted and Joe go around to the front, and no calling to them or pointing to the closer door can dissuade them. They think the closer one is an off-limits entrance for the students.

"Who would care?" I mutter to Brenda, who agrees.

We get inside and find seats behind each other, as it's crowded. When the first group (David's) begins, I can feel not just my smile but my eyes welling up. It's beautiful, far better than what I would have expected for a group of approximately 9- to 11-year-olds. Some look even younger than that. The night continues, and we are treated to a couple of high school seniors playing solo pieces, a female flutist and a male cellist. The young cellist, Alex, is the son of a close friend of my daughter, and he has suffered with many years of serious illness, so it is especially poignant to hear him play. The audience rewards his beautiful cello rendition of Faure's "Élégie" with a well-deserved standing ovation.

Listening to the beautiful music leads me to thoughts of my older brother, who died in a plane crash many years earlier. Bob was a professional musician of the highest caliber: an oboist, composer, and conductor in Europe. Hearing the music on this night, and listening and watching these young musicians, many quite gifted, makes me miss Bob.

Sunday Morning

I awaken at 7 a.m. to the tune of my phone alarm, which is the backup reminder for Ted to take his medicine, particularly the seizure drug. But because it's Sunday, I am out of bed promptly so I can get ready for church. Ted doesn't feel up to it. He'll stay back with Brenda and Joe.

I feel his absence. I hear myself start to worry about little things. To scrutinize myself for things that, to a friend, I would say, "Oh, don't torture yourself with that—you're allowed to be human." The kind of reassurance I have so much trouble giving to myself.

So many times, during mass, I am stung by the realization he isn't here next to me. What I am paying attention to, between the sounds of mass (*concentrate, concentrate,* I keep telling myself) are thoughts of Ted. After communion (why always then, I wonder?) all my worry thoughts give way to a deep sadness. I think of our young cellist friend, who has a struggle ahead, regardless of how effective his new treatments may be. And, of course, I think of Ted, of how I am missing him in just this one hour. How much more so will it be if he doesn't make it? There's a tug and tightness in my throat that is nearly unbearable. Tears are coming up, and I give in. I scramble for the piece of tissue I'd grabbed from the ladies' room during mass, when my neurosis told me to wash my hands before receiving communion, to *not* get sick, to not expose Ted to something in his state of reduced resistance to germs. Then I recalled sitting in a room full of families the previous night at the concert. Worries and anxieties bubble up and over and I weep quietly, surprised by the tears that flow, as the gospel choir sings of Jesus' washing away all disease, all worry, all pain. Sitting here, I realize that I will be looking to Jesus even more if Ted is not around—a thought that is not comforting enough, but it will have to do.

WALKING CAN BE TOUGH STUFF

March 2012

On the fifth day post-chemotherapy this month, Ted and I have an all-too-frequent conversation, as we make our way through a leisurely breakfast, checking emails, and for me, tending to dog-walking, putting away food, cleanup, and showering.

Me: "Ted, do you feel up to a walk today?"

Ted: "I don't know. Maybe. But right now I'm reading/eating/(fill in the blank)."

Half hour later:

Me: "What do you think about a walk? Should I go ahead, or do you want to go, too?"

Brenda and Joe have left, and when I go upstairs to begin cleaning up, I find the area immaculate. Bless them. I am so grateful. People like Brenda and Joe have nailed it, as have so many, many friends and family members and, indeed, strangers. At this point, I am writing in my journal about what seems to help—or not—in this situation of illness. Ted knows I've started to write, that it might someday turn into a book. He's OK with that. In fact, he's been writing down his thoughts, too. Once we realize that we've both been writing since his symptoms started nearly a year ago, we begin to discuss the possibility of merging them together, putting the two accounts together.

This day goes on, with little intent on the part of either of us to do much more than process the visit with our friends, write to another couple who wants to visit us at home later in the spring, and do a few idle tasks.

We lie down on the bed, as he needs a midmorning rest, and we talk about whether I will work at my part-time job when we return to Maine.

"I don't think I want to work now," I say, lying next to him, watching the mound rise from his belly with each breath. "Maybe I can get more writing assignments, but I don't think I want to do my regular job. I just want to be with you."

Normally, I would feel very weird saying those words. I'd spent my whole adult life working, other than time off when my children were babies and toddlers.

We lie there, and then he asks:

"Would you still want to stop working if you knew I'd be alive in ten years? Or are you thinking I might not be around much longer?"

"No, I am not thinking you're on your way out," I say immediately, my fears surfacing within.

I can't state my truth, which is tearing my heart out of my chest.

Around 1:30 in the afternoon, I start making noise about a walk again, and Ted wants to go. He looks less steady than a week or so ago. Now, the full poisonous but hopefully positive effect of the chemotherapy has taken over. I hate how the medicine, though presumably helping in the fight against tumor cells, also kills off so many other cells in his body, as evidenced by the decreased platelet and red blood cell counts. Fortunately, his platelets have made something of a recovery, even if a late one, each month, so that he can continue to be barraged with more chemotherapy. I know—we know—instinctively and by experience, that his body will rally, given another week or so, at least for a while. Still, there is always a slight doubt in my mind, and, I'm certain, in his. We haven't talked about this fear that goes through our minds. Just this morning, he started to trip, early in the morning, coming out of the bathroom. I didn't hear it or see it, but he told me about it later.

By 3 p.m., we park our car and start to walk down Middle Street in New Bern, in the sweet, older part of town. We continue up over Broad Street and keep going. Every block or two, I ask Ted which way he wants to walk, or how he is doing.

At one point, he says, "I want to walk all the way down to the railroad and onto the trestle and walk the trestle across the river to the other side."

That trestle is about a mile long, a skinny rail track across the river that sometimes has a moving train on it. We're in the middle of a chilly and extremely windy day. He's barely able to hobble along, his right foot scraping the ground lightly as he takes his steps. I'm not sure if he's kidding.

I blurt out something like, "WHAT?!? ARE YOU CRAZY?!?" I mean, for starters, it's probably illegal, I tell him, and for another thing, what the hell would we do if a train comes along?

"Well, you keep telling me to push myself," he says belligerently.

"Not like that," I say, hearing the edge in my voice, wishing it weren't there.

"I guess I'm the bad guy again," he sparks. Ooooo. He knows that gets me.

I'd rather have taken the damn walk myself, I'm thinking. *But no—want to be a good wife, have to be compassionate, to...*

And it gets a little uglier from there, including me pointing my index finger at him, yelling, and saying, "Fuck you. That really hurts my feelings."

"I'm sorry," he relents.

We walk along, me doing my best to ignore him, which is not easy because HE HAS A BRAIN TUMOR. Dammit. My heart aches. I can feel the tears forming in my eyes. I feel so terrible.

It takes me about five minutes to soften up enough to walk beside him again. I purposely walk very close to him. He's struggling more now with his walking. After a couple more minutes, he puts his right hand through my arm. We walk the rest of the way back into town. I apologize along the way. He apologizes again.

We walk back to the intersection of Broad and Middle, and wait, letting cars go by. Clearly, no one wants to slow down. We are halfway across, in the crosswalk, when two more oncoming cars, who clearly have plenty of time to stop, whiz by in front of us, and I mime *crosswalk* and point to the painted lines. As if it will do any good.

We're less than a block from the car when he is really having trouble. Oh—and he had a minor seizure that morning, so this is no easy walk.

We stop. He leans against the nearby building. Again, I offer to go get the car.

"No," he says, "just give me a minute."

Just then, a car that's pulling out from the curb nearby slows down. The driver rolls down her window, with a clear look of concern.

"Do you need help?" she asks.

"No," we both pipe, as if scripted.

"Are you sure?" she asks, now looking more concerned.

I approach the car, but not before I get a quick look at Ted, who, frankly, at that moment, looks his all-time worst: tired, winded, posture slightly crooked, leaning against a storefront.

"He's OK, just taking a rest. We're heading back to the car. Leg problem," I say.

"Can I drive you to your car?" she asks. Oh boy. Well-meaning and concerned.

No. *Worried*.

I move closer to her car.

"He has a chronic condition. It's OK. Our car is over there," I say, pointing. She looks unconvinced. "Actually, he's a doctor, I'm a nurse, and we're OK."

"That makes two doctors," she says, meaning herself. "But he looks…"

I point to my head. What the heck. I'm not about to send this woman off thinking he needs CPR or something.

"Brain tumor," I mouth.

She nods. Looks pained. Nods again.

I thank her, reassure her that our car is just across the street, which it is, and that he has just pushed it too much, that he'll be OK. She looks relieved and drives off.

Ted and I make it across the street, and as he gets into the car, I look at him. He really looks like hell. His nose is running from the cold wind, he is listing slightly to the side as he takes his red fleece sweatshirt off, and he is sighing in exhaustion.

"Want to go around the park now?" I tease.

"No, but I'll drive," he says. I think he's teasing me back, but I don't check. By now, I'm tired myself, and I let myself into the driver's side. The last part of the walk had been tense, as I'd seen him get weaker and finally reach for help. That meant he needed to put a little weight on my left arm. That's the side of my injury, and even the smallest influence can set up pain. That, plus he had been leaning particularly on a spot where my bracelet was digging into my wrist. That part I didn't figure out for several minutes. But these are small things. I'd do them again, and again, many more times, to keep up his level of functioning. Or even increase it.

I think about the nice doctor who stopped to help us. I think about her as we drive the path of our walk, 1.9 miles. Five days post-chemotherapy, he walked close to two miles. That feels good to both of us.

We drive to the little park we've become familiar with. Ted wants to sit on a bench. We make a spontaneous trip to the store just ahead to get a newspaper and some coffee. Inside the store, I spot something our landlord has talked about. It's a southern snack called, as he puts it, "bawled peanuts"—*boiled* peanuts—which sounds disgusting to me, but Ted wants to try them before we leave North Carolina.

I come out to the car, newspaper and two coffees in hand.

"Guess what they have in there?" I ask him, as I hand him his coffee through the door.

He shrugs.

"Bawled peanuts! Want me to get some?"

But he postpones the thrill. Maybe another time.

We go back to the park and sit for a minute or two before he feels too cold to sit there. There's still a cool breeze, despite the sunshine.

"Let's get you home," I say. I help him back to the car, navigating the path and grass. He's still sipping his coffee on the drive home. We talk about the little quirks we've discovered about the area, about the South, this Bible Belt filled with snacks and a way of life that's somewhat foreign to us, yet typical of any given region with its own brand of life.

In the evening, I resurrect chicken stew from the freezer, adding more vegetables. It's the stew I started a week earlier. Like the "friendship" bread whose base batter gets passed around friend to friend to make new loaves, this stew is in its third nonconsecutive day on the dinner menu. We are home and warm.

We sit on the sofa catching bits of *Judge Judy* during *Jeopardy* commercials, eating chicken stew, salad, and some rosemary focaccia toast with butter, happy to be together, putting the earlier difficulties behind us. He kisses me and thanks me for dinner.

"I love you," I say.

I move closer to him, and we sit together like a couple of high school lovers on the family sofa in the living room, just happy to sit close together.

That night, after he goes to sleep, I walk the dog, get myself ready for bed, and do a little writing. One last time for the night, I check my email.

There's an email from Ted's brother Kendall, announcing that while they are waiting for their first grandchild to be born, another is on its way. Amid the angst of Ellen being ill, both of their daughters are now expecting.

A few minutes later, I say my nightly prayers, which include a list of people in my life who are ill. But tonight, it starts differently. In contrast to us older folks, who are battling various ailments and troubles, I pray: *Thank you, God, for new life.*

CONTEMPLATION

Tuesday, March 6, 2012
A sunny but cool day. We go for a walk around town for 30–40 minutes, early afternoon, then have lunch at the Baker's Kitchen, then come home to read and write and watch the sunset, which is spectacular. Kathy asks me some questions about my writing, about how personal I am making it, and I don't know how to answer. Words simply pour out of her fingers into the keyboard, and for me it seems so much more difficult. I feel so constipated. I want so much to get out what I hold inside, but it doesn't seem to happen. And I am so fearful that it never will, and I will die still full of words and thoughts.

Tonight, we watch a video of the movie *Shoot the Moon*, Albert Finney and Diane Keaton, a solidly yuppie couple, with four kids, wrestling with the death of their marriage. It's beautifully done—the writing, the direction, the acting. Very real, very painful, and reminds me so much of the latter stages of a previous marriage. Reminds me too painfully of what an angry, bitter man I used to be, and how badly I treated the people around me.

And it puts me into such an isolated, lonely, sad place. Then I start to think about my tumor. I am now about six days post-chemotherapy, and my energy is beginning to return. Kathy tells me I am doing better, better now than, say, six months ago. She says she notices that with every round of chemotherapy, my rebound is stronger and faster. Maybe she is correct, but I have doubts. At my best I can manage to walk about two miles, but in the second mile I am unsteady and tired and weak, and some of the time I need to hold on to her or to some other support to avoid falling. And that leaves me angry and sad, and I inevitably start to think about dying. And if she is correct, that overall my condition is improving, then for how long can that go on? Won't there come a time when it starts to go the other way? What way will that be? How rapidly will I go downhill? Will I lose my ability to speak? Will I lose entirely my ability to walk? Right now, I'm doing pretty well. I hardly ever fall, even though I stumble frequently, and I walk as if I'm drunk a lot of the time. What if my speech slips away? What if I can no longer think straight? Already I am crippled and dependent on Kathy for so much that I used to be able to do just as second nature.

I'm scared. Really scared. I do not want to die so young. (I'm two months shy of 72 years old, and I guess many people would not consider that "so young," but inside me, I feel young.) I do not, especially, want to die in some lingering, quasi-vegetative state, wordless.

There are some reasons to believe that I may survive for longer than many others with this disease. The genetic markers in my tumor suggest that it may be unusually susceptible to the temozolomide I take. So far, the MRIs indicate improvement, or at least no worsening, and that seems backed up by the continued stability of my physical status, which, even given the ongoing weakness and instability of my right leg and hip, does not appear to be getting worse and does still manage to carry me from place to place, however awkwardly at times.

But there is never a day when I do not contemplate dying, and wonder about how it will come to me, and how soon, and how awful or not it will be, for me and for Kathy both. I'm thinking here not only about the parting, which is by itself too painful to consider. I'm thinking, rather, about deterioration, degradation, disintegration into a pained and pathetic leftover of myself. I'm thinking of her having to endure that, as her wonderfully boundless love and empathy is torn apart in her attempts to comfort me and make my days as good as they can be. Because that is who she is.

There are no answers in the back of this book. Only questions.

Friday, March 9, 2012
For the last few days, I have found myself increasingly sad, tense, and irritable. This seems to happen every time I am coming up on an MRI. My next MRI is scheduled in a couple of weeks. Right now, Kathy and I are relaxing and enjoying our time in North Carolina. But it seeps into our consciousness that we have less than a week more to spend here. We will leave on Thursday morning. On the way north, we will visit with her uncle Al, then go on to Brooklyn to see her daughter Sally and quite possibly to see my niece Leah, who is due to have a baby that weekend. Then we will visit my mother for a day or two before returning to Maine. Overriding it all, however, is the MRI, which will be accompanied by some blood tests and then a visit with my oncologist, Dr. Evans. Even though my physical status seems to be, if anything, improved, and even though in general I have been feeling quite well, and even though I tolerate my medications, including my chemotherapy, without any difficulties, the MRI and the visits with the physicians make me and Kathy enormously anxious, every time. I am always waiting for the other shoe to drop, for the doctor to say that the MRI, or some aspect of my physical exam, indicates a progression of my tumor and that I should begin to prepare myself for either a change in treatment direction or, worse, deterioration in my condition and the likelihood of early death.

March 10–13, 2012
Toward the end of our stay in New Bern, Ted's sister Susie comes to visit. I mention to her that a celebrity lives in New Bern. Everywhere we go, we look. Our luck isn't very good, even though we eat at, supposedly, one of their favorite restaurants, which is one of our favorites, too. It seems like every place we go, if we ask about the celebrity, we get the same answer:

"Oh, they're here all the time. Just here yesterday, in fact."

"Oh? You just missed them!"

I'm beginning to feel like it's a big ol' New Bern joke played on visitors.

Aside from keeping our eyes open for the good-looking celeb, during Susie's visit with us, a weird thing happens.

We are in the backyard together. I should mention that she is only here briefly—just a few days, and she has flown here from Florida. We usually only see her once a year, if that, at Ted's mom's house on Long Island, NY. So our time together is precious.

We're sitting on a wide swing out back, overlooking the river, talking, getting a little closer emotionally than in previous family visits, which tend to be hectic and are loaded, happily, with a dozen or more family members. Here at the river, it's sunny and peaceful. But that quality is rudely intruded upon by a 50-something, heavyset, very casually dressed man who bounds over to us from the front yard, with no regard for the fact that he is on private property.

He introduces himself, thrusting out his hand, and tells us he's from a rescue group. He's asking for money.

It takes us a few minutes and some questioning to figure out that he's going door to door soliciting money to help a local fire and rescue department, an appeal we later find out is done annually.

I'm clear with him about the fact that we are only renting the cottage and "give" at home to our own fire company (which we do) back in Maine. This guy will not take no for an answer. He offers a portrait sitting for us as a thank-you for a donation. We say no. He tells us what a good deal it is. We say no again.

"D'y'all have your fire permit for burning?" he finally asks us, in a serious tone.

Of course, we are not burning anything. We are just trying to have a darned conversation.

He continues: "If you had a fire, you'd be mighty happy to have us show up!"

We finally get rid of him, and he is none too happy. We spend the next four days worrying that we'll need them in case of emergency, and that no one will show up. Or worse, that mysteriously there'd be a fire at the cottage… which, thankfully, does not happen.

During Susie's visit, we tell a lot of family stories. One of the days she is visiting, I take a walk to the gas station to get exercise and pick up the newspaper. When I reenter the cottage, Ted is playing my late brother Bob's music for her. He begins to weep. It's very emotional having her visit; she'd tragically lost her son years earlier. Our time together is a lovely combination of good laughs and somber, rich memories. The underlying illness of the sort Ted is experiencing seems to put all of us in a sort of vulnerability that is hard to describe—a combination of fear and anxiety mixed with gratitude and sensitivity for the fragility and beauty of life. Perhaps this is what is called grace.

At the end of our last dinner out together at a favorite spot, Susie reaches across the table to me, phone in hand.

She shows me a picture she took of someone at the table just a few feet away:

Our celebrity.

MOREHEAD CITY

During our time in North Carolina, my son has called me several times. He usually calls every week or two, or, if I haven't heard from him, I call him. In the last couple of years, the conversations were largely around the stress of his work, occasional updates on plans he and his friends were making, plans to come to Maine for a vacation, things like that. Although he is clearly under a lot of pressure in his job, which involves long hours with seldom a day off and constant traveling during parts of the year, overall, he has been doing well. Now, the focus is on his medical problems.

Since his diagnosis with Crohn's Disease, none of us are settled with that. In fact, we are encouraging him to get a second opinion, either for diagnosis and/or treatment options. I do not like his doctor in New York. It occurs to me that maybe I am blaming the messenger, and the doctor may be right on target, although I don't like his manner. He is hell-bent on making sure he was correct on his initial impression of Crohn's. Despite his waiting room full of framed newspaper clippings about himself and how great people think he is, the doctor seems oblivious to how Will has become pretty depressed and anxious. Will describes a recent visit with this doctor in which, while sitting in the waiting room (yes, the one with all the accolades of Dr. Wonderful on the wall), he became anxious and felt his heart "just pounding through my chest." Poor kid. He went in to see the doctor, and his blood pressure was elevated. Big surprise. The doctor then intensified Will's anxiety by stressing that this was dangerous, and he needed to have his PCP check his blood pressure as soon as possible. I am furious when I hear this. The man's approach could not have been less helpful. When Will sees his PCP the following week, his B/P is near normal; she reassures him and says they will follow it, that it is not an emergency, that he should cut back on his salt. We are all very relieved.

With this swimming in the back of my mind, as Will is waiting for further test results, Ted and I take a real day off and decide to drive to the coast.

We pack up Rebel and head out. It turns out to be just the thing to get my head out of my anxieties about Will. By the way, by now that funny little eye thing I'd recently experienced has not returned.

We head toward Morehead City, then continue to Beaufort, passing the familiar big-box stores on the main route and tiny, family-run businesses in between. On smaller roads, we note more churches, some within a block of each other. Small brick square churches, white wooden larger churches, large brick churches, multi-building and definite standouts; tiny garage-converted-to-church churches. By 4:00, which seems to be our new lunch hour, we drive back to a restaurant in Morehead City, where we'd had a fabulous meal a few weeks earlier. Now, we laugh about a couple we'd seen while walking along the street on our last visit there. We'd stopped them to ask if they knew of any restaurants they would recommend. The man had taken a long look at our Maine license plates.

"Are you Patriots fans?" he'd asked.

"You bet," Ted answered, noting his Boston accent.

I added an enthusiastic, "Yeah!"

"Well, in that case..." and he'd gone on to tell us about this good place just up the road. I shudder to think of where he would have sent us if we'd said no.

Now we are back at the same good restaurant.

As a woman of habit—or, better put, an anxious and fear-filled non-explorer—I order pretty much the same meal I tried at our first visit, which I'd really enjoyed. The food is delivered, and after that, the server never shows up again. The green beans, a side dish wonderfully prepared last time, taste very funky, like someone had accidentally spilled something on them that didn't mix right at all. I get up to find another server, who then finds mine, and the beans are returned to the kitchen with an apology that "maybe you didn't care for the spices—he uses onion in them." Sorry. That is not onion. Unless it's rotted. But anyway, no harm done. Then I notice the salad is just drenched with bean juice at the lower part—the beans are part of this dish, but it shouldn't have that much bean juice—sloppy prep, which just makes me feel miserable when I'm trying to have a lighter day.

That's disappointing, but not the end of the world. Then Ted, who is very much enjoying the fish he's ordered, sees a TV screen that's in his clear view behind me. He starts talking about what's on TV.

"...pretty blonde..." gets my attention.

I turn around to see the newscaster, a 20-something model-type. I make a few bitchy remarks, and then feel terrible. I've ruined a memory for us. Dammit.

This thought, which comes to me with some frequency, really haunts me. I do not know how to reconcile being truthful and real with being loving, supportive, and cheerful when the reality is that life does not always feel loving, cheerful, and supportive. Being real is a huge challenge. Considering that we never know how much time Ted has here, how much time is left for us as a couple, the last thing I want to do is gripe. Yet, show me someone who is always even-tempered and never grouchy and I will show you, well, at least the *appearance* of the young, smiling blonde on the TV news. In other words, acting. I must work hard at not letting a moment's harsh words overpower what has been a truly wonderful getaway, in spite of Ted's illness, and one in which we have shared so many lovely moments.

CHAPTER 32

A FEW MOMENTS FOR MY SOUL

One clear and sunny day, we go to The Chelsea for lunch. Afterwards, Ted is too tired to walk. He happily stays in the car by the waterfront to read and nap while I go for a walk. I wind my way around the river, near the Hilton hotel, and continue walking down side streets, gaining a freer momentum, passing street signs, and eventually, at the far end of the historic section, where the land once again meets the river, I come to a place where I stop by the railing. I feel my cell phone in my pocket, out of habit. He's got his phone on him this time.

I give way to the sounds of the river, soothed by the rhythmic rippling and gentle splashing. Now alone, less involved in the task of helping Ted navigate the road or sidewalk, I take time to look around, to sense my muscles, to breathe, to settle my soul for these few moments. A few hundred feet to the right, at the end of a long dock that juts out from a brick housing complex, several workers are constructing a gazebo, the sound of the nail gun punctuating instructions from the foreman. Gulls fly across the river, and closer still, I hear chirping from nearby birds. I'm aware that my shoulders are lowering, relaxing, and I take a few deep breaths.

HOW LOVE SOOTHES

Ted always loves having his head rubbed, getting his hair all messed up, and I've been happy to oblige. Sometimes when we were sitting on the futon watching TV, or lying in bed at night, I would spontaneously rub his head, and he'd gently moan with pleasure. I think he might be part puppy.

Eventually, a motorboat on the far right interrupts my temporary calm, and I realize I need to move on. Ted will probably be asleep by now, the dog settled in his crate in the backseat. Although chances are good that when I return, Ted will awaken and say he's fine and ask me what time it is, part of me realizes it's been long enough. I head back, and he's doing fine.

I am the youngest of four children. When I was in kindergarten, my mother would take me to breakfast every morning after the older kids went off to school. We would go to a little luncheonette called Viebrock's and sit at the counter. My recollection of this happy, cozy time is that Mom would order coffee and an English muffin for herself, and I would have chocolate milk and a "regular roll," which I pronounced "wegulah woll," according to family lore. It's what New Yorkers understand to be a hard roll—a crusty white sandwich-size roll—a *bulkie* in some places—and we would sit happily for probably a half hour or more, she with her newspaper, me eating my breakfast and giving an occasional slow spin on the stool at the counter. Those were among my happiest childhood memories…carefree time alone with just me and my mom, very relaxed, quite special. Now, in New Bern with Ted, I've developed a similar warm feeling. I wish I could wrap a big blanket around us and keep things safe forever.

GETTING READY TO LEAVE NC

We are in our last few days in New Bern. The weather is quite warm, flowers are starting to bloom, the mosquitoes are out doing their thing, and we are apprehensive.

It's been a time of real joining for us, and of simple yet significant revelations for me. I want to hold on to that feeling, to seize it and bring it home with us. There is something about the water that makes everything feel safer.

During one of the last days, Ted and I are down at the waterfront at our cottage. A small amount of beach is present, a path several feet wide, and we are walking along when out of the corner of my eye, I notice our landlord, Nick, walking over.

"Do you see the sharks' teeth?" he asks.

"Sharks' teeth?!?" I gasp, ever the knowledgeable one.

He comes over, and with minimal effort uncovers dozens of little black sharks' teeth that have been on or just under the surface of the riverbed, along this strip of beach.

Picking some up, he places a few in my hand. I show them to Ted, who takes them from me. Now we both eagerly look for more.

"When kids stay here at the cottage, they love to look for them," he says. "These things are over 10,000 years old."

He explains the science behind the beautiful, slender rock-like formations we hold in our hands, a testament to longevity despite worldly changes.

A fully relaxed feeling comes over me.

I look at these beautiful black, graceful objects, and absorb the words he has said, 10,000 years. Later, reading about them, I learn that they can be anywhere from 10,000 to tens of millions of years old or more. And here we are, so many, many years later, holding them.

Something, not even anything I can put words to, begins to make sense. It's a feeling similar to when Ted and I stood inside the enormous Sagrada Familia, Gaudi's temple in Barcelona, years earlier, and I felt comforted by feeling so small in a place so big. Protected, in a larger sense.

That these objects we hold in our hands are so tiny but so strong and can last over so many, many years gives me hope that indeed, there must be some master plan, in whatever evolution or form it takes. I feel God directing the universe, reassuring me that all is well in our very small part, that we are and will be taken care of by the immensity of the universe. It soothes my worried, anxious soul.

LAST NIGHT IN NEW BERN

On the last night we are here, Missy and Nick invite us over for a glass of wine, apologizing for waiting so long to do so, but of course, there is no need for an apology. They've been the kindest of landlords, and we have become quite fond of them. Missy and I have had some wonderful early-morning walks together. Now, we sit on their lovely porch that overlooks the river, chatting lazily, enjoying the last of our visit.

The unspoken truth is that, in most respects, this has been a true retreat of sorts. Here, Ted and I have shared a closeness that seems harder to reach in Maine, amid the busier daily activities and obligations, and more frequent medically scheduled lives. As much as I hadn't originally wanted to leave Maine, now I don't want to return. Neither does Ted.

I rationalize that we will certainly adjust, that it will be great to see our friends, to go back to singing in the church group. But the thought of caring for the big farmhouse is daunting. At this point, we've decided to get it ready to put up for sale.

The next day, with feelings of sadness and gratitude, we begin the journey back, a journey which will include family and friends along the way, while we cope with knowing Ted will be plunged back into the medical world of MRIs, chemotherapy, and fatigue.

MAINE

Wednesday, March 21, 2012
Well, the 21st comes and goes. I have an MRI, although it's almost cancelled because at the last minute they realize they need to have a new CMP lab screen done, in addition to the CBC. A CBC is a simpler test, the basic blood lab values. A CMP (Complete Metabolic Panel) includes electrolytes, etc. Before an MRI of this kind, in which dye is injected, it's important to have kidney function tests. We are made aware of this when we get a phone call just as we are driving up I-95 just south of Portland. Bargaining, we make a deal that maybe we can drive over to the lab right now, if they will wait for us. It is already a bit past 5 p.m. We head that way, but by the time we get there, the lab is closed. Another phone call: If I come to the lab first thing in the morning, say, around 8, maybe they can draw my blood and maybe get the results processed in time for the MRI, scheduled for 9:30. But probably not.

I go to the lab at 8 a.m., but then they tell me there is no way to get the blood processed in time. My MRI is re-rescheduled for the end of the day, around 6. Disappointing, but more than that, because without the MRI results, there seems little point in meeting with Dr. Evans, the oncologist. Nonetheless, I go to the oncology office, where I get the first good news of the day: The MRI is back on the schedule, at 9:30, and I can then follow up with Dr. Evans. So, back to radiology, through the list of questions ("Do you have any metal fragments in your eyes?") and into the tube that makes all the peculiar noises. I meet with Dr. Evans somewhere between noon and one. The news is good: The MRI shows the tumor is smaller and less dense than before. Dr. Evans is very optimistic and encouraging. Kathy says it's the first time she has seen him smile this fully.

Kathy and I have different, almost diametrically opposite reactions to news like this. She becomes very enthusiastic and optimistic. I tend to get depressed instead. I do not believe in happy outcomes. We argue. She gets mad at me. I get mad at her.

OF JOY AND SORROW

We are home, settling in.

On the morning of March 28th, our little great-nephew, on Ted's side, is born. We had spent an evening with the baby's parents in NYC on our way back to Maine, eagerly anticipating this first baby of that generation in Ted's family. We are very much rejoicing, as this will be a wonderful event for all of them, and the grandparents will be able to see and get to know the new baby, whose grandmother Ellen is dealing with cancer, and we are so glad she will know her grandchild. We are on a high from this news, thrilled with every piece of information regarding the birth, pictures, and so on.

At night, however, we get devastating news.

I am on social media when something catches my eye. I see the post of a former high school classmate of Will's, a post that extends condolences to the family of Ted's young flute teacher, Beth.

What, what, WHAT???? My brain is screaming. *What is this???* Heart racing, I send a quick question to the young lady who has posted this, and her immediate and subdued message back to me is that Beth has died in a car accident that day. I can't breathe at first. I remember yelling "Oh, God, no! Oh, God! No, no, *no*!!!"

Ted, who is at his own computer just a few feet away is now asking me what's wrong. I cannot answer. There is no way to tell him. I'm nearly hysterical, shouting, crying, shocked, Ted asking me over and over, and all I can do, finally, is shout "Beth! Beth—was…oh, my God—" and point him to the page I'm reading, crying and yelling and trying to breathe.

We are beside ourselves. It's unreal, like a terrible trick someone has played. It can't be possible. She has been more than a flute teacher to us. She's come to our home nearly weekly for over two years. She is like a part of our family—our *little Bethie*—with her young, energetic presence—joyful and lovely. She'd been so sympathetic and supportive about Ted's illness, carrying on with his lessons, flexibly adjusting to his energy level and episodes of weakness. She'd routinely caught us up on her life—family, boyfriend, work. She'd had two half-time teaching jobs at schools some distance away, but loved them, and was such a terrific, bright, all-around young woman—who even played dodgeball regularly. Dodgeball—a game I shrank from as a kid. If I'd made a big batch of food, we'd given her some to take, and she was always so happy to receive it. Or vegetables from our garden. We'd given her food, but in a more important way, *she'd* fed *us*. She was always so grateful for everything. And now, at just 26, she is gone, leaving aching hearts in her family, boyfriend, and friends who loved her so much.

I cannot make sense of this. Just days earlier, we'd talked about calling or emailing her to restart Ted's lessons.

As awful as Ted's condition is, this grief over Beth is more searing. She was 26. She had a whole lifetime in front of her. 26. Ripped away from so many people. I have not yet met her family, but my heart just breaks imagining what they are going through. As much as Ted and I cry and talk and cry some more about this, we cannot make sense of it or settle with it in any way. I cry myself to sleep. Crying about Beth becomes far more extensive in the weeks and months to come. Will I have enough faith to find God's love in this? I'm not sure at all.

I cannot reconcile God's love for us and the way we, as humans, are made to have such a huge capacity for love, only to lose. My religious beliefs are being stretched to the limit. My prayer list for sick family and friends, and now those in grief, is getting bigger and bigger.

Reliving the memory of past losses, the realization hits hard, over and over, so many times each day, over the loss of this beautiful young person. We go to the visitation at the funeral home and cry some more, as we see her flute displayed, dozens and dozens of pictures and so many memorabilia of her young life, grieving young people flooding into the funeral home, and we meet her family. Upon introducing ourselves, her parents rejoice that we have come. They say they had tried to figure out how to reach Ted, her oldest student, but hadn't been able to yet. But here we are, and this seems to give them a fleeting, momentary lift in the midst of this nightmare. We wish dearly that we could give them back what they need most—their beautiful Beth.

I am unable to recapture the North Carolina feeling. Is it the burden of the big house, with its continual need for repairs and cleaning? What is it with this place? It really does seem to make new dust every day. Or is it the return to more medical appointments? Certainly, our grief in losing Beth is ever-present. We both feel overwhelmed and unmotivated. Everything seems more complicated. I yearn for the days of getting up lazily, writing, coffee…meals that seemed more casual…walks that took center focus as a challenging activity in and of itself, not just something that had to be "fit in." Little by little, unpacking and putting things away, we tend to the tasks at hand that might make it possible to sort things out, downsize, and get the house ready for sale.

Is it the riverfront we're missing? Could something so simple as that make such a difference? Are we busying ourselves with too many things? It seems that the days fly by with less meaning.

We are heavily grieving the loss and tragedy of Beth. As much as I have theoretically put my trust back in God's hands, my faith feels quite fragile since her death.

It would be nice if this were all neatly wrapped up in a spiritual package—to never have to think about it, never have to worry, never have to doubt. But this is not my reality. I try to hang on to the many lessons learned from our time away in the South. I remind myself that I'm not responsible for the tragedies of our world, nor for the course of Ted's illness. I can walk through this with him, and that might be enough. I can pray, to hand it all over to

God to tend. But it is hard work to do this, particularly after the death of a young person so dear to us.

I wonder if it's possible to recover joy.

Ever since we came back from North Carolina, life seems very busy, and not a lot is getting done. We have the traces of mice in several closets and cabinets. The house is still full of clutter of various kinds. Our list for our handyman is growing by the day.

Apparently, the door between the house and the garage had been left open at some point before we arrived home from North Carolina. I go to the hardware store to buy the kind of mouse traps that completely close so if any are caught, the whole thing just gets thrown away.

"Don't you feel bad for them?" asks a friend.

"No."

"How about the kind that keeps them alive, and you just release them into the woods?"

"Why? So they can come back to play?"

I make a mental note to call a contractor or my handyman to see how to seal the basement better, even though I don't think that was their entry. As if there isn't enough going on...

We've been wondering, out loud, why life seems so much more hectic and busier since we've come home. True, in North Carolina we had no agenda, no schedule, nothing to do each day except what we chose to do. But there seems to be more to it than that. And then it occurs to us, both, that it's been almost exactly a year since I first got sick, and for much of that year, neither of us expected me to survive until now. Or at the least we expected that by now I would have deteriorated seriously, that I'd be essentially a total-care patient. Unable to walk, to feed myself, to bathe, to go to the bathroom alone. So, in North Carolina, we made the most of what we had. And with every experience, every event, we would say to each other, silently, that maybe this was the last time we would be able to share this experience. Maybe this was going to be our last Christmas. Kathy did not say these things to me out loud. I did not say these things to her out loud. Both of us had them in our minds.

And now a year has gone by, and although my walking is unsteady and my right side is weak, I am still here, and I don't show any signs of going anywhere anytime soon. The MRI machine and the physical exams indicate that my condition is what they call "stable." So far, so good.

Which changes the equation, hugely. We, each of us, can no longer count on my dying in the next few months. That could still happen, but it seems less and less likely with each passing day/week/month. And that, which ought to be, and is, a blessing, adds to the busyness and complexity of our world. It makes things more, rather than less, complicated.

April is filled with some normal life, such as haircuts, a date with our dear Meryl and Fred, and for me, a coffee date with my magazine editor.

Then something alarmingly unexpected happens. One day I'm helping Ted in his shower. He's now sitting on the shower chair we had previously purchased, negating its previous function as a plant holder. Normally, I hover near him in case he needs help. Today, I go to the bathroom sink to do something that will take but a moment, and no sooner do I reach the sink when Ted, like a missile being launched, is thrown out of the shower onto the bathroom floor, barely missing hitting his head on the porcelain toilet bowl. We're both completely shocked, and later, can only figure that in leaning slightly, he and the shower chair slid. Not good. He's pretty banged up, and I call for help to help him up. No permanent damage is done, physically, but after that I never leave him even for an instant while he's showering, something that annoys him terribly.

At the end of April, an amiable man named Dana comes to the house to talk to us about rails for the outside stairs.

Our study nurse, Debbie, whom I now call friend, comes over with her husband, Brad, to install grab bars in our bathrooms and at the top of the stairs. *Just because.* Talk about your professional installation: Debbie, an experienced and expert RN, and Brad, a surgeon—doing this task for us.

At the beginning of May, Ted and I take a trip to Macon, Georgia, as I am to receive an award for humor writing from the National Society of Newspaper Columnists. Ted and I are both thrilled. This is big-time. And I have him by my side. It's a great trip, in every way, opening a whole new "family" for us.

May 2012
Actually, I have nearly recovered my physical strength and agility, although not quite. I still have to be careful, e.g., on stairs, but not that careful. I don't really have to think about it much, the way I did a couple of weeks ago.

It's a bit difficult for me to account for my physical improvement over the past several weeks. Sometimes it's tempting to begin to think it's all been a big mistake, the diagnosis is incorrect, I feel too good. The seizure meds really work, I hardly have any tremors at all anymore, and I've adapted even to the energy-sapping of the medicines, mostly.

But several times a day either Kathy or I, or often both, fall into the bad places: What if I really don't live much longer? Holy shit, you know! Our life is so happy now and we, as she put it the other night at the graduation banquet for the hospital psychiatry residents, we have become "Kathy and Ted." Or is it Ted and Kathy? We...we just are! It's a permanent feeling, a sense that we have known each other and been a part of each other since before there was time—and going on forever. The thought that either of us might leave the other is impossible. And horrible, and tears come, and sobbing, and there is no consoling, and we have learned that we have to avoid "going there" very much...some of it cannot be avoided...and have to push to make every day we are here the most enjoyable or fulfilled or whatever it can be.

After all, do we have any choice?

The wall calendar on May 9th reads "8:15—Ted Dentist" in decidedly shaky handwriting, another outward sign that his brain is not functioning as well as previously.

On May 17th, Dana puts up the outside rails. We are, at last, both pleased. Dana does a great job, and he's just about as nice as they get.

May 18, 2012
I'm on my fifth day of Temodar, fifth out of five. I haven't the energy to hold my eyelids open, but I go for an hour of physical therapy, which may have been too much. And we have a dinner date this evening with Fred and Meryl, and old friends from out of state are coming to visit on Monday (this being Friday). I do not know whether I will be able to do

these things, although I want to. I'm also nauseous. That's a known side effect of Temodar, but one that has not affected me until the last round of the drug, somewhat over a month ago. It hasn't been too bad this week, until today, but right now it's pretty awful. I told Kathy, and she is asking me if I want to cancel the dinner. She points out that it's my decision, which I guess is true, but I hate to screw up everyone else's evening over this kind of thing.

When I feel really sick, as I do now, I also begin to slip into a kind of despair. Kathy continues to reassure me. Frankly, I am never sure whether she is attempting to bolster my spirits or her own. She says I am doing better now than I was six months ago, that I'm stronger and have better physical control. I had an MRI five days ago and a visit with Dr. Evans, and the report was that my tumor appears smaller and less dense, a little, than it has been. My walking is steadier, at least when I wear my ankle brace. Yesterday Kathy and I walked probably 1-1/2 miles, in a hilly neighborhood. It was exhausting, but really satisfying, too.

But today I feel awful.

June 3, 2012
This week the New England Journal of Medicine published one of their Case Records of the Massachusetts General Hospital. It was all about a man, 54 years old, healthy until a couple of weeks before he showed up in the hospital with some focal blindness, and it turned out he had a large glioblastoma in the left occipital lobe of his brain. He underwent the same treatment I'm having, pretty much. He ended up dying in a hospice 28 months after his original diagnosis. I read and reread the article, feeling more and more scared and sad as I went along. Showed it to Kathy, who read it thoroughly and then did her best to reassure me: That's only one case, you have been in excellent condition, your mother's genes, your doctors are very optimistic about you, etc. Didn't help much, other than to reinforce how strongly she is there at my side, which does help a lot.

Everyone says I look wonderful. Trouble is, they say it with a tone of surprise. And except when I'm in the middle of chemotherapy treatments,

I feel pretty strong and healthy, at least if I don't try to walk too much. Walking reminds me instantly of how much I've lost, and I do not expect to get much of it back, if any.

June 8, 2012
This morning I see my neurologist. He pops my latest MRI up on his monitor and lets me see it, the first time I've seen one of my studies in at least several months. Amazingly, the tumor does look smaller and less angry than before. There is very little, if any, sign of edema (inflammation), also. We discuss whether I can do without my dexamethasone but decide to leave well enough alone. The trouble with the dexamethasone is that it puts weight on me, about twenty pounds since last summer, and it also has lots of other side effects including bleeding and loss of bone density. But as long as I'm doing well, there's little argument in favor of changing any course of treatment.

Ted's illness seems, temporarily, stable. My thoughts turn to Beth daily. I have the privilege of being able to be of support to Beth's parents, Kathy and John, who are still living in Maryland and can't be in Maine full-time yet. They had purchased a house here and had intended to move. Ted and I go to Beth's grave, which is nearby, tend to it a bit, and report back to her parents in between their visits to Maine.

Beth's death has hit hard. Somewhere very deep down, I am sure that she is OK, in a sense, that she has joined God in His Heaven. But the ache of not having her on earth and the tremendous heartache we feel for her family does not leave. And for everyone who has ever uttered the phrase "He/she is in a better place"—well, that may be an interesting philosophy, but in my experience, it's one of the least helpful things to say. For to the grieving left behind, the better place is here.

Some months later, Ted and I get a boost when we hear from Will that he is moving back from New York. Once back in Maine, he applies for and gets a job at a nearby college, and he soon finds a terrific gastroenterologist who is expert, kind, and knows how to explain things in a way that make good sense, and it is well worth the three-hour drive for appointments. He is in good hands.

September 8, 2012

Last Thursday we drove to Boston for a meeting with the social worker/psychotherapist at Mass General whom we had first met when I was newly diagnosed in May 2011. In that first meeting with her, we were reeling with the news that I had a malignant tumor in my head. Based on everything we had been able to find out up to that point, both Kathy and I expected that my life expectancy was going to be very limited. There is no way to describe how we were feeling. Words like *devastated* and *overwhelmed* don't begin to capture the terror and the sadness and the pain and grief that we were both experiencing. Fifteen months later, many things have changed. Comparing notes, Kathy and I realize that when I was first diagnosed, and based on all the conversations that we had with the various doctors and nurses, neither she nor I expected that I would still be alive at this point, that is, in September of 2012. That's the good news. The bad news is that Kathy and I in some ways are not getting along very well. It's not that we are overtly fighting, exactly, but there is an underlying tension that is unavoidable. We are hoping that meeting with the social worker might help us get back on a better footing with each other.

We drive into Boston in my BMW. Our meeting is scheduled for the middle of the day, and the traffic in Boston is very, very heavy as we make our way through the North End and over to MGH. We are late and in a hurry. Suddenly, the cars in front of us stop. My foot accidentally slips off the edge of the brake pedal and onto the accelerator, sending us crashing into the car ahead.

Crashing is an extreme word. It is more like bumping, with no apparent damage, but it's enough to scare us. An unexpected piece of luck: The people we hit seem to be OK and don't care about following up. It is not long after this that Ted and I switch driving most of the time, me at the wheel and mostly using my Honda Element to take us places. In Ted's defense, his car has a revved-up urgency to speed up while at a stop, and I think this could happen to anyone, although it concerns me that he may have less control over the right foot than we have been assuming. We have our appointment, which turns out to be most helpful. We are OK. Maybe better than OK. And we make an appointment to have the car looked at.

We soon find out that the long-awaited annulment has been completed and approved. On October 7th, Ted and I have our marriage blessed in the Catholic Church by Father Jim—a short but sweet private ceremony. I think it gives us both a boost. We love each other, and now we feel that extra grace.

CHAPTER 33

GAMES PEOPLE PLAY

How do a psychoanalyst and a psychiatric nurse amuse themselves? Early on, Ted and I sometimes played a game when we were driving somewhere together.

"They were driving along on a Sunday afternoon," one of us might say, "...lazily gazing at the road ahead, a road lined with maple trees and evergreens..." and the other would pick it up: "...no way of knowing that one particular tree up ahead, a tree over 150 years old, recently damaged by a storm, was starting to crack..." And so, we would build a story of doom. There were any other number of stories that we made up as we went along, enjoying our ride together and companionship, predicting potential disasters that could befall anyone, not realizing that we had one before us. We continued this game even when we knew his illness would likely be fatal, that reality hidden away, successfully at times, by the victorious denial compartment of our collective mind.

2013

In early 2013, Ted and I head south again for a couple of months, this time already knowing and looking forward to what New Bern holds for us.

Once there, I continue walks with Missy, as we had started doing last year. Ted and I make trips into Greenville to see the kids and spend time with each other in the mild weather of New Bern, with small day trips and indulgences in lots of treats.

New Bern is now familiar to us. We know the lay of the land. The best walking paths. The mass schedule at St. Paul's. Restaurants, donut places, even a place in New Bern that makes excellent *real*—aka New York style—pizza. We head back toward the end of March, after seeing our grandson David perform a violin solo during a youth orchestra concert and our granddaughter Emma in her school production of *Guys and Dolls*.

In March, once back home in Maine and settled, Ted and I make a more ardent attempt at getting the house ready to put on the market, as it's way too much upkeep and too big for us, but we change our minds during a particularly difficult stretch for Ted. There's only so much stress we can handle, so the house-on-market idea goes on the back burner.

MARKS OF ILLNESS

Here's another symptom of treatment I discover: skin breakdown. This is caused by the steroid, dexamethasone. After a while, when you've been taking dexamethasone, your skin becomes like onion-skin paper. Here's what happened: Last weekend I was walking my little twelve-pound dog through the living room. He pulled me to the right and I lost my balance. I threw out my arm to catch myself from falling and my right forearm scraped against a door frame. It tore off a patch of flesh about one inch by three inches, down to a depth of about 1/8 inch. That's pretty deep. It bled like hell. It hurt like hell, too. I washed it and got the bleeding stopped. Kathy and I covered the wound with antibiotic ointment and gauze and hoped for the best.

Turns out the best wasn't good enough. When we removed the bandage the next day, it tore away the new skin and left a burning, bloody mess. We have a friend who is an ER doctor and wound specialist, so we called him and ended up going to his home. This was about 9:00 on a Saturday evening. He fixed us up with a collection of specialized ointment, vaseline-impregnated gauze, roller gauze, and some other supplies, and some good education about wound care. So, for the following week we dressed and redressed my arm, which gradually began to heal, although it remained raw and painful.

Then, by Thursday afternoon my arm was beginning to itch. A lot. The wound was turning pink around the edges, although overall the size of it had been reduced by about half. The itching was driving me nuts. I called to see if I could get in to see my primary care doctor. He had no openings on Friday, but his office staff arranged for me to see someone else in his office. That doctor was very pleasant and very knowledgeable, and said immediately on looking at my arm, "You've been on steroids too long." He did not mean that as a comment on my cancer treatment, but only to say that dexamethasone makes the skin so thin and fragile that it tears at the least insult. He also said, "You need to be more careful," and I could only reflect that (a) that's what I hear so often from Kathy, and (b) I don't know how much more careful I can be if I am to go on living any kind of reasonable life.

In general, he was reassuring that my arm would recover, so long as I don't go on tearing it open. He recommended leaving the wound, now partially healed, open to the air, without a bandage or dressing.

This injury is only the latest and the worst I've had, but there have been many others, probably several each week. It takes only the slightest bump or scrape now to tear my skin and start it bleeding. Yesterday I tried to remove a small strip of tape which was securing a bandage to keep it from sliding up my arm. The tape was only about an inch long by ½ inch wide. Ever since childhood I've known that the least painful way to take adhesive tape off my skin is to grab one end and pull as quickly as possible, so that's what I did. The tape came up right away, bringing the underlying skin with it, setting off fresh bleeding and leaving Kathy to yell at me for being stupid.

Most of these scrapes and bruises are on my right forearm because I am right-handed, so that's the arm that gets into trouble. Why couldn't I have had a tumor on my right side, so the disability and the injuries would be on my left? Both of my brothers are strongly left-handed, but I am not. I fantasize that I would deal better with weakness and instability in my left leg than in my right, but that is not the way God dealt the cards.

In any case, at this point my right forearm is an ugly mess of tears and bloody splotches. There are also a few on my left arm, but only a few.

I guess the doctor is correct. I need to be more careful. But I am not sure I can do that, or even want to.

There are times when I walk through the TV room and see Ted lying down watching sports, and I look at him—puffy, yet thinner-limbed, scrapes, bandages, and scars up and down both arms. And it breaks my heart. I hate so much seeing him suffer in any way. It's terrible to watch someone you love in this condition. I look at my Ted, with his wounds, and think of his bravery, which he would balk at, and I think of Jesus, weakened and wounded. I do not tell him this.

Ted has intermittent semi-reprieves from his symptoms and goes to lunch with a doctor friend from our previous workplace, who meets him at a funky café downtown. I drive him there, go do some errands, and pick him up afterwards.

I belong to a lay organization called the Associates of the Sisters of Mercy. This year, my wonderful Sister Mary Gratia, the contact Sister who brought me into the Associates back in the 1990s, lies dying in a nearby nursing home. I go to see her. She is comatose, peaceful, resting in her nursing home bed, tended to by caring nurses, the other Sisters and visitors keeping vigil. I whisper to her, up close, that I love her and thank her for being such an important part of my life. In a way she'll never know, she has given me an important message—that we need not be perfect. Sister Gratia had been my RCIA teacher. RCIA is a program for adults entering the Catholic Church. During that time and beyond, Sister Gratia and I had many down-to-earth conversations on a wide range of topics, and these talks put a lot of things in perspective for me. I learned the importance of thinking through many things that I had not previously or deeply examined, especially that we are allowed to be human. As I came to know her, I remember being relieved that this wonderful and kind older Sister was also, well, real. And wise. One time we were discussing Communion, and she said we should not be worried about being good enough to take Communion but rather that we weren't good enough *not* to receive it and the blessings that would follow. I loved that, and it often relieved me of frustration and worry. Caring for Ted during his illness would indeed produce times of difficulty, in many ways unexpected. I invite anyone who disagrees with this to take a trip in a wheelchair sometime.

When Sister dies later that day, on March 28th, the same date as the anniversary of Beth's passage to God, I know that I will never forget her or the deep mark of love she has left on my life.

And our sweet dog, Rebel, passes a couple of months later of chronic illness, including kidney failure, despite expert veterinary care. I cannot believe the depth of sadness over losing him. It's not something that I share with many people, but those close to us know it has happened, and offer kindness and sympathy. I cry and cry and cry over losing him. Ted and I both are sad, and my response surprises me, as this is really the first long-term dog I have had. Previously, I had a dog who was sick from the start and passed quite soon. But Rebel? It feels like a family member gone. Like a child. He was a great doggy, and a funny one, giving us much pleasure. I'll never forget how when our clothes dryer cycle was finished and made a loud buzzing noise, Rebel would race through the house to see what it was—every single time—running and sliding through the tiled kitchen floor toward the laundry room. Ted would always comment that Rebel saved us, again and again, from the dryer monster. It leaves a sharp, painful void to have our doggy gone now.

Through the coming months, there are tears, there is love, and there is incremental evidence of Ted's physical decline on a routine basis. He now uses trekking sticks for balance much of the time.

I find myself very emotional, dividing the world up into two kinds of people: the kind ones and the bastards.

In late spring, Ted and I load ourselves into the car and head to a nearby town to walk around a lovely island that has a trail of about 1.5 miles around in its circular path. Ted used to run it three times, passing me several times, and we joked together because I could never figure out logistically how he could pass me that number of times if I weren't going around three times, too. Now, walking together, he uses his trekking sticks to make it once around, a major feat. The thing about it is that it has a tiny parking lot, maybe twenty spaces or so, but it's a popular destination. At this time, it has just one spot earmarked for handicapped visitors. If one cannot find a spot, the alternative is to park nearly a mile away, if one can even find a spot somewhere without a No Parking sign. Obviously, with Ted's overall condition, parking that far away would mean no walk there at all. On this particular day, the handicapped spot is available, so we park there and get out. With lots of stopping and resting, Ted and I make it around the beautifully wooded island, with its gorgeous water's-edge views. As we are approaching the car after our walk, however, there is a huge paper note taped to the driver's-side window, a note as big as a paper from a legal pad. It is an angry letter about not parking in a handicapped spot without a handicapped tag. I am beyond livid.

I rip that sucker off the window and head to the poor guy at the little parking lot tollbooth. To say I give him a piece of my mind would be the understatement of the century. I am crazed, screaming. He tries to explain that someone had reported our car, and then he had written up the warning and taped it.

"WE HAVE A TAG," I holler, "INSIDE THE CAR, HANGING UP ON THE REARVIEW MIRROR, RIGHT WHERE IT BELONGS!"

"They said there was no placard," he meekly defends himself, practically cowering. He apologizes and again cites the other person's mistake.

"Where are they?" I demand. "Who are they?"

He doesn't know. Or smartly, doesn't say.

"If you ever see them again, TELL THEM WE HAVE A FUCKING PLACARD BECAUSE MY HUSBAND HAS A FUCKING BRAIN TUMOR."

I walk away, this nice man apologizing and telling me that if there is ever a time when there's no space for us, he will give us one of the special (probably employee) spaces behind him.

I think it's a very good thing that I do not see who the complainer was. I am so angry that I don't trust myself to be civil. I am to hold anger for the unknown stranger for a long time to come because, you see, my husband—my wonderful, lovely, brilliant, and cherished husband—has a brain tumor. And that never stops hurting.

Then there are the other kind of people.

In June, Kathy and John, Beth's parents, move to Maine, and we become fast friends. Our social life, though difficult at times, now includes this lovely couple, who also jump right in with what becomes something of a responsibility with being our friends at this point, as we now rely more on friends and family for help getting out. I have become no stranger to routinely asking assistance from anyone nearby who is able to help. At restaurants, if Will or Fred or another close male person are with us, they help out when Ted needs to use the men's room. Otherwise, I do it. I'm seeing a lot of insides of men's rooms lately. At Parker's restaurant one night, when Ted and I are dining alone, he needs assistance. I go into the small men's room with him, so he can use the stall. A moment later, I hear the outer door open.

"There's a woman in here," I say.

"No problem," says a male voice, good-naturedly, and commences his business at the urinal.

"I'm a nurse," I offer, in the way of—I don't know—comfort? He doesn't seem to care, anyway. And he's gone long before we are finished.

One day, we are getting out of the car in our driveway when Ted and I get alarmingly stuck in the car-to-outside-stair transfer. I've helped him out of the car many, many times, but now he can't make it to the first step of the outdoor stairs. He is heavy for me to help move, and recall, please, that our stupid driveway is on a big hill. I can see the neighbors across the street are not home. But I think I spot the neighbor next door to them getting out of his car to head into his house.

"Don't move, sweetie," I tell Ted, hoping he will be able to stay put. I head down our driveway, calling frantically to this fellow, who comes over and helps get Ted into the house. Poor guy. I hadn't realized until he was helping us that at the same time, he's also helping a family member who is ill.

There is something intricately woven with grace when there is illness and when it draws people in. I don't believe, in any way, that we experience difficulties in order to bring love in. But I do see that it happens as a result, if we are fortunate.

Throughout the months of treatment, we are kept in balance through the love and caring of our family and friends. There's a word for the friends who become every bit as intricately part of us as family: *framily*. Two coworkers whom we love very much come to see us many times, bringing lunch to share, as we sit at our dining room table together. They also share their warmth and help us laugh at life, as we remember funny work times together.

And…above-and-beyond-the-call:

One day, I am getting ready to push Ted, in the wheelchair, across Fore Street in Portland, the destination being our favorite frozen yogurt place where it is made in-store from scratch. I park across the street. It's often hard to find an easy spot in Portland, particularly for anyone who is handicapped. They do make up for it in one sense: With the proper tag, a handicapped car can park free for up to twice the allotted time posted. Still, that's cold comfort for anyone who can't navigate the wobbly sidewalks or streets. Next to the sidewalk on Fore Street where I've parked, there is a slight but markedly downward turn at the corner (and cobblestone, to boot). I lose control of the wheelchair and it abruptly starts to lean, horrifyingly so. I am unable to right it, and I foresee a terrible crash which I can't physically control, when out of the fast-walking crowd comes a 30-ish man, diving in like Superman, saving us from a crash through his sheer muscle power. I thank him profusely and he disappears quickly among the moving crowd. There is a true hero walking around somewhere who saved Ted from a horrific fall.

CHAPTER 34

MORE ANGELS

Fall of 2013

Ted is a bit worse, so it's off to the doctor for more tests. He will need more treatment, this time in the form of focal radiosurgery, a precise beam aimed at trouble spots, the left frontal lobe. Rob, Ted's brother, comes up from New York to be with us. The procedure goes smoothly, and afterwards, Ted talks about what a surreal and cool experience it was from his perspective, like being in outer space, hearing people talk but having an other-worldly experience.

"It's perfect," I heard them say, and "Perfect," Ted says, and describes a scenario that sounds like a movie about Martians. He's delighted, and we are optimistic.

Toward the end of October, we get the terrible news that our sister-in-law, Ellen, has passed away. We are filled with sadness for Ted's brother and their girls, ourselves, and the family. Some weeks later, our friend Greg (our dear friend Marilyn-the-gardener's husband) offers to fly Ted to Albany in his small plane, where Kendall is visiting with family, so the two brothers can then return to Maine together for a few days. I drive Ted to a small airfield about a half hour away, and watch as he makes his way, with lots of assist from Greg, onto the two-seater. Although Ted is grieving, he has always loved planes, and was an amateur but certified pilot of small planes back in the day, and I haven't seen Ted this excited in a long time. Greg, who also looks delighted, refuses to take any donation toward gas or expenses. The next day, Kendall and Ted arrive back in Maine, via

Kendall's car. We are all wishing it had not been *only* Kendall with us. It's good for the brothers to have some time together, after the sadness of losing Ellen.

Heading further into the fall, Ted and I make a frankly idiotic decision in November—to join Cassie, Paul, the grandchildren, and Sally at a popular amusement park in Florida for Thanksgiving week.

On the way down, we break up the trip by staying at a hotel, one of our favorite hotels in Newark, Delaware. That night, I call the front desk because Ted takes a tub bath and neither he nor I can get him out of the tub afterwards. Embarrassing for him, distressing for me, but we're grateful for the young men who nonchalantly help him out, with their youth, strength, and matter-of-fact kindness. The tips I give them are but a partial expression of my gratitude. Good guys.

Much of the trip down goes well, but by this point in time, Ted is going to need a wheelchair, a rental which I have ordered to be delivered to our hotel in Florida. He spends some of the time in the hotel there, happy to read books, continuing his physics/God exploration, while I go between him and the various parks with the family. It's crazy. When he goes to the park with us, it's hell among the crowds (lesson learned: amusement parks are ridiculously crowded with families during Thanksgiving week), and the bathroom situation is horrible for anyone with a disability such as his. Family bathrooms are few and far between, and the wheelchair is hard to push in the uphill parts. I get help from my strong kids and grandkids. But the bathroom situation is dismal. At one point, he insists he can make it OK in the public men's room alone, me waiting outside, waiting—waiting—finally asking a man coming out if he has seen a man in a wheelchair in there—and is he OK? The man says yes, he saw someone at the urinal. This kind stranger goes back in for me and a few minutes later, he is pushing Ted out in the wheelchair, and all is well.

But another, more unexpected kind of angel we discovered? Well, several days into the "vacation" (oh, ha-ha), we are at a cafeteria in one of the buildings at the park and are waiting near the restroom and elevator area, probably for one of my grandkids, on the periphery of the cafeteria. I look over and see a man of about 30 or so holding a tiny, beautiful infant wearing a little pink cap. I melt.

"Oh, she's so beautiful!" I say, going over to peek and fuss over her. Turns out she is just ten weeks old. I suspect the dad is waiting for Mom and/or kids who are in the restroom.

"She's just adorable. Oh, God, she's beautiful!" I continue. I can't help it. I'm a real softie for babies.

At that point, the man stands up.

"Tell you what," he says, approaching me. "Here you go."

And he places the infant in my arms.

I can't get over it. I am holding this tiny, gorgeous little baby girl, the dad entrusting her to me. I look at her while my daughter snaps a picture. I can't even tell you how magical this feels, in the midst of the struggle and emotional pain, to hold new life. Somewhere, there is a little girl whom I will leave unnamed, whose kind and generous dad has given me a true gift: holding his precious child. As long as I live, I will never forget this.

CHAPTER 35

WHO OR WHAT'S GOT MY BACK?

December 2013

The pre-Christmas season starts.

In mid-December, I feel itchiness on my back. Within a couple of days, I have a suspicious rash, which is also a little sore.

Shingles. A year and a half after receiving the first shingles vaccine, unfortunately with roughly 50% rate of prevention, shingles got me. (Years later, a new vaccine comes out with a 90+% success rate, which I do—gratefully—accept.) But now, I reflect on the previous weeks of our lives, and am not surprised I have shingles, after our exhausting vacation.

Ted's not doing well. He's having more mobility issues. We don't know if we will be able to go south this winter. I get in touch with Missy about this. She is more

---

STAY TUNED

For years, one of our running gags was our Morning Show. At breakfast most days, we'd sit at the table at our big kitchen window that overlooks the front lawn and busy country road. One day, we spontaneously started a fake "talk show" of our own, a silly thing where we'd talk to an imaginary audience on the lawn. I was the host. "This morning, Farmer Ted is going to comment on a conservation story from the Sunday paper" or "Stay tuned for this important commercial message" when I needed to go turn the eggs over or pour some coffee. We not only had an imaginary audience, but imaginary hecklers and a camera man, "Lou." We made our own fun out of nothing. They were the best of times, truly, just being together with our minds and humor so in sync.

than accommodating, telling us she'll hold the cottage for us, that we can let her know, and she will let us know if someone else is interested in renting it. She'll check back with us, should this happen. Now, this presents the reality of spending the winter in Maine with its snow and ice.

We cannot do this without a lot of accommodation and help.

2014

Yeah, we can't go south this winter.

It's January. Ted needs more treatment, and choices are reviewed. I am interested in the research projects that involve biologics/immunotherapy, but he doesn't want to do that, as it would involve moving somewhere for treatment. And Ted is not in favor of trying a treatment which is still in early stages of experimentation. After more discussion, he agrees to begin Avastin (bevacizumab), a tumor-starving therapy often used when cancer has progressed. This involves weekly IV treatments. His illness and treatment will keep us here, and I send my regrets to Missy, who is characteristically supportive.

On January 30th, Ted's steroid is cut back, due to severe side effects. We are now to find out, by necessity, how he does without it.

We make it through the winter with *a lot* of help from our friends and medical people as well as more thought to where we might need to live or how to accommodate our home. Trips up and down the stairs are becoming more arduous for Ted and more worrisome for me—not to mention the physical toll it is taking on my own body in my effort to ensure his safety. It is not unusual anymore to call 911 to get the wonderful and strong local emergency workers to come pick Ted up when he falls and we can't get him up ourselves. No matter how many months and years pass in my life, I will never lose my deep gratitude for these people. They are the brave ones. They are not celebrities who get much attention. But these humble, kind, even lighthearted folks from Rescue—well, they are the essence of holiness, making a difference.

March 2, 2014

It's Sunday night. We are sitting on the futon watching a Carole King and James Taylor concert on PBS. James Taylor begins singing "Sweet Baby

James," and I am overcome with my love for Ted. I can barely get the words out.

"Want to dance?"

And we do, a small, slow circle of movement, face to face, body to body, breath to breath, trekking sticks and all…the last dance we are to have.

At an April appointment, Ted enters a new clinical trial, during which he will either be getting a new drug, AMG 386 (trebananib) or be placed into the placebo group, along with the continuation of Avastin. He will not be told which group he's in, unless his condition worsens. The nurse in this study is a new one to us, a nice fellow who will see Ted on a regular basis, and Ted will continue his other ongoing medical appointments. He is getting wonderful care.

One day during the spring, Ted and I sit down at the computer with the printouts of our combined manuscript in hand and continue the editing process of what has started to look like a book. The result is a couple of handwritten yellow lined sheets with some questions for Ted to "fill in the blanks" in whatever way he is able. He knows I can be his scribe.

In mid-April, on my birthday, Ted's expressive speech takes an odd turn. He's suddenly jumbling some of his words. We get in the car and head to Dr. Evans's office, once again, but more urgently now. Driving down Forest Avenue in Portland, heading south, in the semi-silence of our drive, I fear that the end is near. Outwardly, I am pleasantly chatty now and then, reassuring to Ted. Inside? Aching and very, very scared.

We are tremendously relieved to hear that Ted has a budding pneumonia, which seems to account for his rapid increase in symptoms. That is the hope, anyway, because that is fixable.

The fact that he is coming home from the doctor's office, after a trip to the pharmacy to get the antibiotics needed, is the best birthday present I can get.

We now look to healing.

Within a couple of weeks, we get some new helpers in place, who come to the house: an occupational therapist, a physical therapist, a licensed therapist/social worker, and a speech therapist. Improvement is slow but steady. Weeks of therapy turn into months.

We are in a fight against time.

Ted's improvement in areas of speech, motor ability, and cognition is in baby steps. I am helping him more and more with daily activities, once done independently. Helping him more in the shower. Helping him get dressed. Trimming his mustache.

He is aware of his speech difficulties. It frustrates him and gives me an unasked-for lesson in brain function. One morning, we are at the kitchen table eating breakfast, facing outdoors, sun pouring in through the large window in front of us. He seems to be having trouble dealing with his mustache while eating. He keeps doing this thing with his lips, where he is trying to clean off one side of his mustache.

"What's wrong, sweetheart?" I ask.

"The window. Fix the window," he says.

I have no idea what he's talking about. He's looking at the window but messing with his mustache. Getting more adamant.

This goes on for a moment or two. I wonder if there is something else wrong.

"Hey, let me see you," I say, and I get more in front of his face. And that's when I see it. His mustache is completely slanted. I had trimmed his mustache on an angle, completely unaware of it until now. Half his mustache was interfering with eating. He is trying to tell me that, but because of his impaired cognition, he's using the word "window" because that is what's in his line of vision. I go upstairs to get the electric trimmer. Solved.

He gets up frequently during the night. Like a new mom with an infant rousing, I am startled when he starts getting out of bed. I hear him move his walker, which we leave on his side of the bed, next to his wheelchair. This is the best setup we've come up with, and it's not perfect. I try to get to him quickly to help. Sometimes he falls, and he gets annoyed at me because I say things like "Oh, no!" or "Oh, dear!" or "Oh, SHIT!" which pours out of my mouth without thought, an automatic response, even though I try to check it. When he falls, he still sometimes flatly refuses to have me call for help. He wants to do it himself. The standoffs are time-consuming and energy-sapping. Rarely can he and I figure out how to get him up. He usually gives in, eventually, and I gratefully call 911. The fine balance of each of our individual agendas is evident. They don't conflict...and they do.

The crying, the frustration…his insistence that he will clean up the mess on the floor, me adamantly not letting him…two people deeply in love in a horrific situation of illness and exhaustion. I'm pretty good at being more stubborn than he is. I hate what this is doing to him. I just fucking hate it. It's heartbreaking and, in a sense, feels like our little secret—how sick he is. It's no small thing to watch someone you love, someone with an exceptionally brilliant mind and an extraordinary generosity and kindness of heart, to suffer in this way.

Some days still have a sense of normalcy. We get out. He gets an occasional massage from our expert massage therapist at her office, who is ever patient and helps him down a short hallway to the bathroom mid-massage one day when I am off doing errands while he gets treated.

And on it goes. Ted's birthday in May. Our anniversary, July 4th. Different, tenderly love-filled, but with now a sadness as we continue, against all odds, to keep living our daily lives. He is failing, and I can only speak for myself when I say that even now, throughout his trial, I still look for a miracle.

I get out for a few hours several times a week with help from my brother Steve and a young man I've hired. It clears my head and is necessary on many levels.

Now, when we can get to the movies, the manager of our favorite theater helps us get Ted inside more easily via his wheelchair, through the theater's individual outside entrances. I drive up to the front, go in and get our tickets, then drive around back, where the manager opens the appropriate door, saving us a tremendous amount of muscle and effort. This is one of the best examples of how the smallest of gestures makes the biggest difference, and if you think that the tiny things in your life do not matter, please remember this story. As Mother—now Saint—Teresa of Calcutta has so popularly and simply said, "Not all of us can do great things. But we can do small things with great love."

If you do something to help someone, even if it takes extra effort, know that you are making a difference. If you are able, do it anyway.

CHAPTER 36

HARSH REALITY

Ted's disease is clearly progressing. The clinical trial of the most recent chemotherapy drug is such that those involved can find out if the patient has been getting the drug or a placebo, if the patient is not doing well. We now find out he's been getting the placebo and he can now avail himself of this new medication, so it is added to the Avastin he is already being given. What follows in the next few weeks, however, is a sharp decline.

A full relationship is a real one. There are unpredictable times that test people's devotion and love. One such moment occurs when, extremely sleep-deprived, I just lose it when, late at night, Ted has an intestinal episode requiring the kind of crew that isn't normally available in anyone's real world. I say something less than kind, he follows with telling me *he'll* do the cleanup (um, *no*), and we rapidly erupt into a brief but very nasty shouting match, ending with us each yelling "I hate you!" and instantly realizing that not only do we not mean it, but quite the opposite, at which point we profess our love, apologize all over the place, and my heart is breaking for anything like a sad moment between us. We are both so damned frustrated—and exhausted—with the physical problems he is having, sometimes worsened by side effects of the medicines he needs to keep his cancer in check, symptoms over which he has no control. We are human. This is one of those moments I feel terrible about for a long time to come. Ted is gifted in that he lets these things go much more easily. Early in the relationship, if we argued over something, we'd soon make up, and I might later say something about how I regretted something I'd said, to which he would respond, "Oh? I don't even remember that."

July 30th

I notice on the calendar that I forgot our "Kissaversary" yesterday, a made-up holiday Ted and I have celebrated since our first kiss years ago. Normally, we'd give each other a card or some greeting. He has a perfect reason for forgetting. Me? Too stressed to see the date and the word "Kissaversary" on the wall calendar in the kitchen?

Feeling guilty and sad, I kiss him.

"Happy Kissaversary, a little late," I say, and he is happy.

I'm so deeply sad. Life is no longer about romantic gestures or deep conversations. It's about terror and missed receptacles. We buy a handheld urinal for him to keep by the bed. In short order, that becomes a nightmare of fumbling and pee spray everywhere. How many people does it take to hold a urinal in place in the middle of the night? More than the two of us, apparently.

Close friends and loved ones continue to love us and help us.

My brother Steve continues to help us regularly, and on a beautiful sunny day, the three of us drive down to the waterfront in Portland, where there is a lovely bayside walkway. The good people at the Visitor Information Center let us park in their lot so we can get Ted and his wheelchair out easily. We have forgotten Ted's hat, and now realize it's extremely sunny out, so I improvise, using an extra T-shirt in the car, to make a turban for him.

"Sahib! We are ready to walk!" says Steve, at which point Ted laughs, and we all have a good laugh. His head is protected from the sun, and we have given him a new character name.

August

One night in August, Fred and Meryl come over, and afterwards, I am made aware—after the meal—that I now cut up Ted's food for him, pretty much automatically. He is still able to use his fork, but the agility to use a knife for cutting is gone. For me and Ted, it's been a subtle progression to the level of help he needs, so I don't even think about it until Meryl mentions it to me quietly and lovingly, in a subsequent conversation between the two of us.

There are times in life when blind hope overcomes fear, and one night this month is one of those nights. Ted and I, unspoken, are both somewhat aware of this, I am certain. It is mid-evening, and Ted is ready to go upstairs to bed. We have done this hundreds of times together. Normally, he heads up in front of me, using both handrails, going step by step up the thirteen steps to the top, where he grabs the wall grips that have been installed. A second wheelchair sits in wait at the top of the stairs. He continues toward the wheelchair, still holding the grip on the left, and I pull the chair over and help him sit. Then I wheel him through our office and into the bedroom to begin the nighttime process of getting ready for bed.

But this time, he is shakier. I see that, and he sees that.

"Are you OK to do this?" I ask, at about step four.

"I think so," he says.

So we continue. He is slower, less sure-footed than usual.

We get to the top of the stairs. He goes to reach for the chair, and his minor touch sends it out of reach.

"It's OK, I'll get it," I say, wondering how to pull this off.

But then a second unexpected thing happens. Ted's right hand becomes rigid, and he cannot let go of the grab bar. In a matter of seconds, he begins to sway. Remember, I am behind him, and much smaller than he is. Now we are both in a panic, as his balance is becoming more precarious by the instant, me trying to loosen his right hand, both of us shouting ideas in an effort to get out of this fix, and all the while I am thinking, *Well, I guess we are both about to fall down the stairs*, and knowing if that should happen, we will both likely be badly hurt or possibly even killed.

In an instant of God's grace, I somehow free his grip, he lunges forward, still holding the left grab bar. I grab the chair, pulling it under him. I don't even know how this is accomplished. I honestly don't know. We are both terribly shaken up. And I know this will be the last night we will sleep together upstairs in our bed.

The next morning, I call one of his medical helpers, with whom he has a home visit scheduled this morning. I tell her what's happened.

"Do not bring him downstairs yourself. I will come over at ten o'clock and help you," she says.

What follows is another miracle of unspeakable kindness. All off the record, she calls her husband and a young adult family member. I contact a discount furniture store and order an inexpensive single bed. She comes over, and together we help Ted get downstairs, slowly and carefully, step by step. At the end of the day, she and her guys pick up the new bed, install it in our living room, and rearrange the furniture around it. At night, I put the large wooden coffee table in between the new bed and our sofa to keep Ted stable in bed once he is asleep, and I sleep across from him, on the sofa. From then on, it's bed baths for Ted and much more limited living. I begin to make calls to see about places where we can stay that are one level or accessible, and then make a call to inquire about getting ramps installed outside in case we decide to stay put in the house.

I am only partway through the decision in the next several days when the decisions become clearer: The third or so night into our arrangement, I decide I want to sleep next to him. By now I have gone to a medical supply store and installed a guardrail on the side of his bed opposite the wall, the side that worries me. This way, he cannot fall out of bed. On this night, I carefully climb in and settle between Ted and the wall. Now, I am not tiny by any stretch, but by now I have stayed at my goal weight for some time, mostly because I am constantly on the move and rarely have time to finish eating a meal. I slide my arms around him, holding him, and we fall asleep. Sometime after that, he starts to get up, and somehow plummets himself around and *over* the guardrail, landing right on the floor with a big crash.

There is blood on his face, but he is conscious. I am terrified and call an ambulance, sadly ending the intended coziness of our night together. I talk to the doctor in the morning, and Ted seems status quo, so we go on.

On Saturday night, our friends Kathy and John are at the house, one of many visits in which we all get take-out food to make it easier to get together. By now, there is a commode set up in the laundry room on the first floor so Ted can use that at times instead of trying to get into the downstairs bathroom, which is tiny and does not accommodate his walker well. This evening, he falls getting up from the commode, and John and I help Ted up from the floor.

About a week later, we have more visitors, and Ted uses the small bathroom. I go in to help him when he is ready, and I cannot get him up. It takes me, our friend John, my brother Steve, and Will to lift Ted, who has essentially become dead weight.

I call Dr. Evans and ask about Ted going into the hospital for evaluation. Maybe there's something we're missing at this point. Maybe, maybe…

"If he goes to the hospital, he won't be going home again," I am told.

"Well, I can't take care of him here," I say, realizing that the risk of *not* having him evaluated, for me, feels worse than the current situation. I am still holding onto a fragment of hope that there will be a fixable explanation for this dramatic decline. Maybe something related to his recent fall? The doctor arranges for him to be admitted the next day.

After a brief hospitalization, during which tests determine that treatment has failed, the doctor suggests a stay at a rehab to see if he can get some strength back.

That sounds hopeful!

After some checking around, we decide on a place that has a good reputation, but which, during his twelve-day stay, turns out to be a disaster. The transfer of information between nursing staff, Physical Therapy, and shifts of healthcare workers is terrible. There are conflicting treatments, and treatment plans not followed. At one point when Ted is having a bad day, I ask the nurse when his last bowel movement was. She has no idea. I figure someone must be checking on the basics, so after I bring it up, she goes to check and comes back.

"Eight days," she says. Well, that could maybe explain part of his struggle.

On another occasion, a nurse comes in to give him his injectable anticoagulant medication.

"He had that this morning. Isn't that a once-daily shot?" I ask.

"Yes," she says, "and he gets it now. Every evening."

"No," I say. "He had it this morning."

She argues with me, then goes back to look, and guess what? Not a time when I wanted to be right. After that, I worry that he's being given other meds wrong.

On the board next to his bed is a schedule of when he should be getting up out of bed to be in the wheelchair, and when to rest in bed. Though his schedule is clearly posted, in large letters bigger than life, again and again I come into the room to be with him and find that the schedule is being ignored. When I point it out, one after another of the nurses or assistants looks at it, totally surprised that it is there at all.

The lack of coordination is staggering. I talk to the supervisor twice during his stay. I tell her about what I've witnessed, acknowledging that there are many caring and kind helping people there.

During the first part of his stay, Dee and Al (of Sherwoods fame) come to visit, Al playing his baritone ukulele, and he and Ted singing old Sherwood songs and folk songs to an appreciative audience of Dee and me.

A week later, our friends Peter and Marcia come to visit from Philadelphia. Peter feeds Ted his lunch on the patio in this facility, dessert first, per Ted's request. These Sherwood people are among the best human beings on earth. They have traveled hundreds of miles to be with us.

UNCONDITIONAL LOVE

It was a scorching hot day in 2007 when Ted and I brought my dad from his assisted living place to the internist's office. Dad had an infection in his leg. At this point, my dad was unable to walk without help, and due to the infectious process, was very weak. Ted bent down and, dripping with sweat, he lifted my dad out of the car, placing him in his wheelchair. This is just one of the many times that Ted voluntarily came through in a big way for my family—whether it was a physical need or an emotional problem, he did whatever he could out of pure love and caring. I loved him even more, if that's possible, for being so wonderful to my family, and especially to my children.

CHAPTER 37

NOW I JUST FEEL LIKE JOB

I now sleep in the empty bed in Ted's rehab room most nights. The young man we'd hired stays with Ted for a few hours when I have medical appointments.

One afternoon, mid-August, I take a couple of hours off to go home. On the way, I pick up a few groceries, with the thought of baking some chicken to share with Will to help him along on his special Crohn's diet. I put the chicken pieces into the oven, and seeing a rare opportunity, decide to go for a short walk in the neighborhood.

In the "country" where we live, down the road are quieter, more suburban-style streets, better walking because I have no concerns about getting run off the road by fast-moving cars and trucks, as on our street, which is a cut-through road zoned at 30 mph. As if.

I start down one of the streets and am only a few glorious minutes into my walk when I pull out my phone and text Will:

"I'm actually taking a walk!"

I'm basically walking in the middle of this quiet street, choosing not to walk too close to any houses, when suddenly there is a lot of barking, and in an instant, three dogs (two of them quite large) are jumping at me, barking, attacking. It's terrifying. A large dog bites me in the hip—hard—one of the most vicious and painful things I've ever experienced. By now I am screaming.

The owner comes out of the nearby house to help. What follows is an evening of phone calls, comfort from a friend who comes right over, and my eventual return to Ted at the crappy nursing home...with subsequent assurances from the dog's owner, who insists the dog has been vaccinated, but days later refuses to take my calls when I need proof as requested by my physician, for my health and peace of mind. I go for a doctor's visit for the "crush" injury.

On August 26th, Ted is still at the nursing facility, not making progress. There is no longer any actual therapy going on that I can detect, even though initially a woman from PT had told me, on just his second day there, that he was doing very well in therapy with her. I come back from a medical appointment, and our helper is trying to help Ted eat, encouraging him. Ted does not seem to want to. I sit down next to him and ask him if he feels like eating. Suddenly, he goes into some weird and frightening kind of seizure. He stiffens up and stops breathing.

"No," I plead, "don't leave! Not this way! Not now!" and I ask our helper to hurry and get the nurse.

A minute later, nurses are helping him into bed, taking vital signs and calling for an ambulance. Ted starts breathing on his own and stabilizes, and he is brought to the hospital.

Shortly after arrival in the hospital ER, Dr. Evans comes in to evaluate Ted. The doctor delivers the bad news, but in a stunningly loving and caring way. He tells us it is time for hospice.

"I would go to the ends of the earth..." he says, if there were any way to fix this, to cure Ted.

We take this in, with silence. Then Ted nods a slow nod.

How many times can a heart feel like it's breaking...and this is one of those times, for me and certainly for Ted, who must be just damned exhausted from his illness. I can see his doctor is pained as well. I am so moved by our lovely Dr. Evans, whom we have come to trust—literally—with Ted's life, who has brought him through nearly three and a half years of a horrific illness, compassionate and honest every step of the way. Our triumphs were his; Ted's decline felt, I am sure, as a personal injury to the doctor's soul as well.

Ted is in the hospital, while arrangements for transfer are being made. Meryl and I make a brief visit to the nearby Gosnell Memorial Hospice House.

Now—remember the dog bite? Well, I've put my family lawyer on the case just to try to get information from the owner, the same owner who had initially seemed kind, repeatedly saying it was a "heckuva way to meet a neighbor," wink, wink. The same owner who is now not returning my phone calls asking for proof of the dog's vaccinations.

I am in Ted's hospital room on the day he is to be transferred to Gosnell when I get a call from my own doctor's office: If I haven't gotten proof of rabies vaccine by now from the dog's owner, I need to go to the ER for evaluation, because the treatment period for me, in case I need rabies shots, is fast approaching. I can't do this. Any of it. It's all too much. I hang up the phone and walk over to the nurses' station.

"Can you call a priest for me?" I ask and go back to Ted.

Within minutes, two women appear at the door to Ted's room: a religious Sister and another woman, who is the Jewish component of the pastoral team at the hospital and who also happens to be a friend from long ago when our children were in preschool together. I hug them and am hugged as I spill out my story to them, met with immediate love and support.

"I have to go to the ER," I say.

"I'll go with you," says my friend. She walks down with me and stays with me the entire time. God's angel.

In the ER, I begin to tell the ER doctor what has happened, and when I get to the part about not being able to reach the dog's owner at their workplace, the doctor quickly gets up.

"Give me that phone number," she says, and leaves the room.

Ten minutes later, she is back.

Apparently when an ER doc calls, they pay attention. My mind's dialogue is going over all kinds of nasty things I would like to say and none of them include being a "heckuva way to meet a neighbor."

The ER doc is lovely, smart, and explains that although the dog is not properly vaccinated (out of date from the last vaccine), it is so extremely rare that a house dog would have rabies that she does not feel there's a need to vaccinate me. She is my hero.

By now, the good and warm and fluffy priest at the hospital has joined us from another duty, and once the doc is done with me, the three of us sit in my ER cubicle and discuss what's been happening. Then, at Father's suggestion, we all join hands, and Father and my friend pray for me, for Ted, and for our family. It couldn't have been more beautiful. My Jewish ancestors would have been so moved, as was I.

Then, freshly blessed and loved, I go back upstairs to Ted, to await further information on the transfer to Gosnell in Scarborough.

I take in this message again: In others' difficulties, just show up. Be present. Say something, or say nothing, it doesn't matter. Touch, pray, hug, grieve, love...that's what makes the difference. And that is all that is needed... all that matters.

PART 4

CHAPTER 38

HOSPICE, ROOM 106

August 29, 2014

We have moved into the Gosnell Memorial Hospice House in Scarborough. As Ted is getting settled by staff, I am given the basics, including that the average stay is just a few days. I am told this by various staff members I talk with who introduce themselves and orient me to services. Ted and I settle in for an undetermined length of stay. I can be here with him 24/7.

The day after we arrive, Denise shows up with a huge aluminum pan of baked pasta, meatballs, and her fabulous chocolate cupcakes—the Holy Spirit in action. She even has the meatballs in a separate container from the pasta, as she knows I don't generally eat beef. Our mini refrigerator in the room is now beautifully stocked.

> **OLD MEMORIES, YOUNG FEELINGS**
>
> When I was in seventh grade, I went steady with a boy in my class. He was my first real boyfriend. Back in those days, a boy gave a girl an ID bracelet while they were together, which was returned after a breakup. At the time, that bracelet was a big thrill. In one of our many conversations in getting to know each other, I told Ted about this. About a year or so later, he gave me a beautiful white gold bracelet à la ID bracelet, but more delicate. It became a permanent and much-loved gift, worn on my right wrist, honoring that cherished part of me that would always feel thirteen and in love.

Gosnell is set up in such a way that an entire bed can be brought outdoors, and I ask Ted if he'd like to be in the gardens out back for a while. He does not.

Although I like the setup in Room 106 and it is bright and sunny, I soon realize that from where I sit (fortunately not in Ted's view, due to the setup and direction of his bed), I see the front entrance: every quiet ambulance or car that pulls up, and every hearse that leaves. At one point, nurse Larry matter-of-factly and quietly pulls the blinds, and I realize why. Like a train pulling into a station, somewhere there is a ticket with my beloved husband's name on it, and a date. The inevitable is too horrible to bear, and still, childlike, I hold on to hope, my inner child sad but ever strong.

I now begin sending out emails to our family and circle of close friends to keep them updated and to reduce the number of phone calls.

9/4/14, 10:45 p.m., Kathy's email:

Ted is a bit more tired this evening.

Randey went back to Philly (boo!), but Ted's family of origin (most of them, including Susie's two adorable Yorkshire terriers) are here till tomorrow, including his amazing newly turned-100-year-old mom.

On another note—Although my dog bite saga is not quite wrapped up, I was reassured by my own doctor today, in a follow-up call, that my chances of getting rabies were about the same as getting abducted by aliens.

"Right now, I wouldn't mind that," I say, "if they're nice aliens."

Ted and I have been having some very difficult but precious and sweet moments. In the midst of all this, I can't help but reflect on all the truly wonderful times he and I have packed into 13 years...with some things left undone, of course. But that's how it is, and although we are still in this life, still present, we probably won't be taking that cross-country trip we talked about or the quick weekend on the coast of England. So, my parting words to you tonight are this: Grab everything you can. If you have someone to love, hold them tight and love them with all your being. Go climb that mountain, eat good food, sing and dance and have lots of sex. This life will never seem like quite enough, but if you plunge in, it will be just right.

9/5/14, Kathy's email:

Had a great visit from Ted's family, who went back to NY this morning. Never seems to be enough time, but they are a very special bunch and cheered us both. (I tried to get Ted's sister Susie to leave one of her Yorkies with me, but she wouldn't budge.)

Sally is now here, so I have a helper by my side. It amazes me how things fall into place. Every time someone leaves, I feel so sad. But then—here comes the next. Grateful.

Tonight's supper was from "Local 188"—Sir Ted dined on flatbread/hummus, gasbacho (I can't spell it, but he liked it), pickled beets, black squid risotto, lemon butter cookies...

We are holding steady. Lots of hugs & kisses help.

Love to all.

In our room is a bulletin board that is filling up to the brim with cards and photos. I probably look at them more than Ted does. I am also cared for here by the staff, so lovingly.

And during this first week of hospice, my dear friend Terry from Boston, who had been such a comfort to me when Ted had his original surgery, tells me that her husband, Richard, an absolutely wonderful guy, has been diagnosed with kidney cancer. I am so sad for them, and begin adding them to my prayers, hoping their journey will have a better outcome than ours.

9/9/14, Kathy's email:

Ted is about the same; not much eating, although he slurped down (and I mean slurped) a milkshake this afternoon. He got a gentle massage from a volunteer massage therapist who has an oncology background. Then she worked on me for a while.

In some ways, subtle, Ted seemed a little better today, but it may be that I'm adjusting to the new normal, which is pretty ill. At times he seems very far away, at other times quite present.

Please continue prayers, and thanks for everything you guys are doing, in ways small & big. Denise, special thank you (& Mark).

Love...

BOOKS AND SONGS

On our first date, I sat cross-legged on the carpeted floor of Borders Books as he squatted next to me, reading poetry to me. Months later, we started singing together in the car, harmonizing. "Lida Rose" from *The Music Man* was a favorite of ours. When we'd visit his mom in Long Island, NY, I always broke into "Marian the Librarian"—also from *The Music Man*—when we crossed over the town line in East Marion driving from the ferry to Cutchogue.

September 10th

The days flow together in a routine no longer of our former life. It is now about medication, positioning, and turning; food or no food; the occasional visit of a massage therapist or spiritual consultant or our parish priest, Father Jim. I have bonded with staff, former annoyances regarding differences in care or practice floating away in a process of peace. I am truly happy to see each nurse, each aide, and each social worker as they arrive on any given day. The occasional volunteer appears, sometimes an odd ingredient in this comfort stew...yet—most of the volunteers? Well, I threaten to take them home with me. Our family and close friends seem to sense the needs we have, although I find myself, on occasion, like a grammar school hall monitor, quieting them or reassuring them and gently escorting them down the hallway, as Ted approaches overstimulation.

We missed Ted's mom's 100th birthday celebration a few weeks ago, something we had both very much looked forward to. My heart aches for her, for she knows how sick he is.

A wonderful young person we know works here as a nurse's aide, sometimes assigned to Ted. When Will is here at the same time, they talk about music, play guitar, and sing for Ted—a great addition to warm and respectful care.

9/10/14, 11:34 p.m., Kathy's email:

Ted had a decent start to the day but grew very tired, had very little food/fluids, and appears to be gaining distance. In the early evening, he had much restlessness but settled down, was given something for discomfort, and is resting very comfortably right now. Sally pulled me out of the building for 15 minutes during the evening while Will stayed bedside. I just don't want to leave him.

At this point, I am trying to keep things very quiet and peaceful in his environment, as noise disturbs him. Text or call if you need to visit. I am trying to stem the flow for now. The best for Ted right now is quiet and prayers from afar.

His eyes are open now, so I will leave this with my gratitude and love for each of you.

My friend Connie, whose wife recently lost a dear friend, thinks that people die the way they live. This concept of the style in which one passes is not lost on me. Formerly, at gatherings of family and friends, Ted would engage, happily and earnestly, for a time. Then, especially at family functions, he'd retreat, removing himself from the hubbub, while avid and noisy Skip Bo players carried on in another room. He might move to the football game on TV. Or read in the living room. But occasionally? Occasionally, mid-evening, I'd wander upstairs looking for him and would find him, fully dressed, napping on our bed, this happening years before his illness. It wouldn't have occurred to him that there was anything out of the ordinary about that—more that everyone should do their own thing.

So maybe, as Ted is learning to die, I am learning to let him go about it his way. For me, I would want parties and people and music and laughter and enough medication to enjoy it. I think. Nobody really can plan these things. Our reality with Ted's imminent transition is clearly that of his own making. My task is to stop second-guessing it. It is his death and his wisdom within. I must step aside. Now follow two to three days for Ted of decreased eating and drinking; staring/looking upward, gazing—no words about what he is looking at.

September 11th
Ted keeps trying to put his left leg over the side of the bed rail. The nurses, at my request, try to see if he can sit on the side of the bed, but it is unsuccessful. He is too weak.

"I can't stay here," he tells me, as he tries to get up.

"You need to do what you need to do," I say.

Earlier that day, with no provocation at all, he yelled, "Shut up!" Out of character. And I understand there is much going on in his head to which I am not privy.

At 5:45 p.m., one of the nurses leaves, after working an hour and a half past her shift, leaving me a note about a book on loss she thinks I may find useful. She lost her husband the prior year and tries to prepare me.

"It's so much worse than you think it will be," she says gently.

I am so heartbroken at this point that I can't imagine it could ever feel worse. That doesn't seem possible. I wonder why she is telling me this. Being next to him, seeing how sick he is, my heart and my soul feel they are breaking right in half.

9/11/14, 9:26 p.m., Kathy's email:

Ted's medication was reworked today so he has been pretty comfortable, overall, sleepy but not as deeply sleepy as yesterday evening. Basically, an easier day for him. He has periods of responsiveness and looks afar a fair amount. I wonder what he is seeing...

September 12th, Friday

> **EQUAL FOOTING**
>
> We had a compatibility that I had never experienced before with anyone, and we had a deep respect for each other as individuals. He never suggested I change my name when we were talking about marriage. I called him White and he called me Eliscu much of the time. Like most couples, we had our "in" jokes. When we were up high someplace, like on a bridge or atop a mountain looking down, we used to say that our "balls were going up" into our throats—even though only one of us owned a set.

SAINT BECKY

Becky's Diner in Portland has been one of our go-to places. Becky Rand has been running this popular spot since 1991. Tonight, Sally drives there to fetch food for all of us, returning with a large bag full of their home cooking.

"Oh. They left out the mashed potatoes," she says, disappointed because it's her favorite part of the meal. I get it. It's a staple at Becky's, far from the New York City food Sally is used to. Becky's mashed potatoes? It's like coming home again, especially now, when things are feeling so sad. Comfort food. At my urging, she calls, tells them about it and asks if next time we order they can throw in some extra mashed potatoes. They are apologetic—does she want to come back for them?—and she tells them we are at Gosnell, so she doesn't want to drive back to Portland tonight just for that.

About a half hour later, I am in the hallway for a minute, and I see someone familiar walking toward our room. Becky. She is as shocked as I am. She did not realize it was Ted who was here. She had not connected Sally with us. And she is carrying a huge bag of food—much more than the replacement mashed potatoes. We hug.

"You didn't need to do this," I say.

"It was on my way," she says.

Much later, I learn that she was on her way to see her newborn grandson, stopping first to give food to someone at Gosnell. Because that's who she is.

NEXT MORNING

Our doctor today is Dr. Cynthia Burnham. I call her the Angel Doctor.

We chat about the various feelings people experience in hospice.

"How can you do this?" I ask her.

"I've gotten very comfortable with the unknown," she says.

Later, when I come to bed, standing next to Ted before lying down, around one in the morning, he reaches over to me and rubs and feels me, very intentionally, like he used to. It is so sweet and so special, not so much a sexual thing, but sensual and deeply affectionate, as if he is saying *I know your body, I have felt it millions of times*...an intensely affectionate and intimate few moments of touch—first my right arm, sliding downward to my right breast, then around to my back, and back again—the places of contact that make me feel that for a few moments, my Ted is back. The next day, as I stand next to his bed, there is a shorter version of it, profoundly familiar.

ON THE HOME FRONT

The next morning, I get a call from Sally, who is still staying at our farmhouse.

"Mom," she says, "is there a problem with hot water in the upstairs shower?"

I lead her on a brief verbal tour of the house. "Go downstairs and see if there's hot water in the kitchen," I say.

As she does that, she hears an odd noise coming from the laundry room, just beyond the kitchen.

The hose at the back of our washing machine has burst, hot water spewing all over the laundry room. And into the closet and storage space, which are packed full of needed items, paperwork, and more.

9/13/14, 11:00 p.m., Kathy's email:

Our Ted is still quite sleepy. A bit of fluids, some smiles. Mostly very tired. Very sweet. Soul-crushingly tender moments. Going through a lot of tissues.

Sally, Will, and Steve are my right-hand team today.

Meanwhile, back at the ranch, Denise & Mark came to our aid in the latest house crisis. Mark installed new washing machine hoses post-flood.

Sally remarks, "I've heard of people having friends like this. I've read about it. But I've never actually seen it until now."

(email cont'd.)

A call to Amica proves once again that they are the BEST insurance company ever. Don't know if this mini disaster will be covered (who cares at this point?), but they will have their field rep call me Monday morning, send someone out to the house, and figure out what needs to be done. The woman I spoke with was so kind. (P.S.—did you guys know you're supposed to replace the hoses every 4 to 5 years? Um, me neither.) So, anyone coming up next week: Bring your own sheets/towels, enough clothes in case the washer is still out of commission, etc. I know Laurie & Randey will be up. At some point, I will be back home, so we will then play musical beds.

Please continue to keep us in your prayers. I've got you in mine. We are in this together.

Love—peace—hugs

Each day I have pockets of peace, periods of tears, and pain. My words to him give him permission to let go. But my soul? I don't think it ever will. He may have to be the bold one. The adventurer. I try to fool myself, remaining in a place of non-change, stubbornly holding on, maybe just 2% of me, to the hope that still, still—suddenly he will sit up and say, "OK, then. Let's go for a ride and go out to lunch."

His near-lifeless sleeping body says otherwise.

His legs, thin from disuse, his arms, dotted with peeling Tegaderm patches covering skin tears, dark, near-black scabs in places, fingers slightly swollen on his right hand, his dependent hand...he is trying to find his peace, as he dozes and then opens his eyes, staring off into something I cannot see. He is gently medicated, something he finally has agreed to. He often, now, refuses any offer from me—to read to him, to take a sip of ginger ale, although one of the nurses was more successful—and maybe now I need to adjust to a reality that he may not need me. I broach the topic of our manuscript, ask him if he would like me to finish it, and he nods and smiles in agreement.

I'm so deeply, profoundly sad.

My nephew Misha, his wife, Theo, and their baby, Gabriel, are here. Misha, a neuroscientist, has cut short a conference in Japan to be here. Theo and the baby have flown up from Virginia. We've not seen the baby for almost a year, not since he was in NICU in a hospital in Virginia. He's progressing beautifully from his preemie birth weight of just 1 pound, 12 ounces.

Across the ocean in Holland, my sister-in-law Eve and niece Lula light candles for us.

Kathy's email:

Ted is quite comfortable. Plenty of sleeping, awakened easily.

We have just passed the 2-week mark here and continue to be warmed by the kindness of the staff, quite special.

Sally is here until Monday morning now, instead of just until tomorrow. Thanks, Jet Blue, for being good humans in time of need! My sister and Ted's son will be coming up Monday.

Thank you for continued prayers—for us and for yourselves in your healing of any kind.

xo

Sunday, September 14th

Ted has had some brief wakefulness this morning, and I ask him if he wants a kiss. He nods and I get a couple of tenderhearted kisses. He then eats a few small bites of a cinnamon roll brought in from a local bagel shop and sips some ginger ale. I take a walk outside the building, on this most beautiful clear blue sunny September day, while the CNAs bathe him. In the afternoon, Father Jim comes in to visit. We now consider him not just our pastor, but a friend, a gentle man of great wisdom.

My niece Kathy is here for a while, catering to us, using the house as home base and caring for it, which is helpful. Kathy is one of the funniest people we know. She gets Ted laughing over and over again at her imitation of the women at the nail salon she goes to, and one morning, when she is feeding him pancakes, tiny bites at a time, she tells him that if he chokes to death "on my watch," she'll kill him, which gets them both laughing so hard they both nearly choke to death.

She and William show up every evening, guitars in hand, giving nightly impromptu concerts for Ted, who at times weakly sings along a bit, often with tears in his eyes. Folk songs, hippie songs, "This Land Is Your Land" being one of the most frequent, with whoever is in the room or wandering by welcome to sing along. Kathy has used up virtually all her vacation time from her role in the Broadway show *Mary Poppins* in New York. William comes over after working all day at his job, driving nearly an hour each way.

9/14/14, 11:02 p.m., Kathy's email:

Our Ted ate a bowl of ice cream tonight (van/choc/straw)—once again defining his reputation as a hospice patient in the best way possible.

Had some fluids, did a lot of sleeping, but also had some wakeful moments. He is comfortable and well-loved.

Sally heads back to NY tomorrow at the crack of dawn. I have so much gratitude for her help and companionship this last week and a half. Thank you, Sally, so very much. (P.S.—sorry about the results of the card game...ahem.)

Randey is coming tomorrow and Laurie (tomorrow or Tues.)—Laurie, there is a vehicle available to use here if you need it.

I believe Ted's mom & sister are also coming up soon for another visit. I am overwhelmed by the generous spirit of all of you—prayers, hands-on help, if I listed it all, you'd think I was making it up.

You are making a difference and allowing me to focus on Ted. Grateful seems an inadequate word.

Monday, September 15th
Denise is here around 10:30 a.m. She brings me breakfast, rescuing me and my craving for a croissant with egg, cheese, and bacon. Then she stays with Ted while I go to therapy. How do I begin to explain a friend like this?

Today, Ted refuses his noon pain medicine. In the hallway, I take some flak from a nurse's aide who insists he is having pain and should be medicated. I am stuck in the middle, not wanting to override my husband's wishes.

Our dear friend Bill comes by around two, and Ted is positively gleeful—laughing, talking, more engaged—a new Ted for an afternoon. Bill keeps him interested, and Ted laughs quite a bit with old work memories.

Afterwards, he is sleepier. Laurie, and then Randey arrives, and Ted is happy to see both. More smiles. Ice cream. Sips of fluid.

I have no idea what's going on, God. Maybe You do.

Ted takes his midnight pain medicine from the nurse. She is lovely, and he is blanketed and tucked in. Time for me to get ready for bed. I pull over the sofa and commence my own bedtime routine of flossing, brushing, and so on, and then get myself tucked in next to him, as I've been doing since his admission here.

9/15/14, 10:41 p.m., Kathy's email:

Interesting day. Ted turned down pain meds earlier, so that may have made a difference, or possibly he just felt better, chicken/egg? Nevertheless, a good afternoon followed by much sleepiness, and arrival of my sister Laurie & soon after, Randey, both of whom Ted seemed very happy to see. Needless to say, it makes me very happy to have them here. Sally is safely home in NY, and Theresa, thank you for picking her up & bringing her to the airport at the crack of dawn. Thank you, Sue S., for that & other offers of help. I feel extremely blessed by the amount of love and sacrifice people have shown these last weeks/months/years. Ted continues to defy the statistics of this hospice facility, even though taking in minimal fluids and food but indulging, once again, in an evening bowl of ice cream. For how long he will hang in there, I don't know. But I do know this. Some force which I call God has the answers and I don't. God is very secretive about it all. The good news is, now I realize I can tell God anything & it will remain between us.

So—God is good, and in spite of everything, amazing humans shine through with love and peace—family, friends, and the hospice workers here.

Our Ted is in good hands, and your good wishes and prayers, being sent in so many different ways, have warmed and soothed me. Thank you.

Love...

My sister Laurie is one of the family members staying at our house. She fills in on the evening shift with me with ease, as she is on "showbiz" time. I find it helps so much, since most of our family is on more of a daytime schedule. It works out well, covering many more hours of support for me, something I very much need. Family and friends give me breaks, practically pushing me out of the room for a few minutes now and then.

Laurie tells me that one time during this week when she is with him while I'm in a meeting, she keeps asking him if he wants his pillow adjusted, or something to drink, anything she can do to help, and he gets angry. He yells at her, "JESUS CHRIST!!!" and she pauses a moment.

"Ted, I didn't know you were so religious!" she says. And he roars with laughter!

9/16/14, 10:25 p.m., Kathy's email:

A more difficult day. Ted has developed a cellulitis in his right arm and will be started on antibiotics.

He has had almost nothing by mouth today, and has rested/slept most of the day, in part from pain medication, which he needed. So he is comfortable but not the perky Ted we saw yesterday afternoon.

Not much more to say. I am at his side, just taking a moment to write this. Please continue to pray your good intentions for him and for all of us.

Love...

CHAPTER 39

CHOICES

Today, the staff social worker asks to talk privately with me. It turns out that Ted is now considered generally stable—although terminally ill—and they can no longer justify to Medicare that he needs this level of acute care. This is a big surprise to me, that hospice is considered hospital-level care. I'd never given it any thought. She lays it out carefully and gently. They will not kick him out, but it is time for me to consider our options: Keep him right where he is, but we pick up the tab for room and board ($300+/day) if they are not at capacity; move him to a nursing home; bring him home with caregivers in place. The choice is easy for me. Bringing him home would require moving him again, plus finding two round-the-clock caregivers, a big expense and not necessarily reliable. Nursing home? No way. Not going through that again, and not putting my Ted through that again. I go into Ted's room to make sure I am not making a decision he is unhappy with. I lay out the news lovingly, and hoping he will say, "I'll stay here," which is exactly what he says. I am tremendously relieved, and unconcerned about paying the bill because frankly, finances are the last thing I'm worried about right now. I'll figure it out later. The social worker assures me that for now, it's fine for him to stay, and that I shouldn't feel rushed about an alternative, even if beds start filling up. That thought does lie there in the back of my mind, but two days later, it is revisited when things change. I am soon to learn that his eligibility for hospice-level care is no longer an issue.

9/17/14, 11:20 p.m., Kathy's email:

Ted had a reasonably comfortable/sleepy day. The priest (whom I had met in the ER post-dog bite) was here seeing another patient & stopped in to see us. Lovely man.

Randey & Laurie & Denise hung out here today, and Ted's mom & sister Susie are heading up tomorrow from Long Island. (To our helper) I think you said you were coming by Thursday to say hello. Give me a quick heads-up first. I think he'll be happy to see you.

Thank you for the notes & texts (Connie!!! xox)—cards—etc. You guys are all so awesome.

Yes, Sally, people like this really do exist. I know. It's amazing.

On the house front: ServPro was in today, assessing damage to laundry room & surrounds. They will be coming in tomorrow with the "big stuff" to dry wall interiors & pull up linoleum & subflooring. Apparently, I am supposed to have a laundry room flood every couple of years...

Sue S., it was nice to wave to you. Will talk soon.

Love...

Ted's mother and Susie stay at our house and visit Ted every day. I can't help but think that in this case, it is not a blessing for his mother to have lived so long, as she is now seeing her oldest child in his dying days, with another younger son in the family now having a serious, life-threatening illness as well. She sits by Ted's bedside, holds his hand, talks to him. Susie, who faithfully brings her here every day, is not only here to support Ted and all of us, but also to take care of their mom.

A DIFFERENT KIND OF DAY

Friday, September 19
Before he leaves for Philadelphia, Randey gets Ted laughing, recalling old stories. Randey has visited so often that he's used up every minute of vacation time, and maybe beyond, sometimes driving up from Philly, sometimes

flying. Today, Ted has refused pain medication. He is very present, and engaged, to his capacity. Ted is back! My heart is so happy. I am still holding onto that miracle fantasy, that he will somehow—*somehow*—get better. That his essentially strong body will fight back and kill the cancer.

We have time alone midday. He starts crying. We hug, we cry, talk (mostly me), but it is odd, unlike anything I have experienced, as if we don't need words but we know what we are saying. He touches me, caresses me gently, gives me something like hugs with his left arm, and we kiss over and over again—soft, heartfelt, loving kisses…

He has some food at noon—a bit of pot roast, mashed potatoes, tiny amounts of broccoli, just small soft bites I've basically mashed for him—and he really, truly enjoys it, with quiet *Mmm*s.

I feed him just a bit more food and drink later. Then, at midnight, he asks for pain medication.

During the night, Ted begins to have some spasms that cause spitting up and later, vomiting. I am given instructions for handling it, for helping him through it. The spasms become hiccupping, with difficulty breathing; the nurse is back, and in the early morning, the doctor comes in. Ted's medicines are changed. There is no longer a choice. The oral Keppra will have to be replaced with IV or subcutaneous Ativan, plus the morphine and dexamethasone (Decadron). There is talk about decreasing his Decadron, but the covering doctor ends up keeping it in place, my preference. A subcutaneous port is inserted just under the skin in his abdomen, a tiny, permanent entry point for medication to be given without future need for an injection.

9/20/14, 6:50 p.m., Kathy's email:

It is Saturday, close to 7 p.m. I am next to Ted, who is sleeping deeply and peacefully. During the night last night, he took a turn for the worse, after a really wonderful day in so many ways. But in the night, he had a lot of breathing trouble, probably related to seizure/neurological activity, so this morning the doctor came in and discussed…the best route for his comfort is now getting medication through a subcutaneous port. Because of this, and the fact that his swallowing now would represent a real problem, he is on slightly different medications for seizure control. Thus, the deep sleep—but also, more regular and less problematic breathing. None of this will shorten his life—but it will keep the respiratory issues at bay.

He is approaching the time of transition. His sister Susie and his mom were here all day—William, Laurie, Denise & Mark, Fred & Meryl...a quiet grouping of loved ones, who also represent other loved ones. Our wonderful priest was in as well, with prayer and blessing and the Anointing of the Sick.

Heartbroken? Yes, I am, so much so. But it is better that he is peaceful than struggling for breath.

Please continue prayers for peace—for all of us.

Love...

Now starts a week of decreased response to almost everything, but Ted seems comfortable. It is vigil time. Every night, through these days at Gosnell, I pull the sofa up to his bed and make the two into one bed so I can hold him.

If I hold him, maybe he will stay.

I know he is safe and secure in this bed in Room 106. And still I hold out hope for recovery.

"Can we start IVs to help him?" I ask.

I am told that, at this point, his organs are shutting down. I know that. I see that. When they tended to him earlier today, they tried to get a vein to give him his medication, but it was not possible. It was necessary to put a port into his abdomen for medication administration. His urine is blood-tinged. I know what is happening, but the core of my being will do anything to save him.

Every night, and often during the day when we are alone, I say prayers, mostly the prayers given to me by the priest whom we'd met so long ago during the Sherwoods week. These prayers comfort me, and you know, it's all I can really do at this point. To be present and to pray. I feel very close to my God right now. Very close.

September 20
Father Jim comes in to visit, a scheduled visit. This time Ted is, for all purposes, unconscious. He makes sounds occasionally, sometimes when turned. His breathing is slow and relaxed. Now and then, it appears he stops breathing for a few moments. Then he starts up again.

Father Jim and I sit on the sofa next to the bed. We chat, with silences for stretches of a few minutes at a time. It is a quiet room right now. I look down at my feet, socks and sneakers, and realize I am wearing a wonderful pair of socks my son Will gave me last Christmas. They read: "Fuck This Shit."

"Sorry about the socks," I say.

He reads them and chuckles. It's good to laugh. Maybe Ted can hear it.

I barely leave Ted's side, unless booted out now and then by someone in our inner circle to send me to walk around the building a few times, during which time I glance toward the window with each round to make sure everything looks status quo.

Randey comes in to be with Ted. They tell each other "I love you" and when Randey heads out, heading home to Philadelphia, I promise him I will call if things change.

September 24
When Dr. Burnham comes in today, she has a suggestion that, at first, seems odd. It is a thought that has come to her in the middle of the night.

"Open a window, and the doors," she says.

Then she explains that in answer to everyone's rhetorical question (including mine) as to why Ted is still here, she thinks that because he loves nature so much, that maybe opening the room up to the outdoors will help his soul move on.

I tell her I like the window idea because there's a screen.

"But it's still really buggy out there," I say, nodding to the doorway and corridor door just beyond, so I nix the idea of leaving the room door with the door to the outside wide open.

She's OK with the compromise. I keep it in mind but don't act on it today.

That night, one of my favorite nurses comes in at 11:00 for the night shift. I have a strong connection with her, and tonight she shares a near-death story, a story I need to hear, a story that gives me a boost of hope that there really is something after this life.

Randey is on his way back up to Maine.

September 25

Time continues in a vacuum at Gosnell. Nurses and assistants periodically come in to wash Ted, to move him, and to check on both of us. I am given a tremendous amount of love and support by these people, including warmed blankets for my comfort, and am still supported by close friends and family every single day. I have now become addicted to the cook Norm's cookies, freshly made daily here at Gosnell, which I savor, quietly, with tea at night. A nursing assistant stops by frequently in the evening on her way home from her shift, hugs me, prays with me, hugs me some more as I weep.

I have opened the screened window a bit, letting in the mild evening air.

The family and I have talked about how I am to notify them when Ted is nearing death. I need only make one call, and a rapid phone chain will be put into play. At the house now are Laurie, Sally, and Randey. Ted's mom and Susie are staying at a local motel.

Tonight, as third shift staff comes on, I find out that last night's nurse is here, but assigned to another wing. I'm disappointed, and a little anxious at not having her maternal, soothing presence nearby. Our nurse will be Larry, a nurse Ted has had maybe just once, an amiable fellow whom I don't know very well. Much later, I will recall he's the nurse who gently shielded me, previously, from seeing a hearse in the front of the building. He seems kind, but…I was thinking last night's nurse would have been assigned again to Ted. But this turns out to be one of those times when God seems to know best.

9/25/14, 6:40 p.m., Kathy's email:

Dear ones,

Tomorrow will be four weeks here at hospice. Ted's journey is drawing closer to his transition. He is having some chest congestion and is being medicated for that, but there is no doubt his overall status is progressing. Only God knows when he will be ready, but Ted is comfortable and has been surrounded by love all day long.

Please keep us in your prayers—for peace and strength.

Love...

September 26, 2014
Early Friday morning on September 26th, we awaken to the CNAs coming into the room at about 5:30 a.m. for routine morning care. Ted begins breathing rapidly, shallowly. They send for nurse Larry. Ted's pulse is very weak. He is clearly struggling, continuing rapid, shallow breathing. His morning medication is given. Soon, his breathing calms and is no longer labored. I call home to set the notification chain in motion.

"Come now," I tell them.

Nurse Larry is standing next to the bed.

"Do you want me to stay here, or do you want to be alone?" he asks me.

"Stay, please," I say, needing no internal dialogue about it at all.

He stays with us, quietly sitting by the bedside. He is present, but unobtrusive.

The window is still slightly open. Sunlight begins to open our part of the world, and the gentlest of breezes blows through the window. It is just after dawn.

I talk gently to Ted—words to be swallowed up by the heavens for a visit in another lifetime, in another realm.

"*I'll always love you. Nothing will keep us apart. I love you, my Ted. I love you so much...*" I quietly tell him, as I gently cradle him around his head and his shoulders.

Then, Ted takes maybe four small, very calm, quiet breaths.

And as I whisper to my beloved in this sacred moment, he leaves us.

FROM GOSNELL TO GOD

I'm still holding him. I begin to weep, exhausted, then transition seamlessly back to the mystery that cocoons us. The calm presence and kind words of Larry, nearby, comfort me. I am to take all the time I need, he says.

After an hour or so of family coming in to pay respects to Ted and to see me, it is time to start packing up our items. Every little thing Ted has touched has meaning. Razor. T-shirts. Soap.

The nursing staff comes in to wash him before he is transported to the funeral home.

"Do you want to stay here?" one asks.

"Can I wash this area?" I ask, pointing to just below his right shoulder, that area of his chest where I have laid my head so many, many times. They encourage me to do so. After that, I think I may want to continue washing him, but once I begin, it doesn't feel right, and they take over for me. I move away, not needing or wanting to remain for this part. Not the first time that I've learned that there is no guideline for life and its circumstances.

After Ted has been tended to, they ask if I am ready.

He is then covered, the funeral home people come in, and we make our way, slowly, down the hall toward the front door. As we head down the hallway, Randey is rushing toward us and comes right up to me and gives me a kiss and a hug. It is to be one of the sweetest memories I will ever have. We all emerge into the soft September sunlight, where Ted's gurney is lifted into the hearse.

I am surrounded by my loved ones.

"Turn around," someone close by tells me.

And as I turn toward the front entrance of Gosnell, I see it. Dr. Burnham. Nurses. Aides. Volunteers. Norm. Receptionist staff. All the faces who have loved and cared for us these 28 days, standing at quiet, gentle attention. Kindness embedded on each face, God's grace in the flesh. It is extraordinarily moving to take this in. They stand in testimony of a valuable life lived and transitioned.

Sometime later, some of us go to a local family restaurant very familiar to us.

I eat nothing.

I cannot live without him.

I don't want to go on.

Nothing will ever be OK again.

This is so, so much worse than I could have ever imagined.

PART 5

CHAPTER 40

REALITY

As peaceful, gently paced, and grace-filled as Ted's transition was, I am now facing the numerous decisions and funeral-related tasks that must be done on something of a reasonable timeline. Thankfully, I am not alone.

During the next couple of days, my sister Laurie goes to the funeral home with me. I am angry, and every suggestion she makes annoys me, even as I realize how kind and helpful she is. I don't want to be picking out a coffin for my mate. I would rather be doing anything else. We choose the simplest of coffins, as we intend to honor Ted by continuing a family tradition my sister started when our mom died years ago. Prior to the funeral home hours, family and close friends will gather to write notes and paint pictures and write messages on the exterior of the coffin in which Ted will be placed, a personal farewell captured for all time.

There are so many questions that come up that Ted and I never discussed. You don't know what to ask or think about until it happens. The funeral director asks me about Ted's wedding band. Leave it? Remove it? I have no idea. This becomes the first of so many decisions for which I am unprepared. I talk to my family. To close friends. I even go to the jewelry store where we purchased our rings.

"Some women keep the ring and wear it on a necklace."

No, I don't want that. My daily necklace is the small cross Ted gave me.

My head is spinning. I remember how much Ted loved wearing his wedding band. He would want it on. I leave it on, relieved to have made that single decision.

I have much help from family, friends, and Father Jim regarding the funeral mass that is being planned. The song group will sing. My niece Kathy will sing. My grandson David will play violin. My granddaughter Emma and my dear Meryl will do readings I have chosen. Randey asks to give the eulogy. Steve helps with music planning. Meryl connects me with a lovely fellow who helps with reception planning at one of Ted's and my favorite waterside restaurants. These blessings spill forth at a time when I can't even eat a piece of toast in the morning. My tears are nearly nonstop.

Several days pass. A few family members and friends and I paint and write notes on the casket, our love expressed with acrylic paints and pens. Words, drawings, love notes. This will be displayed at the funeral home, with a chance for others to add their expressions of love.

The funeral home visiting hours are well-attended, and after a while, we sit in a circle and Father Jim says a prayer. Then follows impromptu speeches, then a few songs from the Sherwood "men in green." There are so many people, among other family members and friends, who have traveled from great distances to be here. Will and my niece Kathy sing and play guitar. Ted's brother Rob speaks. After the funeral home hours are over and most leave, the coffin is opened for a few of us who wish to see Ted again. The box of ashes of our pup, Rebel, are placed inside with him for all eternity, along with notes and trinkets from me and others. One of his sisters leaves a small bag of coins. I leave one Blue Man doll in the casket with him, keeping the other with me.

The next day, the funeral is beautiful in every way. Held at our large, resplendent stone church, Father has readily agreed to a full mass and fully welcomes all to participate, no matter their faith. The song group is filled with both current and past members. I'm overwhelmed with the love pouring out.

Meryl and Emma are, I discover, well chosen for their roles in readings. I am comforted by Randey's words, as he honors his father in a beautiful eulogy and speaks of the happiness Ted and I found in our years together. The music is gorgeous, and we end with choruses of the spiritual "Amen," with niece Kathy singing the descant above it. I cry and I sing. I am clapping to the rhythm as we exit the church to go across the street to the cemetery. I probably look psychotic. Maybe I am. Maybe I need to be.

There are a few brief words from Father Jim at the cemetery. Shortly after, people start to leave, many heading to the restaurant reception. I stubbornly wait until some of the dirt is put over the coffin before I leave. I just don't want to leave him.

Finally, finally, I agree to leave, and Randey takes me downtown.

In the weeks that follow, Cassie and Sally take turns staying with me for a week or two at a time. They keep me company and get me through the day. I have no idea how or when they figure this out. They alternate their visits, as Cassie lives in North Carolina and Sally in New York. It's so comforting to have someone here, not too far away on the huge, sad bed at night. These days are a cloud of unreality. There is crying, hugging, more crying, and probably enough food to stay alive. Blue Man, later recognized as a transitional object, is my constant companion. I talk to him and take him with me as I go about each day.

Some weeks after my daughters leave, I feel some vague chest discomfort and go to Dr. Emery, who does a careful check of heart, lungs, etc. and then simply sits with me while I cry—on and on—for probably 20 minutes. He is so kind.

I feel very close to God through this time following Ted's death. Others in a similar situation may feel completely abandoned by and angry at their God. Both, I believe, are normal. God can handle it all.

I have discovered a new type and sound of crying that I thought only occurred in wild animals. It seems to happen a couple of times a day, very intense, almost like howling and then, when over, I feel a bit better. Until next time.

I have trouble getting out of bed each morning. I often lie there for hours at a time, a talk-radio station droning on next to the bed. I wonder what time it is, too exhausted and sad to turn and lift my head to look. Other days I feel better and am up and about, the loneliness giving way to something of a fantasy state, during which time I am dreaming of someday falling in love with someone, usually somebody unattainable. At some point in the fantasy, I get such a deep, sharp emotional pain from the loss of Ted, I can't see any way out of this, ever.

Intellectually, I know this is not true.

I know in my head that I may be able to love again, or at least live more fully again without Ted. But I don't feel that in my gut. I don't know what this phase of widowhood is supposed to be like.

Each day seems as hard as the one before. Each day, I think the next one will be better. Sometimes I have a stretch of a couple of days, usually when I'm distracted or away from home somewhere, when things do seem a little bit better. But in my old routine, in my bed, in my kitchen, in my car, there is something missing—something so significant that I can't comprehend how any day will ever be OK again without him.

Now, in the recesses of my mind, I remember the hospice nurse telling me it would be so much worse after he's gone. At the time, I did not appreciate the message she was attempting to convey, but now I'm very glad she said it. It was one of the most important things anyone told me. In my lowest moments, I reflect on it, and in some odd way, it's comforting. It gives some sense of normalcy to what I am experiencing now, when it seems like life will never be normal again. It affirms that I am not alone in grieving to this extent.

A couple of months later, I'm watching a movie starring Diane Keaton, a movie I haven't seen before called *And So It Goes*. Maybe I have seen it before, I don't even know. So much escapes me now. I tell Heavenly Ted, aloud, what I consider a miracle of sorts: "Look at me, Ted—I can work the TV just great now—I'm switching remotes and everything is falling into place just the way you used to do it." I'd had so much trouble with those damned remotes in the years before he died. There were at least three of them, a complex system that could have been simpler, I would guess. And pressing the wrong button would mess up the whole thing. Now I go through the motions without even thinking, as though Ted has somehow performed a brain transplant from him to me, one more moment which I attribute to the concept of an afterlife. It's magical and gets me giggling. You see, he'd written, years ago, a two-page instruction sheet on how to coordinate the remotes and had gone over all of it with me more than once. Even with that, I was completely unable to figure it out. At the end of the two pages, he'd made one last humorous comment: "Do not let Sally try this." Sally was even less familiar with the system and electronics, at the time, and she and I had giggled over his remark.

So—I start the movie and the first song that comes on blindsides me, a song by Joni Mitchell: "Both Sides Now"—one of the songs Ted and I used to listen to. I hear the notes and words start. It grabs me in the gut, and all over again, I can't believe he's not here and I can't stand it. I just can't bear it.

I'm back to the level of horror crying like when we received Ted's initial diagnosis. Only now, I don't have that person to turn to in mutual grief. The one who previously walked with me through almost every situation is no longer here to help me, to be with me. I am in close touch with my family on a regular basis. Friends reach out to me, but it is never enough for the void that now envelops me. Can never be enough. Again and again, I think I can't go on without Ted. Again and again, I wake up the next day to repeat the grief.

I pull myself out of bed, force myself to have a cup of tea or coffee, put myself through whatever paces are necessary to finally shower and get dressed, put socks and shoes on, my insides desperately wanting to hide in a cave somewhere. A small part of my brain pushes me to walk out of my home, eyes brimming with tears, leading me to understand, on some level, that he is gone, but I am still here. At night, sometimes I lay little Blue Man on my face, gently holding and hugging him until I lay him down against Ted's pillow.

Over the next weeks, my close friends stay present. There are frequent phone calls. Denise listens to me, day after day. Her most frequent comment is a heartfelt "I'm sorry"—which is just right. Meryl tells me to call any time, day or night, and listens to me cry and talk and cry some more, commenting with an occasional, soft "yes." Consoling me is very helpful. For Meryl to do this at one in the morning is heroic. Kathy and John continue to ask and coax me to meet them for dinner, even though I am no longer a "couple." I see them regularly, and it comforts me. Friends send cards. These are the things that keep me going. Nothing is enough to even begin to resurrect my life as I once knew it, yet every kindness is a salve, even if temporary.

I begin weekly grief counseling with Carol from Hospice of Southern Maine. She understands and validates my thoughts and feelings, as crazy as they seem to me. I trust her to tell me if I am, in fact, going crazy—because it feels that way so much of the time. I bring Blue Man with me everywhere, including to these weekly sessions. Carol takes it in stride. I find that others close to me accept this, as well. The fact that they do not judge me is relieving. I know it's out of the realm of what I would previously consider normal. And in some way, it's irrelevant, other than that it's an outward sign of my intense grief. In fact, during a visit with my niece Kathy in New York, we get into a silly mood and have "Bluey" dance to some music—his solo debut—at our table in the middle of a busy NYC café. It gives me some good, much-needed laughs.

GRIEVING PEOPLE

...are around us all the time.

Usually you don't see how very, very troubled they are within themselves. As a species, reasonably civilized, we have a major group denial and also give a false image to others. We wish for everything to be better and pretend that it is. This, I think, is the basis of all the ridiculous, yet often well-meaning utterances of others when faced with a grieving friend:

"He's in a better place."

And much, much later: "Two years? That should be enough time to (date/feel fine/fill in the blank)." In other words, "Get over it." But it doesn't usually work that way.

Within a few months of Ted's death, one of his siblings asks me about a handmade microscope that an uncle had created many, many years earlier. I know this item is a family possession, but just hearing the request and the timing of it feels harsh. That, along with the picture of "Grandfather"—a painting that is meant to be in the hands of the oldest male of the family, which I will also give back, along with much paperwork and research that Ted had done on his family history to share. I let them know I will keep these items safe until I see them next. And I'll look for the family's childhood toy train set.

I still haven't gone through any of Ted's things, these months later. A few people give suggestions, including what to do with his favorite, often-worn

T-shirts: Make them into a quilt, or pillow, or teddy bear. I understand these ideas come from a place of caring. I find them dreadful.

A few months after the funeral—maybe sooner—I go to the office of a stone maker in a nearby town, the stone maker who had made my parents' headstone years earlier. I start to explain to the owner why I am there, and every time I start to talk, I start to sob. Finally, I squeak out that my husband has died, and that I will come back another day. "Another day" happens three more times over the coming year before I can ask even the preliminary questions without having to leave the office mid-visit.

I wander a lot. In the Old Port area of Portland, I walk by our Butterfly Corner in hopes of something miraculous happening. There is no magic there now.

Ted's brother comes up some months later to help me sort through Ted's old slides. We divide them into categories, and he takes the early family ones. A handful are earmarked for duplication so we both will have them. The microscope is given to him along with, unfortunately, a snarky comment from me.

I had not expected to feel hurt by the simple requests for items, and I doubt that if the shoes were reversed I would give it a second thought, that it would be any different. But without Ted here, these requests to look for such-and-such an item and send it back to a family member builds a bit of a wedge for me between what I'd thought of as my family, too, as if they'd better grab it before I do something with it and it's gone for good. I'm aware of their deep grief in losing their brother. But I can't see my way out of my own deep mourning, and I'm operating on a preteen level, at best. I've written a note to one of Ted's siblings twice already and put it aside, not knowing if I should send it or not because it talks of feeling pushed away by the family. The second rendition of the letter is much gentler than the first, so I need to decide if I'm sending it or not. If I send it and it results in hurt feelings, I am pushing myself further away. If it does the opposite and they reach out to me, I will feel better. I think. Unfortunately, there's nothing much that will make me feel better because Ted is gone. I have plenty to do each day and at the same time have never felt so fucking unfocused in my entire life.

> **LOVE NOTE—PEOPLE**
>
> Ted was extremely kind yet had so much honesty of character. Imperfect, like everyone, but so wise.
>
> "People will disappoint you," he once told me.
>
> That single sentence has gone a long way in helping me to forgive people. Including myself.

I stop in, again, at the cemetery office, to ask the same question I've asked a dozen times. I ask about our three plots.

"Which one is Ted buried in?"

"Plot number 36."

Each time I go back or call and ask, it's still Plot 36. All the plots are numbered. I will be in number 35 someday. We will be kept apart by the cold cement vault, and I am heartbroken about not being able to truly lie together underground. Maybe there will be no concrete wall separating us in Heaven. Plot number 34 is empty for a mystery person, whom I hope to never have to know about in this lifetime. I hope our children will sell it. Or just leave the space for grass to remain.

Double stone for me and Ted?

Separate stones but on the same base?

While we were together, we were so very connected. I want us to be together in the next life, which is what Ted wanted so much. Always and forever. I call my daughter Cassie for the millionth time to ask her opinion. Finally, and with her helpful input, I settle on separate stones but on the same base. Cassie tells me they will design mine.

"Why don't I design it?" I ask. "I mean, all you have to say on it is Best Mom in the World."

No. They will design it. Not knowing and giving up control is so tough.

December 2014

It's early December. Cassie calls me from North Carolina.

"Come down and stay with us for the winter. We'll take care of you." Those are the sweetest words a mom can hear. I begin to think about making the trip in January.

I deal with the upcoming Christmas holidays by overdoing everything. I've vowed to keep things simple for Christmas, yet I find myself pushing to near exhaustion, shopping, making preparations and possibly reparations to others in this time of distinct weirdness. I use any excuse to take care of myself in terms of treats for myself and others. I feel awful, and the more awful I feel, the more I go to the mall.

Donation requests from charities to which Ted had given in the past pour in, addressed to him on the envelopes. Most receive a check from me because I see it as a tribute to him. To toss them away would feel like tossing him away. Money flies out of my checkbook.

Christmas itself is a mixed blur. My close people stay connected. Denise and Mark come over and lovingly, beautifully decorate the house with indoor lights, which cheers me, more lights than I've ever thought of putting up. It's gorgeous.

I buy a small but very pretty artificial tree from a local store, which looks old-fashioned, and I set out Ted's Christmas stocking, which I had made a few years ago for him, along with those for Sally, Will, Steve, and myself. I write Ted a love note. I buy a tiny dollhouse-size gift for Blue Man.

I am constantly aware of Ted's absence. At the same time, I continue to get little messages which seem to be from him. I'm slowly chopping some vegetables one day when I feel a hand on my shoulder for a few moments. But that's another story, maybe for a different time. Any perceived contact from him is immeasurably comforting in the void.

At church, floods of memories both haunt and console me. Some days, I remember funny things about Ted, offering a momentary reprieve from the harshness of grief. Those are welcome moments, although I'd be lying if I said they feel truly lighthearted. Maybe someday they will.

LOVE NOTE—HIS HUMOR

Ted and I had taken some very cool trips together over the years. Oftentimes, when seeing the ocean, or a huge expanse, as on the apex of a mountain, he'd look out and jokingly say, "Somehow I thought it would be bigger than this." Lake Tahoe? "Somehow I thought it would be bigger than this." On the shores and vast expanse of the Pacific Ocean in California? And from the forever view from the top of Mount Washington in New Hampshire? "Somehow I thought it would be bigger than this."

CHAPTER 41

PLODDING ALONG

January 2015

I am still inundated with paperwork—legal, financial, so many places to notify post-Ted's death. Meryl spends afternoons sitting with me.

"OK. Give me something else," she says, every few minutes, and calls places on my behalf, relieving my burden, call by call.

One afternoon, I call American Express to close his account. The only charge made for quite a while is a recurring bill of around $20 to $30. They are understanding, kind, and helpful.

"So, what I owe you should just be the most recent twenty-something," I say.

"No, actually the balance is $264," she says.

Turns out someone in Corpus Christi, Texas has recently charged hundreds of dollars of food and related gift cards. More lots-of-calls later, I have done what I need to do to report it. American Express does not charge me for the theft. But I am angry and hurt that there are shitty people in the world who steal.

Mid-January, I pack up for North Carolina. I try to remember how to prepare the house, including the lamp-at-window notification system that allows Sue and Sam across the street to see if the light goes on, indicating a drop in heat in the house. I plan out the drive ahead, which will include some brief family and hotel visits, spreading the trip down south over many days so I am not doing too much driving on any one day.

Cassie and Paul open their home and hearts to me. I live in their spacious home, live there through my first Valentine's Day without Ted when a gorgeous bouquet of flowers arrives from Denise and Mark, along with cards from friends, including a precious, handmade Valentine's card from Dee, of "Dee and Al," our Sherwood hosts of past years.

Here in NC with Cassie, Paul, and the kids, Cassie makes a major event out of Valentine's Day, which is quite a fun spectacle (that's my girl!), and I enjoy it despite my ever-present inner agony, especially on this day, missing Ted so much. I begin a tradition of sorts, buying him a Valentine's card, and I leave it out with my loving words for him, open, in the guest room where I'm staying. In case he can see it.

I stay with Cassie and Paul and the children for a couple of months. Partway through, I get a call from Sue and Sam, back home in Maine. The special light in the kitchen that is sensitive to any decrease in heat is on. I call Michael, our handyman, and meanwhile, Sam goes over to investigate. Turns out I had left the lamp too close to the outside window. The house temperature has not dropped, which is good news. Sam and Michael adjust the lamp so it is still visible, but not too close to the chilly outside window. Close call...

I find a "home" church in Greenville—St. Gabriel of Our Sorrowful Mother—a lovely, simple church that is quite culturally diverse compared with my church back home. I am comfortable and delighted by this mixture of warm congregants—Black, Hispanic, and White. It's a vibrant community, with many get-togethers. Sometimes there is a breakfast set up in the lobby for after the morning mass, and as one is heading to communion, the smell of sausage wafts through the church. One day, there is a small tent set up just outside the front door, where several people are selling tacos. The music director—just a really nice woman—invites me to join in special masses in which the St. Gabriel's choir sings. I'm challenged by some of the hymns that are in Spanish, but Cassie coaches me. I think of Ted, who would have loved this. He often wanted to sing the hymns back home in Spanish, having lived in California for 30 years, in communities of many Spanish-speaking people.

I plan a day to go to New Bern, purposely on my own. It's exciting to drive there and pass so many familiar places, remembering, remembering...

sentiment mixed with amusement. I meet with Missy and Nick for lunch, then I wander around, visiting little shops, reminiscing some more: the place where I took a picture of Ted sitting next to a life-size papier mâché bear, across from the Visitors Bureau; the waterfront; Kristof's, the restaurant at the Hilton where we spent a Valentine's Day dinner; various restaurants we'd enjoyed together; the store called Beach, featuring a full-size faux Elvis Presley out front; and the Pepsi store. The last year we were here together, toward the end, a new Indian restaurant had opened. I'd gone in to look at the menu and I'd talked to the manager, wanting to take Ted there because he loved Indian food. It didn't happen.

But it's been a happy afternoon, and I'm shocked when I burst into tears on the way back to Greenville.

Had my subconscious thought I'd be bringing Ted back with me?

BACK HOME IN MAINE

2015

It's early spring, and I'm back home in the farmhouse.

I was up until four in the morning last night, in bed at two but I couldn't sleep, a mixture of grief and energy and sexual energy and, oh God, missing Ted so much. In and out of sleep for about two hours, up and down, sleeping, not sleeping, and a couple of times in my half sleep, I hear a man's voice—Ted's?—but at such a distance it's distorted—saying, "I love you so much." Yes, I hear those words. Today, I'm just a fucking mess. I can't stop crying even while I'm doing the normal things like eating and cleaning and all the stupid details of life. I can't bear not having him here.

Just yesterday I was talking with my neighbor Sue, outside, and I was feeling fairly good. She remarked that she thought I had turned the corner. But last night and this morning I feel like I'm right back in the throes of deep grief. Right now, it is the worst it's been in a long time.

I walk through the cemetery, through the back area with older graves, the graves of so many children who died between 1918 and 1920, likely from the influenza epidemic.

I am in rough shape emotionally, all over the place, and I have this thought: I want to get roaring drunk. I don't even drink. But I just want to get blasted. Or high. I don't do either, but I have this wild energy mixed with sadness, so deep there isn't even a word for it. I can't tolerate the feel of a normal life anymore, whatever that feels like.

I talk to Will by phone and tell him this and he understands.

June 2015

I may be delusional, but I'm going to drive to Indianapolis to a yearly conference of the National Society of Newspaper Columnists (NSNC), a conference I've gone to many times, always held in a different city. I will be six days on the road, not driving more than about 3½ to 4 hours a day, driving part of the trip on the Lincoln Highway, a cool road with some old-timey motels and murals and statues devoted to Abe Lincoln, that starts at Times Square in NYC and ends up in San Francisco. Ted and I had talked about doing this kind of drive together, and now, with trusty Blue Man as my cohort, I'm going to give it a try, picking up the Lincoln Highway in Pennsylvania and taking it through a couple of states to get the feel for it. If I don't do it this year, I may never do it. I don't want my world to get too small. I need to push myself. Using Sally's handmade Christmas gift of a dashboard car seat for Blue Man and a tiny "baby" that my sister bought from the same Fisher-Price series, they are wrapped together on my dashboard, remarkably and strangely keeping me company. I navigate hotels, roads, restaurants, and then, at NSNC, I experience being alone without my Ted, yet comforted by and excited to see my old pals and meet some new ones. One night, hanging out with my friends after-hours, I start to feel sad and out of place, my grief peering out in yet another situation. I say something that makes me feel like an idiot—my default setting—and I quietly slip out and go back to my hotel room. I cry for a few minutes, then think some. About twenty minutes later, I decide to return to the social gathering, and one of my friends greets my return immediately with arms open for me. I cry onto him as he simply holds me.

THE UNIVERSE AS WE KNOW IT

One day, as I wander through the house, I sit down at Ted's computer. I recall how he would call me over, saying "Look at this!" and show me—in gorgeous, enhanced color—the beautiful photos of the universe from the Hubble Site web page. We'd watch the pictures together, enthralled by the beauty of the galaxies. Now, this gives me an idea.

With calls to and permission from the Hubble Site people, and coordination with my stone maker, I choose a gorgeous photo that can be transferred, via glass art, to the back of his stone, crediting the Hubble Site at the bottom of the stone. Imprinted also will be Ted's own words: "Somehow I thought it would be bigger than this." I chuckle as I know how Ted would love the humor. There's a tiny satellite at the top of the photo, barely visible, in which I picture Ted as he flies through the universe on an adventure.

I find the right words for the front of the stone. Meryl, who is an internationally recognized artist in ceramic and fabric art, readily agrees to design a kayaker on a lake with trees on the side to partially frame the words. It's going to be quite special. Finally. It's a relief, and I feel good about the choices, which took a long time but feel just right. As right as it can be. The Hubble Site people ask me to send them a photo for their records, as it's apparently the first time anyone has ever done this, to their knowledge. This feels amazing. Ted will now be immortalized in their archives. He'd have loved that.

I begin to make a plan to have a few people over to the house for dinner, the first time I will do something like this since Ted's passing. It's been many months since he left. Part of me wants to feel like everything's so much better, that I can host this small gathering as a thank-you. The reality is that I pretty much haven't even cooked dinner for myself during these past many months. Once I notify people, I suddenly feel like I can't do it. Not yet. I postpone it, and they understand.

Some friends seem to have fallen away, especially some couples. I'd been warned that this might happen, and now I see it and feel it. I don't understand it. Maybe it's hard to be around someone who is grieving. Maybe widows don't fit in well with social plans. Whatever the reason, in some way, they choose to move on, even though I desperately want things to stay the same. One friend sends cards and makes overtures, but for reasons unknown, I cannot bring myself to connect much, like being stuck in an inertia bubble. I understand that for all kinds of reasons, people move on, friendships become distant, and in some way, I am now aware that widows (and probably widowers) in our culture are often a forgotten group of very hurting people. Time moves on. My steadfast couples remain, a huge gift. In this way, Ted remains my partner. Nothing needs to be fixed.

There's still the crying. Every day. More than once a day. I cry while driving, grocery shopping, in the shower, in bed, watching TV…I cry so much I have trouble understanding how my body can make so many tears.

My loving family continues to check up on me. So much is still a blur.

"Do you miss Ted, too?" I occasionally ask someone. It feels important to know he is still missed, that it's not only me who misses him.

Meryl remains like a sister to me. One day, feeling brave, I tell Meryl she no longer needs to take care of me, as she had promised Ted in his last weeks. It isn't entirely true that I don't need her help, but at the time, it's important to me to feel less dependent. Meryl tells me she is going to train to become a hospice volunteer because of Ted. I can't think of a better tribute.

CHAPTER 42

ANNIVERSARY IN HEAVEN

*F*all 2015

Approaching the first anniversary of Ted's passing, I see an opportunity to honor him in a way that will hold meaning: Pope Francis is coming to America. Ted used to fondly refer to the Pope as "Frank." I call Maryellen, who lives just outside of Philadelphia, and we make plans. I end up having a deeply meaningful and beautiful weekend with her and the crowds of the faithful in Philly, where, at one point, the Pope passes by us, about ten feet away, waving. The next day, I join thousands of others in an outdoor mass, and in a personal and spontaneous triumph, I find myself, post-communion, on my knees on the litter-lined streets of Philadelphia, praying and filled with gratitude. The significance of this is that, as a nurse, I normally would not be messing with whatever bacteria and street filth might be below my knees at that point. Ted would've been proud of me.

Back in Maine, I face something I've been putting off. It's been a year or more since I've been to "our" Japanese restaurant in Portland. I go there with Fred and Meryl. We all know it will be difficult. We'd spent so many wonderful times there, the four of us. Now we walk in and are greeted by one of the servers who has been there for quite a while.

"Just three of us," I say, and her face falls. Her sadness is evident, and within moments, several of the other staff become aware and offer condolences. The table is ready in a few minutes. When I begin to walk up the three small steps that take us to the upper level, this kind woman reaches out and holds my hand, walking beside me as I take one step at a time. I will never forget this. The sheer simplicity of this outward gesture of deep caring leaves a permanent imprint.

Once seated at the table and looking over the menu, Fred, Meryl, and I talk about what Ted would have ordered, in a lighthearted way. Always the adventurous one, Ted would never miss an opportunity to order the spiciest or most exotic special of the day, and he would always carefully follow instructions from our server regarding sushi, when the platter was placed before him.

"Use this sauce for this" or "Nothing on that," the server would gently instruct. Ted would nod his head, taking it in. I've never been so adventurous as to try raw fish. It even goes beyond that. In one of our pre-dating outings with our coworkers, Ted had talked me into trying fried calamari. I took one bite and spit it out.

"It tastes like rubber bands!" I said, much to his amusement.

Now, with Meryl and Fred, we draw out enough warmth and laughter and memories to enjoy our meal together, minus one.

A month or so later, I plan that chicken dinner again, the one I have postponed several times. This is the first time since Ted died that I am having company for a meal—Will, Meryl and Fred, Father Jim, and my brother Steve. I'm trying to be casual about it. It doesn't seem to be working well. I hope I don't break down in front of everybody. I'm so sick of crying all over the place.

I give Father Jim a quick house tour. When I show him the upstairs bathroom, which is large and cushy, with a separate walk-in shower and whirlpool tub, I say that I'll miss it if I decide to sell the house.

"Well, someone else will enjoy it," he says.

I have trouble taking that in. I'm not that selfless right now. I am currently three years old mentally, having an internal temper tantrum much of the time.

"Yes, true," I say, trying to sound like a grown-up.

The dinner goes well. I have many mixed emotions throughout, but I put on a good enough face, I think. I might have a little crush on the good Father. Eh. Safe enough. And in therapy, I realize this, along with other similar eye-openers, is part of my mourning process. It breaks up the grief for a moment.

Facebook posts show couples my age having wedding anniversaries. Everywhere there are couples. Is the whole world a couple? It feels that way.

Contrary to the few months following Ted's death, I no longer rejoice in public displays of affection. Now, I'm just angry.

One mild autumn day, I hike up the gentle trail of Bradbury Mountain, a small mountain nearby. I sit at the top, looking out at the wilderness, people all around me, couples and young families, small children in my peripheral vision. Couples with their adult athletic legs walk past my sitting spot, and I'm irritated. *Do you know how lucky you are?* screams the heartbroken child in me. I'm lonely and feeling extremely sorry for myself, in a self-imposed limbo here on top of the mountain, watching the groupings of families come and go and winding their way around everyone. Coming close, then wandering away. Like the ache in my grieving heart.

At the same time, I think about a friend of mine who is physically unable to do much for themselves. I sometimes help them with small tasks, like writing a letter. That's how it is in life. We think we don't have what we need or want—but then, at a different vantage point, we realize we have so much or have had it before.

I tell my grief counselor, Carol, that when I see couples my age holding hands and looking happy together, I want to punch them.

"That's better than a year ago," she says.

She reminds me that soon after Ted's death, I told her how happy it made me to see people in love.

"You were one of the most numbed people I'd ever seen," she says.

I thought that because I was crying so much I was doing well with my grief. Now I see what she means. A cloudy mixture of love and crushing sadness had colored everything. I wonder if, in my mourning, this had been my childlike psyche bargaining with God.

If I admire other couples in love, will you bring Ted back to me?

Some weeks later, I get a gentle nudge from my grief therapist. I would gladly keep going to Carol forever—but I need to make my own way a bit more and give my spot to someone else more currently in need, as this service is normally offered for about a year. I am beyond that now. I've claimed that year-plus fully, so grateful for Carol and her unconditional support and wisdom.

I will continue with my regular therapist, who I can rely on to help me process life in my new reality.

November 23, 2015

The Monday before Thanksgiving, I fly down to North Carolina to be with Cassie and Paul and the kids for the holiday week. They are wonderful to me, and yet now something new emerges. I feel like I don't have a home anymore. I have a house in Maine which does not feel very much like home without Ted. I have passed the God-awful one-year mark since his death. During that first year, compassion flowed freely from others. Now, it feels like everybody is back to their normal life. Except me. Intellectually, I know that's normal, expected, and not even necessarily true in many cases. But it's how it feels within me. Forgotten. Lonely.

The start of the second year, although not consistently filled with crying, feels harsher in a way. He is not coming back. I know that now. Yet I still have a spontaneous, intrusive thought: *It's not possible he's really gone.* I simply cannot believe it.

Then one day, my thoughts are: *I can't believe he's gone. I just can't believe it. Unless...maybe he's not really gone, in some way.*

Maybe he pops in now and then. My experiences since his death would point to that, and that's something I track for myself. Not necessarily coincidences maybe. There have been messages that are extraordinary, and I tuck them into my memory for when I feel doubt that there is something beyond this life.

CHAPTER 43

JANUARY 2016, SOUTHERN WANDERING

I'm back in Greenville with Cassie and Paul and the grandkids for part of the winter. While I'm here, I sign up for a grief group, which, though not always easy, offers some insight into the acceptable, normal craziness of my emotions and thought process. This is a weekly group. Nice people, each with their own story of loss and sadness. Besides this, I just do the best I can, reaching for some sense of normalcy. In these past several months, Ted's wonderful and talented brother Rob and my dear mother-in-law have both passed. I no longer know what normalcy means. Ted's family has endured so much sadness. And my own heart is heavy.

One day, I decide to take a walk. It's one of the more difficult days of missing Ted. Behind my sunglasses, I'm fighting back tears, and not doing a very good job of it. I already look like a fool walking from one shopping center to the next in this section of Greenville, where almost everybody drives. Crossing the four-lane, fast and busy streets, I walk on grass next to curbs where there are no sidewalks. I'm not sure where to go, not sure what direction to take, looking for comfort that does not exist, for answers that are elusive. I walk and walk, and I have no idea where I'm going to land and I don't even care. The reality of this second year hits like the cold wind that is now coming across the parking lot where I'm walking, in front of an abandoned store, once a lively supermarket. Why must everything change?

I cannot stay in North Carolina. I will not be able to stand it. But where to go? Where to be? I feel like I've developed a personality disorder. They told us in the grief group that we would feel crazy at times.

I keep walking, to another nearby shopping plaza across the busy four-lane road, again, heading to a large supermarket.

I am still in relationship with Ted. I discover this every time I say something to him aloud, chuckle quietly to an imagined or retrieved joke or conversation like the ones we used to have. I make a remark that I know he would have smiled at. I do half of a high-five in the air. All this sounds rather strange, I suppose, but it is real. Love does not die. And still, grief dominates my being.

Today it happens in aisle 7 at the supermarket. I'm looking for dried ramen chicken soup. Then I head toward frozen foods. Overhead, the store music switches, from something unrecognizable to "Glory of Love" by Peter Cetera. My tears hit the air before I can count out the first measure. I'm stuck with my emotions and grief so overwhelming I wish I could hide. The music continues, sharply hitting my heart. All I can think of is you, Ted, of wanting to dance with you, to move with you, to smell you. My mind flashes back to our last dance together at home to the music of James Taylor, and now I'm frantically searching my pocketbook for tissues. It doesn't help any that as I turn to avoid being seen crying, the automatic freezer lights shine through the glass doors right onto me, a spotlight on my self-conscious grief.

A little later, while waiting for my daughter to pick me up at Barnes & Noble, I head toward the wrong vehicle until I see that it's not my daughter at the wheel.

When Ted was sick, I thought about how awful it would be to lose him. But the thought that never occurred to me was how it would feel, after he was gone, to lose myself.

SPRING, SUMMER, AND ONWARD

It is Spring 2016, and I am on my way home from NC in March when I get a call from Terry. Her husband, Richard, who had been fighting cancer for the past year and a half, has died. I am in the NY area at the time and pack up to go to her. It breaks my heart. She is younger than I am, and none of it makes sense. It's not fair—and should not happen to these kind and loving people, though my rational brain knows that there is no connection. When I land at her home outside Boston, I see her grief-stricken face and hug her tightly, wishing I could make it better, and knowing what the time ahead will be like for this dear friend of mine.

HOME AGAIN

Back home in the spring, our house now has a warm sterility about it, with its terra cotta color scheme in the kitchen and dining room but lacking the trinkets and photos that identify the inhabitants. I slowly prepare to put the house on the market, with ambivalence. It's a spacious country property in the outskirts of the city of Portland, with stone walls and gardens that still flower, though not as well as when Ted was here. When Michael, my handyman, cuts the grass and I put in a few hours of gentle gardening, it's so pretty it hurts to think of leaving. I have no idea where I will go if it sells. But it is big, too big for me, and expensive to manage alone. Finances have changed, plus I need to do many things by hire that Ted once did.

All family pictures are put away, part of the staging process. Occasionally, I bring flowers in and manage to keep them going for a week or more until the edges of the petals turn brown. I save them in stages, cutting, trimming, throwing out the bad ones and keeping the good, in different vases, until there are not enough to put them into the smallest of vessels.

One day, I take myself to lunch at a restaurant we'd frequented in South Portland. The hostess learns that Ted has died. This is the first time I can bear to go in there since his passing. As the hostess stands by my table, she reaches for my hand, and holds it continuously as we talk for ten minutes or more. She says little, but listens to me with intense eye contact, occasionally asking simple questions.

"What happened?" and "I'm so sorry." This is the embodiment of being present, so gently. The ease of generosity and kindness she shows is remarkable.

There is an annual September celebration/memorial in downtown Portland that I attend: Twilight in the Park, with its thousands of luminaries lit at night, people milling around, music, crying, hugging... In many ways it is beautiful, and at the same time, I feel so very alone and sad again that I can barely stand it. Back in my car, I call a friend I've recently met, and when he answers I begin to cry. He coaxes me through it, and suggests I join him for some supper at a nearby restaurant. It helps to see him. It is then that I start to see, in a new way, that there are no right or wrong ways to grieve. The ceremony had been just too much for me, alone. A burger with a friend? Better. I just never know what's going to be helpful or soothing or worthwhile—or not—at grief-related gatherings.

Some weeks later, I take the house off the market, as nothing much has happened with it, and we are heading into the fall. The very next morning, at the kitchen sink, looking through the window at the woodsy backyard, I'm surprised to be filled with happiness and relief that I am still here in our farmhouse, able to look out any window and see the beautiful woods. For that moment, I forget about expenses and tasks and am just happy to be surrounded by nature and to feel peaceful.

My good friends periodically lend hands. I hire a couple I know to attend to some house and yard repair, and Kathy and John, Beth's parents, are ever available, including me as a welcome "third" in social dinners out and family events. We go to the cemetery together often to be present for each other as we mourn Beth and Ted. My friendship with Kathy and John feels like family, and we often tell each other how much we wish we had met under different circumstances—a wedding, not a funeral.

I find my people in places like the nearby Starbucks, where I always get a hug from the sweet manager and the other baristas. My favorite grocery store cashier, whom I now consider a friend, always gives me a hug, and we chat and catch up on our lives. These human angels come up out of the universe and connect in a world that is now, for me, devoid of Ted's affection. The hugs make a genuine difference as I navigate daily life. Not for the first time, I mentally log in the many and simple ways God reaches out to comfort through human contact. In my Catholic faith, this is one of the "threes" of the Trinity—the essence and power of the Holy Spirit.

One day, I am sorting through papers, including writing projects, and come upon the manuscript for this book, which I have not looked at for a very long time. As I skim through it to assess how much editing needs to be done, I come across those two sheets of yellow lined paper. They contain notes I had written for Ted as we sat together, more than two years prior, in the dining room, discussing the areas he needed to fill in. These notes sit undone, as it was just shortly afterwards that his cognition began a slow but certain descent. Now the answers to these questions I'd posed are irretrievable. "Unfinished business"—a term I have come to detest—takes on an additional meaning. I put the papers back into the three-inch binder and put it away, yellow lined edges loosely floating outside those which are bound, just enough to taunt me. I begin reading the manuscript, but it is too much to take, emotionally.

Many months later, I take out the binder again. It sits untouched for two days on my dining room table. Then, in a massive cleanup, I put it away again. Sometimes I can't remember where I've put things, and rush around looking, usually locating anything of importance locked up in my dad's old gun cabinet, which is now used as special storage in my bedroom. It will be my winter project, I decide. I envision sitting in a room in North Carolina, typing away, crying. There is now, occasionally, a tiny element of glory in my widowhood, a silent badge of courage, much like a soldier who returns from war with a missing lower leg but can still make his way into town to eat a gravy-laden meatloaf lunch at the diner, receiving warm admiring words and smiles from others. As I amuse myself with this image, I am also aware that there is something called *healing* that is under way, something of a forward movement amongst the shaky steps.

I get together with my new male "burger" friend here and there, sometimes working on our individual projects in coffee shops,

> **STAGE SETS**
>
> Years ago, we hiked at Caples Lake in Northern California, Carson Pass area. We stayed at a small roadside motel, and when we looked out the window in the nighttime, we saw one of the most glorious settings we had ever seen, with a magnificent evening dark-blue sky filled with almost surreal twinkling stars, trees surrounding the lake, mountains in the distance—it looked like a colorful Hollywood stage set. Ever since then, when we would travel or drive somewhere and saw a stunning scene we would say, "Wow! They did a really great job on this one!"

sometimes watching a movie, allowing for some jokes and the occasional flirtation between two lonely people. It reminds me I'm still alive and gives me moments of reprieve—a laugh or temporarily seeing things differently than through my darkened lenses.

For now, I do what I do best: filling up my day and night until 2 a.m. with current writing promotions (for my humor book—finally published in 2015 after ten years of work) and breakfasts out with church friends. Somewhere around 1 or 2 a.m., I force myself to lie down in our big, lonely bed. I say my prayers, say good night to Bluey and the three babies—yes, the "family" has grown—and transfer a tiny kiss onto Ted's pillow.

A testimony to the individual nature of grieving is that I dwell very little on Ted over this Christmas. Oh, there are many thoughts of him, but little in the heart-wrenching category, possibly because I don't stay in one place very long to think. A few friends seem to make an extra effort to reach out to me throughout the holidays with concern—sweet and now ironically irritating all at once. These very kind people are doing what we all try to do—the best we can.

In loss, nothing or everything feels right. And nothing or everything feels wrong.

My daughter Sally is here for the week. She arrives from NYC two days before Christmas. The first part of her visit is filled with fun, punctuated by some tender moments of reminiscing. She reminds me about a time when Ted was at Gosnell and a hospice minister came into the room to visit. The minister had referred to Sally as "your daughter" to Ted, and she and Ted made eye contact and let it go, in a private moment of humor and sweetness, for Ted loved her like a daughter, and Sally loved Ted like a dad.

Sally will probably stay until New Year's Day. I say probably because we finally have a talk that I am certain neither of us consciously thought about having. I try to sort out New Year's Eve possibilities and things become a little tense. Turns out she and my older daughter have, for the past two-plus years, been figuring out together how to support me emotionally, especially at holiday times. Neither one has checked with me to see what level of support I need. Nor do I, at any time, say, "I'm doing OK. I am rebuilding my life. You can stay with your friends/other family members this time/etc." We open a conversational door that has been not only shut but sealed. Now pried open, I tell her I might want to spend a little time with a male friend of mine before she and I go out later in the evening. The tension dissipates, and freedom becomes our mutual goal, and we make plans. We laugh about how, under normal circumstances, our usual pattern of visits is that three to four days is perfect, after which we need a gentle break from each other. Our fun is fierce, but we are both independent personalities.

It is the day before New Year's Eve. Yesterday and today, I think much more about Ted. New Year's Eve has always been the holiday of romance for me, ever since my teen years. It's part of me, regardless of how it landed there. I can't deny it any more than I can deny that I am now wearing my mother's hands—capable, softly wrinkling, and a bit worn from years of real life, tending babies, and endless hand-washing.

Ted was never a New Year's Eve person. But for my sake, he would play along and enjoy going to dinner with our closest people. Then we'd lazily head home together. Somewhere around 10 p.m., he would start dozing. There was a sweetness to hearing that soft snore next to me on the futon, the television set to the standard mainstream New Year's Eve fare, as I went about simple tasks—getting my calendar or appointment book set up for the coming year of birthdays, the next dental cleaning, or my annual GYN appointment. I enjoyed going through the time-honored task of using a paper appointment book and wall calendar, where I would happily transfer birthdays and other noteworthy annual events from one year to the next, a cherished activity for me. He'd occasionally awaken on his own, or mumble "Jesus Christ" at a loud local car dealer commercial, then lovingly reach out to me, warmly stroking my leg or arm. Eventually, we would call it a night, some moments after midnight, and find our warmth together in our marriage bed, two happy, sleepy bears snuggling.

Now, suddenly, I miss the physical connection terribly. I am deserted on an island, starving for the adolescent sensual fabrication of New Year's Eve. For just one hormone-stirring midnight kiss. For arms to encircle me, for just a moment.

And this is where I move—from scared, torn, enraged, half-dead—to a flicker of life—for just a moment—crazily ignoring any preconceived vision of myself, possibly to the consternation of others who would cast me as the forever widow, a broken, weak shell left by a disaster called cancer, to begin to close the gaping hole with just a single kiss in the dark from someone who has been present for me emotionally. A brief ceasefire in battle.

    Ted is not here. But I still am.

CHAPTER 44

EARLY 2017

There is healthy soothing and questionable soothing. Widowhood can be very, very lonely, so early in 2017, I begin to look at dating apps. It's disastrous, but at least provides for some material for the humor column I write. I'm lonely, but not desperate. I may never want to fall in love again. But maybe a flirtation, or a distraction?

I struggle with this and find I have very few friends or family members to talk to about it, so I am cautious. After three disappointing coffee dates, I give up. I'm not interested, and it feels like more energy than it's worth.

Weeks later, I am back in North Carolina for an extended visit. It is filled with the grandkids' zillion activities, racing around town near constantly, school activities, getting together with friends of my daughter and Paul, movies...a hectic pace for me, and thank God for it. In between my underlying sadness, it provides a very welcome distraction. Family—in all its ups and downs—is a true blessing. I work on some writing here and there, have a book signing for my first novel, spend money, and eat too much. There's a café here called The Scullery in downtown Greenville, which has, hands down, the best blueberry pancakes in the world. When I ask Matt, the owner, about them, he shrugs and says, "It's simple. Just pancakes from scratch."

I also frequent a small frozen yogurt store, which supplies me with a fix for something sweet but not too decadent. Their product is good, there are lots of fresh toppings, and the Christian music playing overhead does not bother me at all.

I am a frequent visitor at St. Gabriel's. I've discovered noontime masses a couple of days a week. I also participate in a Lent preparation class that is Ignatian based, in which we are encouraged to meditate on various Gospel passages, putting ourselves into the imaginary experience of being there.

The pancake, egg, and sausage breakfasts at St. Gabriel's continue about once a month. I remember the first one I ever attended. I'd felt quite awkward. The second time, I felt much more welcomed. There are two people I will particularly miss when I go back to Maine: Father Romen, who is very kind and sweet, and was the reason I initially joined the breakfast. I had quietly told him that I was really missing Ted, and he invited me to stay to eat. The other person is a woman named Lucille. Lucille is probably in her 90s, a tiny little African American woman with a demeanor that embodies the Holy Spirit. She is intensely interested in everyone and everything and the kind of woman who tells you she'll pray for you and always adds, "Please pray for me." She tells me to invite my granddaughter to mass.

"I'll ask her, Lucille, but you know, she's not Catholic," I say.

"Tell her to come visit anyway," she says.

I tell Emma that Lucille is the cutest tiny little lady in the entire world, but I don't think Emma will go there. I mean, she's a teenager.

FRUSTRATION AND GRATITUDE

Spring 2017, Maine

Here's a new one for me: crying over a screen door. No, obviously it's more than that. But SHIT. Where is Ted when I really need him? I wake up to a beautiful day, open my front door to see what the weather feels like, and WOW! There it is. A gust of unfettered fresh air, where the screen used to be. The upper screen has somehow completely rolled up into the door works at the top, no way to get it down. Four phone calls later (big-box hardware store, a national window company, then two calls to a company that has replacement parts), I get an understanding woman who says she'll send me a screen replacement and email me a video of how to install it. I explain (OK, complain) to her that just reaching up to feel the screen induces neck pain from an old injury, so I will find someone to replace it for me...and then I tell her (because I can't keep quiet when I'm about to cry) about my husband and how he used to be able to fix all kinds of things and she says she's sorry and I say thank you and hang up and think, *Well, I'm lucky I have a house and a front door*...which makes me feel even worse for crying over a screen when people are starving...but here's the thing: I am, again, heavily grieving for my husband. I don't know why, I don't even care why, I just miss him. I miss the person I love. That person who had my back, literally and figuratively—that capable travel helper and companion when I was getting ready to visit someone and couldn't lift my darn suitcase...grieving feels like being on the edge of a breakdown in the most unexpected ways and places. Definitely not a straight line.

Within a week, the part for the screen door arrives, and Will, ever the good sport, comes over on the weekend and the two of us, with lots of laughing, cursing, and joking, get the damned thing on and working.

fall 2017

I spend some time in the South again. In North Carolina, I take out our manuscript. Now, I can begin editing and filling in the blanks. It's a very emotional process, and I can't work on it for very long. I wish Ted—my buddy—was here to help.

On the drive back to Maine, I notice anew more of the scenery of the area, views I had taken in when Ted and I first started spending winters in NC. With fresher eyes, I take note of the road out of North Carolina and into Virginia, which holds a constant string of billboard signs—*Ruby's Peanuts*, RV camps, *Robbie's Cigarette Outlet Fireworks*, and other cigarette and fireworks outlets. And I'm leaving behind the broken-down tiny shacks on this road which have already started to meld with the earth in their brokenness.

I head toward the Virginia border and recollect the minutia of the last day or so: the details of packing up to leave, packing the car and wondering if I've left something behind. I do feel that I have indeed left a little something of myself behind at St. Gabriel's. What's important to me will be waiting for me at my church back home. In this emotional reverse transition to Maine from the nest of North Carolina, I get a catch in my throat as I drive past town after town. Suddenly, I'm daydreaming and recalling how Ted or I would read short pieces of writing or a poem to each other, and now, with tears surfacing, I get a sense—a "step-in"—from Ted. He could never get through reading aloud a piece of writing—something that touched him—without tears welling up and getting a shakiness in his voice. I loved that show of emotion. Now, I was loving him all over again. Aching for him.

COLD WEATHER COMING

It takes a long time to sort through and figure out what to do with Ted's bureau and closet, still near full. My son had accepted a coat and some other pieces of clothing early on. I'd needed to know they were being used by someone who loved Ted. Currently, there is a local drive for warm clothing following the devastating Hurricane Maria in Puerto Rico. We have a group of people who have arrived from Puerto Rico, now living in Maine, who need help. That's a positive way to pass on clothing. Ted would like that. Each piece of his clothing, every trinket, holds sentimental value to me, a part of my dear Ted. It's easier to give things away when I have an eager or needy recipient.

Beyond this clothing drive, even non-clothing items feel like a big decision. He'd left no instructions. I had not asked. I suppose that's usually how it is. So, I must decide what to donate, sell, keep, or throw away. I end up keeping his most often-worn work suit, complete with shirt and tie, and leave it hanging in the closet. I can still picture him wearing it before leaving for work, and how happy I felt seeing him in it at the end of the day.

I keep his Sherwoods jacket and hat. His guitar, and other similar items are still in wait. Understanding that these items are Ted's and not Ted himself helps to relieve the unwelcome guilt of selling a few things. I sell his kayak to a 40-ish schoolteacher who is very excited to get it. It makes me happy to think of someone who loves kayaking, as much as Ted did, using his kayak.

I move my wedding and engagement ring to my right hand. I move it back to the left almost immediately for a couple of months more, until it finds itself on my right hand again. It will be years of switching back and forth. The ambivalence and complexity of loss is not lost on me.

CHAPTER 45

LOVE, GUILT, CHANGES

2018

It's taken about four years to be able to override my inner conflicts in making certain decisions, substituting "what would Ted want?" with "what do I want?" without guilt motivating the decisions.

Guilt. What was I feeling guilty about?

That we didn't go to Indian restaurants—one of his favorites—more often? That we didn't take that trip to Costa Rica? I'd been the hold-back because I have a lot of medication allergies and was afraid I'd react to the preventative malaria pills we'd need to take. Held back because of fear. When I talked with him about it in the last year of his life, that I had regrets, he'd responded, so Ted-like: "I could have gone if I'd really wanted to."

Was I feeling guilty because of some arguments we'd had? Or was it simply that I couldn't save him?

In the final analysis, I think guilt blocks positive thoughts and actions. And yet, in some way, it has its place in the process. Ironically, I've noticed lately how the smell of Indian cooking is just wonderful.

I am now actively working on this book. I have tried to keep all of Ted's words, making only the most minor changes of tense or typographical errors. I cannot stand to erase any of his words, as it feels like a betrayal and another loss.

When someone you love dies, the relationship does not end. I thought there would be a fading away of love over time. Life's distractions do soften the edge of the pain after a while, but the love remains, the longing, the dull ache, the frustration of not being able to touch, feel, to hold or be held by that person. Or simply to ask them a question.

Now and then, I need to make an executive decision about something in this manuscript, like cutting out an incident or shortening something. At those times, I look upward.

"Ted? If you wanted to help me with this part, you shouldn't have left." And recalling one of our many running gags, I add: "Too bad for you."

During a visit to North Carolina in the spring, Emma and I visit Lucille at her home, arranged by Veronica, a woman I met at St. Gabriel's. I don't think Lucille will be around for very much longer. Her grasp of time is iffy. I am not sure she is 100% with us, but her warmth and kindness are very present, as is her faith-teaching. She is one of those people I wish would always be here, sitting in church up front, in her same spot in the pew, receiving and giving love and hugs and kisses to virtually dozens of people before, during, and after mass. In our visit with this sweet woman, between somewhat disjointed thoughts at one point, Lucille refers to the well-known "Footprints in the Sand" poem—something that is lost on Emma until later, when I tell her about it. Later, back home in Maine, I buy Emma a little wallet card with the poem on it and send it to her.

In the summer of 2018, nearly four years after Ted's death, I put our house back on the market for a second time, and it goes under contract in four days. The place I want to move to will not be ready for several months, so I look at a few other places and make a temporary move to a one-bedroom in an over-55 apartment building a couple of towns away, but within easy driving distance of my old turf. I figure it will serve me well enough until I find someplace more permanent.

Things move quickly. A week after the move, the impact of it hits me hard, partly because the task of packing up and moving from a huge farmhouse to a tiny apartment in 90+ degree July heat does not do a lot for my general constitution. I am dehydrated and exhausted, even with lots of help from Cassie and others. But I recover quickly, physically.

I don't particularly miss the house itself, but I am missing Ted so much, it feels almost unbearable. Brief, seemingly "normal" situations intensify the feelings: arriving at my same church in Portland to sing, yet feeling out of place. New faces, different song leader. I am introduced to a married couple who sing together, the way Ted and I used to. It's a searing pain, seeing this middle-years happily married couple in front of me at mass, remembering when Ted was singing at my side. Time has marched on, as it should, but I have not caught up. I spend the entire mass trying not to cry, leaving early and going across to the cemetery where I sob and sob until I can catch my breath long enough to call my sister, who provides the comfort and wisdom I need.

Two days later, I go to our old workplace to return Ted's pager that I'd found in his top drawer when I packed up the farmhouse. After I leave it, I get back into the car and realize I'm in for an evening of tears. I get out of the car again and head back toward the building. One of the managers is coming out.

"How are you?" they ask, and I blurt out that I'd found Ted's pager in the move, had just returned it, but I wasn't so sure now.

"Get it back. Here, I'll let you in the building," they say. I am moved by their kindness and understanding.

They let me back in.

"I understand," adds the sweet young security guard. I can tell he does.

If you've been there, you get it.

FALL REALIZATION

One day, after living in my new place for a couple of months, I realize something that stops me cold. I am putting my key into my apartment door, and…I am smiling. There is a calm happiness within. I have a long way to go to sort through things, make the apartment compatible for living, to work on my writing, and so on. But I've begun to meet some people in the building—nice people—and suddenly, it feels like I have a new start.

I tell my kids about the people here, and Cassie starts referring to it as "the dorm." I am cozy, slowly settling in, figuring it out. The care of this new but tiny apartment is a piece of cake. And just steps down the road is a wonderful specialty grocery store that, in fact, has excellent cake. I am a quick five-minute drive to my favorite beach, and because I'm old enough, I get a free parking pass for that beach and two others nearby. The other tenants in my building are mostly single women, widowed or divorced, a few males who are like brothers, and a few couples. It's a good lot.

I think I have found my people.

CHAPTER 46

2019 AND BEYOND

In January, I learn from Veronica that Lucille has passed. St. Gabriel's will never be the same. I wonder at God's plan, which feels so heavy at such times. I remind myself that I am not privy to the answers in this world, but it doesn't stop me from wanting to get a bigger picture. I tell Emma about Lucille, and we are both sad, but glad we knew her. And we agree she was the sweetest, cutest little lady ever.

I talk aloud to Ted daily, and still compile notes of the tiny reminders I get from Heaven. I put Post-it notes on my kitchen area wall that say things that are Ted-reassurances. My son, now 31, fights through yet another autoimmune medical battle in the early months of 2019—successfully, but not for the better part of the year, as it turns out. In the early process when I am terribly worried, I hear Ted's voice in my mind's ear, something he's said to me several times: *Your baby boy will be just fine*, and I write this and post it in the kitchen where I can see it often.

When I go to the cemetery, I whisper "I love you, always and forever"—his words to me so many times—remembering the dozens and dozens of cards he wrote to me over the years, cards I rediscover periodically as I sort and rearrange the house's stored leftovers. I meet Kathy and John at the cemetery frequently. We visit each grave—Ted's and Beth's—then take a walk together, Kathy and I chatting incessantly about the state of the world, as John walks by our side, giving us plenty of girl-space. Sometimes when I am there alone, I take my beach chair out of the car trunk and sit and read next to Ted/Ted's stone, sipping iced coffee. Just having a relaxed visit, close to him.

I think Ted is still around me now and then. I tell him I'm OK. I don't want him to worry about me. I want him to be free. I have this theory about Heaven. I think if you want your loved one to be truly able to enjoy Heaven, then you need to eventually get to the "I'm OK" stage, or close enough, to release them. It's just my theory, probably bullshit. Hopefully, God has our collective back on all of this, that we are taken care of after death. That we can trust God. I mean, if not God, then who? But I do want Ted to be free in the next life. And that seems to be the best way to love him now. So, I fill my days—often overfill—with everything from meeting friends for coffee to writing to walks, mundane errands, and tasks of life, including baking breakfast bars that are healthy, with blueberries or dark chocolate chips, and playing canasta with my girlfriends in the building where I live. I visit family, meet for outings and vacations, and am involved in lots of church activities, often wondering to myself why I get involved in some things that are frustrating to me. Ted used to tell me he didn't "play well with others," and I know what he meant. I feel that way at times. I want the world and my various communities to do things my way.

My gentle husband Ted was one of the most tenacious people I knew, but that didn't save him from his cancer. I loved him more than I ever thought I could love a man, but that wasn't enough to stop the cancer either. Together, we lived fully. Now, there is a letting go on many levels. Not complete, but enough to clear a path for me to keep going.

In some way, in my new apartment, my life feels freer. I am still in love with Ted, and though I joke about finding a handsome 50-something "younger" man to take me to dinner, it's hard to imagine being in an actual relationship. But there is plenty of room for old friends and new ones. After these several years, I feel my steps getting lighter, even with the issues that come with aging.

I know that this is not the end of processing Ted's death. There are still enough times, predictable or not, when the tears flow and I am aware of a terrible ache in my body and soul. But there is movement, erratic as it is, and I am now able to live with the pain as well as the beauty of what we had.

March 29, 2019

Easter approaches. I'm doing a lot of praying. It's been a rough go emotionally since Christmas. William is finally stabilizing medically, although it is to be many months before he is declared out of the woods. Sally had been sick and had to cancel a trip south, where we were going to meet at Cassie's a couple of months ago. I couldn't find my sea legs, with two of my adult children so ill. Now, with both recovering, it's a little quicker, a little easier, to find my way back. I can almost feel the cortisol still coursing through my system. I am so aware of how anxious and stressed I've been. Times like this, I really need Ted. I discover the added blessing of Will's girlfriend, Katie, who is wonderful and lovely, and has been taking care of him while he's been sick. I am not the only one who can help him pull through these kinds of things. I am filled with gratitude for her, this kind person who gives her love so freely, even during adverse circumstances, and makes him so happy. I am hopeful that they will be a forever couple. I can't really say that to them at this point. But I can think it, and be grateful that this is how it is, at least now.

I find Sally to be extraordinarily resourceful, and I check on her frequently by phone, knowing that even though I hate the long flight from the East Coast to the West Coast where she now lives, if she needs me, I will go. It takes her several weeks to get past a rather complicated respiratory situation, but she does. She's a real fighter.

When I moved to this new town last summer, it was weeks before I could consistently figure out my driving route into nearby Portland, because I was driving there from the south instead of the north. (Ted and I had been living just slightly north of Portland in the farmhouse those years back.) But recently, after enough times of getting on the turnpike and heading the wrong way, I now catch myself and quickly move into the correct on-ramp lane. So it is with handling my children's ups and downs, illnesses, and with my yearning for Ted. There's something of a recalculation, a different way to approach things so as not to get so completely entangled. I've also come to rely on something greater than my daily concerns and anxieties. Oh, the worries are there, believe me. Yet beyond that, calling to me rather loudly, is a line from a beautiful piece we are rehearsing at church for the Easter vigil, "Most Holy Night" by Dan Schutte:

"God's mighty love is stronger than death."

Near the end of April, I begin a two-day drive to Pennsylvania. Ted's younger granddaughter, Samantha, is expecting her first baby, who would have been Ted's first great-grandchild. I have not yet met Samantha's young husband. En route, I have dinner with my longtime high school friend and long-ago babysitting charge, Carla, who lives just outside New York City. The next day, I continue to my destination, a sportsman's club in a remote town close to Blue Mountain. I am somewhat anxious, as I have not seen some of Ted's family much, and here I am doing this on my own and feeling it. I am greeted warmly by Maryellen, Samantha and her sister, Vic, and their happy and excited mother, Stephanie, who is a soon-to-be grandma for the first time. I meet Samantha's husband and a bunch of others who are new to me, a happy group of family and friends, and I begin to relax and enjoy the lovely party. Over the next couple of hours, we all play various shower games, and watch Samantha and her husband open gifts. We chat and refill our plates from the overflowing buffet tables of delicious food.

Maybe some things have come full circle.

For, as I sit here at the tablecloth-covered folding tables, with cupcakes and leftover plates of chicken and salad and baked beans, as I talk and laugh with family and new friends and admire Samantha with her youthful energy and her full belly of baby nearly ready to enter this world, I take in the connection to something greater. Reassuring. Peaceful.

Later, as I start the long drive back to Maine, it hits me…that God's way of healing is so, so much smarter than I could've ever imagined.

EPILOGUE

In life and in nature, we see renewal. There's always an inbox and an outbox. We eat, and we excrete. We breathe in, we breathe out. In daily life, the mail arrives, is processed, and leaves in some form. The tree leaves turn color, transform, and fall off their branches in the autumn, and new buds form in the spring. Human-based destruction aside, there is virtually nothing in our natural world that does not renew in some form, in some way, at some point in time, nothing that doesn't hit the inbox and the outbox again and again. So somewhere, in some energy form, whether we call it Heaven or a consciousness or any other number of vague or specific ideas, Ted does live.

And now, his story and mine live together, a testament to the love bestowed upon us by so many, by each other, and by this force of power, healing, and love I call God.

Surviving loss is as complicated and individual as each human being is. Yet it's also simple, when watered down. We survive by learning to listen to what we need, seeking it, and being meticulously tolerant of ourselves. The only answers are those within us. We learn to forgive ourselves and forgive others for being human, for being angry, jealous, proud, self-indulgent, fearful, for whatever needs forgiving. We learn to forgive the one who has left. To forgive God for making a plan in which people do not last forever on this earth. To realize that it's OK to be stuck for periods of time. The concept of closure is a meaningless present-day term. Grieving is a process without form, without rules, without predictability. It just *is*.

In August of 2022, I take a long-awaited family trip to Portugal. It's wonderful to be with them all, but I am woefully out of condition, having recently completed several months of PT for my back and surrounds.

Walking the big up-and-down hills of Lisbon and Porto knocks me back into lots of pain and lots of sweat, like I could never have imagined. My family patiently waits for me, adjusting their pace and helping me again and again, and we end up taking more Ubers than expected, and that's OK. During one of the last days in Porto, I take the morning for myself while they go off, planning to meet them in the afternoon for a relaxed tuk-tuk tour. The one thing I want to do before I leave Portugal is visit a church and light some candles for people who are ill and for those loved ones who have gone, including Ted and Beth. I finally find a church. It's closed but set to open at 2 p.m. I walk around, pick up a few souvenirs nearby, then end up walking to an ATM, as I have run out of Euros. I go back to the church. Still not open. Although it is not exceptionally hot out, I am, once again, pouring sweat in all the uncomfortable places. I feel the trickles go down my back. I'm perspired, exhausted, discouraged, but when the church finally opens around 2:15, I go in. It is very beautiful and set up with stations of devotion to various Saints—with lots of candle-lighting opportunities. I light candles at the feet of the Holy Mother for those gone from us and for other special intentions, and then go sit down in the middle of the front part of the church. I can feel the dampness of my clothing and my hair, and my face is greasy just a couple of hours after my shower. I'm hardly dressed for any kind of appearance in a church. I am exhausted after what I consider to be a week of boot camp, physically, although certainly the joys, laughs, and sweet times of being with my family overpower that in a big way, and Portugal is beautiful. It's been a wild and crazy ride, this week of traveling and all the waiting, crowds, and standing in long airport lines. As I sit here, I realize this is how we come to God best. Discouraged. Frustrated. In pain. Sweaty. Angry. Grateful. Loved. And isn't that the way we have a true connection? In a real relationship, not holding back. Expressing, feeling, and listening. Listening to that eternal voice that says we are loved and valued in our most frail, fragile, grimy, imperfectly perfect selves. Not dressed up, not pretending, not putting on a show about who we think we should be, but putting our raw human selves out there—and still feeling the love and peace that comes to us from these moments we are able to be true to and lovingly accepted by the universe and our God. That is my lesson from Ted's difficult trial, and my own: God is here. Unconditionally and always. Not magically fixing things. But here, to walk with us.

I don't think I will ever be at a point when I don't yearn for Ted's warmth at night and humor by day. But I have memories and an ever-present connection with him that makes me smile and laugh, and I continue to feel a deep love for him—a link that cannot be broken even through physical death.

So often, Ted and I talked about writing something together. Well, Ted?
   We did it.

ACKNOWLEDGMENTS

Writing and organizing a manuscript written by two authors is no easy task. It took a tremendous amount of time and research, and it could not have been accomplished without the assistance and support of the following people:

Thank you to my wonderful expert editor, Genie Dailey, whom I trust with any of my book-babies; to my talented and patient graphic designer, Michelle Hodgdon; and to the entire staff at Maine Authors Publishing in Thomaston, Maine, who make book publishing easy. You are there every step of the way. Thank you, Nikki, Molly, Dan, and Nadia.

I give loving gratitude to internationally recognized artist and friend Meryl Ruth for reading the rough manuscript and giving title to this book.

Special thanks go to The National Society of Newspaper Columnists and its twice-weekly writing space led by Suzette Standring. This workshop space is responsible for getting me on task through the pandemic and beyond, and I credit these good people with my ability to complete our book. They totally rock!

I am also grateful for the support and warm friendships from the South Portland "Gather" group, which is part of the Maine Writers and Publishers Alliance.

Thank you (in alphabetical order by first name) to Cole Imperi, Cheryl Gillespie, Dave Lieber, Judith Blanchard, and Suzette Standring for reading our manuscript and writing blurbs. It is no small thing to spend the time and effort to do so. You are all professional and personal heroes of mine, and I thank you very much.

Thank you to Dan Hudkins, my dear friend Susie's husband, who came to my aid more than once during tough computer issues.

Thank you to famed, amazing songwriter and musician Dan Schutte, who willingly and easily gave me permission to use a line from his song "Most Holy Night." His work is simply gorgeous, and he is a huge blessing to me and to many others with his music and generosity. Thank you, Dan, so much.

Thank you to Rod Pierce of "Math Is Fun" for consulting with me on the ancient chicken/fox/grain story.

And our story itself? Well, there is no succinct way of conveying the depth of gratitude for the hundreds of people, companies, and medical facilities that walked with us through the difficult experience called brain cancer. This book itself is a loving acknowledgment of those who were part of our story. The following is a mere sprinkle of our gratitude, because there were so many, and nearly every day I recall more people and places who made a difference—a wonderful problem to have.

We are deeply grateful for our family members. Our children and their spouses listened and gave support in the most generous ways: Cassie, Paul, Sally, Will, Randey, and Maryellen. They drove, flew, and came to our aid, sacrificing their own daily lives and plans, again and again. After Ted's death, they patiently and lovingly endured my tears, often late into the night. "Thank you" seems inadequate. Our deep gratitude to Ted's mom, Margaret, who has since passed, and to our awesome siblings, nieces, nephews, cousins, and grandchildren, who seemed to know just what we needed to add to our joy during Ted's life and to my comfort afterwards. Susie, Little K, Laurie, Steve—and so, so many of you, including our 2020 bonus—Will's wife, Katie! I hope you all know what a difference you have made. You all brought the best gift: yourselves. We hit the jackpot when it comes to family.

Our friends were there through all iterations of the illness and its aftermath of grief, with food, physical lifting and legwork, painting, hauling boxes, helping dispose of trash, and offering hugs and reassurances—and we quite literally could not have gotten through as well as we did without their strength of body and generosity of spirit. We have given testimony to many, but again, the limitations of a manuscript became apparent in the long editing process. That does not diminish how much your caring and involvement mattered. To our many friends and colleagues: We are immensely grateful that you showed up. You made a difference, and "above and beyond" especially, in no particular order: Meryl and Fred, Denise and Mark, David and Theresa, Sue and Sam, Kathy and John, Marilyn and Greg, Debbie and Brad, Sandy and Denis, Al and Dee, Leora, Roz, Jeri, Bob and Ruth, Jack and Birgitta, Peter and Marcia, Terry, Brenda and Joe—the list goes on and on. You were heroic. Thank you.

We give special thanks to the Sherwoods, Ted's treasured Cornell singing group. You and your partners held us in friendship and song.

Thank you to my dear Sisters of Mercy and Mercy Associates, who offered kindness, love, and prayers, and to the following parishes that offered abundant care and welcoming: Our Lady of Hope, Portland, Maine; St. Paul Catholic Church, New Bern, North Carolina; and St. Gabriel of the Sorrowful Mother, Greenville, North Carolina. Thank you to all the priests, staff, musicians, and parishioners who contributed to our well-being with prayerful words and hugs. Special thanks to the former song group at Our Lady of Hope, "On a Wing and a Prayer," who sustained us for over twelve years with song, laughter, and dinners out, sometimes bursting into song in public places to the joy and/or irritation of others. Thank you, Louis, for your leadership, inspiration, love, and piano and vocal chops.

Special heartfelt thanks to our "Good Samaritan" on Fore Street in Portland who saved Ted from a terrible wheelchair accident, and to the lovely dad in Florida who handed his baby girl to me for a few moments. To do these things for a stranger is the true meaning of love.

Thank you to my young friend who has been there for me through some rough times. You have helped me survive with lots of laughs. Bravo, Sir! Thanks.

Thank you to my new treasures in the senior community where I live, who gather in the community room and around the canasta table with frequency, where we share the healing benefits of wisdom, laughter, homemade cookies, vegetables from our community garden, and the best chocolate ever from Len Libby Candies. You are all blessings in my healing.

We were extremely fortunate to have medical providers who were expert, kind, trusted, and so very human. Medical people for whom we are especially grateful include:

Mass General Hospital; Dr. Will Curry; Dr. April Eickler, Dr. Oh, and our social worker at Mass General Cancer Center: Neuro-Oncology; Dr. Peter Emery and staff at Intermed, Portland; Dr. Devon Evans and his wonderful staff of nurse practitioners, nurses, and adjunct staff at New England Cancer Specialists; Dr. Rodger Pryzant and Dr. Cornelius McGinn, MaineHealth; nurse Debbie Cushing, MaineHealth; Dr. Christine Lu Emerson; our friend Dr. David Getson; our therapists, psychological and physical; Ted's in-home outpatient therapists; the entire amazing staff of Gosnell Memorial Hospice House, Scarborough, especially Dr. Cynthia Burnham and nurse Larry Robinson; Hospice of Southern Maine; and the priests and pastoral counselors at various hospitals and parishes, including John Kearns at Mass General and our Father Jim. And special big thanks and acknowledgment to grief counselor Carol Schoneberg, whose wisdom and love should be enough to win her a Nobel Prize. We were so very fortunate to have had these people in our corner. Their caring, kindness, and devotion were unparalleled.

Thank you to Ben who helped us with household tasks and kept Ted safe, and to Michael for keeping our house intact. And Katrina from Servpro? You're on the road to sainthood.

Thank you to the good folks at the New Bern Visitor Center in North Carolina who provided information, maps, answers, and encouragement. Special places and people gave us joy and good food and were certainly a part of our story. There were many, but favorites include: Becky's Diner, BenKay, Foreside Tavern, the former Imperial China, the former Parker's, and the former GoBerry—all in the greater Portland, Maine, area—and The Chelsea, China King, and Baker's Kitchen in the New Bern area. And my special thank-you goes to The Scullery in Greenville, North Carolina, where pancake dreams and manuscripts come to life. Thank you, Matt. You are among the very best of humans.

Our thanks to NASA's Hubble Site Telescope people for providing joy to us with their gorgeous photos for years, and for giving permission to use one on Ted's gravestone; to Amica Insurance company for coming to our aid during TWO floods. Thank you to Starbucks and Dunkin' and other places who made our lives easier due to their many locations with easily accessible, one-person bathrooms that accommodate an individual and that person's helper.

Thank you to the bookstores who carry this and other books, especially the wonderful books by Maine authors. People love reading, and you make it fun. A heartfelt shout-out to Maine's many wonderful independent bookstores. I love you.

And lastly: Thank you to each of you who has read our story. We hope that in some small way, it has comforted or enlightened you.